NEW COVENANT THEOLOGY

BOOKS BY

TOM WELLS

CHRISTIAN: TAKE HEART
COME HOME FOREVER
COME TO ME
FAITH: THE GIFT OF GOD
GOD IS KING
A PRICE FOR A PEOPLE
A VISION FOR MISSIONS

BOOKS BY

FRED G. ZASPEL

THE CONTINUING RELEVANCE OF DIVINE LAW
THE THEOLOGY OF FULFILLMENT
JEWS, GENTILES, AND THE GOAL OF REDEMPTIVE HISTORY

NEW COVENANT THEOLOGY

Description
Definition
Defense

Tom Wells & Fred G. Zaspel

5317 Wye Creek Drive, Frederick, MD 21703-6938

Phone: 301-473-8781 or 800-376-4146 Fax 301-473-5128
Website: www.soundofgracebooks.com
Email: info@soundofgracebooks.com

New Covenant Theology

Copyright © 2002 by Tom Wells, Fred G. Zaspel

ISBN: 1-928965-11-3

Scripture quotations are the authors' own translations or are taken from the following:
Holy Bible: New International Version®. Copyright © 1973, 1978, 1984 by the International Bible Society. Used by permission of Zondervan Publishing House. All rights reserved.
Holy Bible: New King James Version®. Copyright © 1982 by Thomas Nelson, Inc. Used by permission. All rights reserved.

Chapter 2 by Fred G. Zaspel and chapters 3, 4, and 15 by Tom Wells originally appeared in *Reformation & Revival* journal; used by permission.

All rights reserved. No part of this publication may be reproduced, stored in a retrieval system, or transmitted in any form or by any means—electronic, mechanical, or any other—except for brief quotations in printed reviews, without the prior permission of the publisher.

Printed in the United States of America

02 03 04 05 06 07 08 09 // 10 9 8 7 6 5 4 3 2 1

The authors wish to thank all who have helped make this book possible. We especially want to express appreciation to Douglas Moo for his generous foreword, to Donald Carson, Thomas Nettles and John Reisinger for reading the manuscript and urging others to read it. A special thanks also goes to New Covenant Media for the interest they have shown, including the untiring work of Carrie Bates. We are also grateful for the cover design done by Paul Osborne.

When two parties, both submitting in principle to the authority of Scripture, strongly disagree as to Scripture's meaning, and when the issues are complex and intertwined, is resolution a forlorn hope? Must the two sides merely dig themselves into defensive positions and lob theological mortars at each other? At very least, if there is any hope of a meeting of minds, let alone of a resolution of the issues, it takes time, patience, intellectual humility, a willingness to be corrected, and thoughtful and empathetic listening combined with accurate and understated articulation of each party's understanding. And those are the values of this book. Wells and Zaspel will not convince all of their opponents by their understanding of "new covenant theology," but they deserve to be treated with the respect they extend to others—and perhaps, in the mercy of God, we will discover, in time, that some genuine steps have been taken toward theological agreement.

D. A. Carson
Research Professor of New Testament
Trinity International University
Deerfield, IL 60015

One of the great necessities of Christians who agree on so many vital issues is to find a way not to separate over ambiguous differences. Two things are necessary in order to maintain discussion in the context of brotherly love as well as godly zeal for truth. One, channels of clear communication must be pursued so that the points under contention and the way that they are framed by contending parties become clear in the process of dialogue. Two, the implications of the differences, properly understood, must be worked out fairly as part of the corporate discussion so that no one will be maligned or declared heterodox unjustly. Particularly in a controversy over biblical Law we must not bear false witness against our neighbor. Tom Wells and Fred Zaspel have moved us along the road for this kind of profitable discussion. They have related New Covenant Theology to recent evangelical scholarship in a way that shows that their canonical hermeneutic is not quite so idiosyncratic as might appear with a restricted reading of that literature. They have showed that NCT has undergone a process of seeking to streamline its vocabulary and relate constructively to its critics. They have shown unity with their contending brethren on many points while making clear the leading principles of NCT and setting in bold relief some of the major implications of those principles. Some of us who may not agree with all aspects of the position as articulated here, nevertheless hope that this book gains a wide and respectful reading. Careful interaction could prompt an important dialogue that ultimately concerns the excellence of the Gospel and the glory of Christ. These concerns are earnestly sought by all parties in the discussion with the hope that they may be displayed more fully and purely by our common witness.

Tom J. Nettles
Professor of Historical Theology
The Southern Baptist Theological Seminary
Louisville, KY 40245

New Covenant Theology
Table of Contents

ABBREVIATIONS

FOREWORD by Douglas J. Moo — xiii

PREFACE
Approaching a New Covenant Theology — 1

CHAPTER 1
The Christian Appeal of a New Covenant Theology — 7
Tom Wells

CHAPTER 2
A Brief History of Divine Revelation — 33
Fred Zaspel

CHAPTER 3
The Description of the New Covenant (Part One) — 43
Tom Wells

CHAPTER 4
The Description of the New Covenant (Part Two) — 59
Tom Wells

CHAPTER 5
Matthew 5:17-20—A History of its Interpretation — 77
Fred Zaspel

CHAPTER 6
Matthew 5:17-20—Contextual Observations — 91
Fred Zaspel

CHAPTER 7
Matthew 5:17-20—The Messianic Mission — 109
Fred Zaspel

CHAPTER 8
Matthew 5:17-20—The Law of Christ in
  Matthew 5:18-20 and Related Passages   123
  Fred Zaspel

CHAPTER 9
The Continuing Relevance of Divine Law   139
  Fred Zaspel

CHAPTER 10
The Meaning and Source of Moral Law   161
  Tom Wells

CHAPTER 11
Critiquing a Friendly Attack (Part One)   169
  Tom Wells

CHAPTER 12
Critiquing a Friendly Attack (Part Two)   187
  Tom Wells

CHAPTER 13
The Sabbath: A Test Case   211
  Fred Zaspel

CHAPTER 14
The Sabbath: Some Critical Texts in Paul   239
  Tom Wells

CHAPTER 15
Our Creeds and How They Affect
Our Understanding   259
  Tom Wells

APPENDICES

1 The Relation of Law to the Work of Evangelism   271
2 The Relations Between the Biblical Covenants   275
3 "Covenant" and its Cognates in the NT   281
4 The Promises of the Abrahamic Covenant   285

5 A Table for Studying the Decalogue as Commanded by God in the NT	289
6 John Bunyan on the Creation Sabbath	293

BIBLIOGRAPHY 295

INDICES 307

ABBREVIATIONS

ANF	Ante-Nicene Fathers
BAGD	*A Greek-English Lexicon of the New Testament and Other Early Christian Literature*, Bauer, Walter, William F. Arndt, F. Wilbur Gingrich, and W. Danker
BibSac	Bibliotheca Sacra
ECNT	Baker Exegetical Commentary on the New Testament
JBL	Journal of Biblical Literature
JETS	Journal of the Evangelical Theological Society
LXX	The Septuagint
NASB	New American Standard Bible
NIC	New International Commentary series
NIGTC	New International Greek Testament Commentary
NIV	New International Version
NTS	New Testament Studies
TDNT	Theological Dictionary of the New Testament
TNTC	Tyndale New Testament Commentaries
SJT	Scottish Journal of Theology

Foreword

What a great time to be a biblical theologian! Few periods in church history have witnessed such a concern among scholars, pastors, and laypeople alike to put inherited ideas and ecclesiastical traditions to the test of Scripture. Covenant theologians are wondering whether some of their cherished doctrines have clear scriptural warrant. Many dispensationalists, under the name of "Progressive Dispensationalism" are recasting their tradition. To be sure, this move toward confessional soul-searching has its down side. Seeing their pastors and teachers questioning long-standing doctrines can lead some Christians to think that theology doesn't really matter at all. And none of us should too quickly abandon doctrines that past generations have passed down to us. But a return to careful analysis of our traditions in light of what the Bible teaches is certainly, on the whole, a welcome development.

This book on New Covenant Theology by Tom Wells and Fred Zaspel is a fine representative of this new biblical theology tradition. While expressing deep appreciation for the heritage of Reformed theology, Wells and Zaspel nevertheless argue that the emphasis on the continuity of revelation in much of that tradition has been overdone. They are convinced that the New Testament claims an ultimacy for itself that is not always respected in Reformed, and especially Covenant, theology. Particularly is this the case when one considers the teaching in the New Testament about the Mosaic law. Wells and Zaspel therefore appropriately devote considerable space to this matter. Wells does a fine job of analyzing some of the historical and broadly theological issues, while Zaspel concentrates on a careful exegesis of key New Testament texts – especially the pivotal Matthew 5:17-20. The combination is impressive and persuasive.

New Covenant Theology does not offer a full-fledged alternative theological "system." But by offering a perspective on what must be a crucial component of any theological system – the nature of the continuity and discontinuity between Old and New Testaments – it makes a basic contribution to the eventual shape of that system. I think the perspective that Wells and Zaspel take on this matter is close to the right one. Their careful biblical argument needs to be taken into account as the task of reforming our traditions in light of the witness of Scripture goes forward.

Douglas J. Moo

PREFACE

Approaching a New Covenant Theology

Every author who sits down to write a book has some justifications in his mind for what he is about to do. Often he is also moved by some event that creates an occasion that seems to call for the book. The men who contribute to this book on New Covenant Theology[1] are not exceptions. It is only fair to the reader to make those matters plain at the outset. That is especially true when the subject of the book may be unfamiliar to many who might profit from reading it.

The occasion that prompted this volume was the publication of a book containing a friendly but serious attack on NCT.[2] Some of the present volume interacts with that volume, but we did not limit ourselves to reviewing that book, since it is time that something more substantial than fugitive pieces appears in print on this subject.

The justification for works on NCT seems to be at least fivefold. First, it has seemed to some of us that if the New Testament is the apex of God's revelation, then we ought to read the earlier parts of Scripture in its light. The point seems self-evident, but for some of us it was nevertheless hard to arrive at. Second, the NT is very explicit in making believers

---

[1] To avoid constant repetition of the phrase "New Covenant Theology," we will refer to it from now on by the initials NCT.

[2] Richard Barcellos, *In Defense of the Decalogue: A Critique of New Covenant Theology* (Enumclaw, WA: WinePress Publishing, 2001).

"slaves" of Jesus Christ. The implications of this are far-reaching; here we simply note the fact. Third, a nagging question arises when OT law becomes too prominent in discussions of Christian morals and ethics. The question is: Which is the higher revelation of the character of God, the Ten Commandments or the person, work and teaching of Jesus Christ? Most Christians, we think, will agree on the answer. We've tried to go a step further and work out its implications according to the NT Scriptures.

A fourth thing calls for an understanding of NCT: the renewed emphasis in our day on exegetical and biblical theology as the source of systematics. This has inevitably called into question the way Christians read their creeds and confessions.[3] Finally, in one of the odd providences that the Lord sometimes sends our way, those who defend New Covenant Theology find themselves falling in with an emphasis that has been prominent throughout church history. It is sometimes forgotten that two alternative readings of the New Covenant, Dispensationalism and Covenant Theology, have developed since the beginning of the Reformation. Covenant Theology was unknown until Ulrich Zwingli called it into service against the Anabaptists.

It came about in this way. Zwingli concluded that baptism could not wash away sin. That had been baptism's traditional rationale. He briefly toyed with the notion that baptism was the badge of Christian profession for those old enough to profess faith.[4] That view, however, played into the hands of those who

---

[3] We develop this point extensively in chapter 15.

[4] "At the outset Zwingli had been intimate with the people who later opened the Second Front [i.e., those Anabaptists later known as the Swiss Brethren]. He had, in fact, to quite an extent shared their views....He had, for example said that infant baptism 'nit sin solle,' ought not to be." Leonard Verduin, *The Reformers and Their*

wanted to separate church and state, a dangerous precedent in an intolerant age. So Zwingli retained infant baptism, but without a rationale for it. What could he do? Faced with these hard choices, he adopted "a completely new hermeneutical approach to Scripture as a whole, i.e., the idea of the unity of the covenant of grace."[5] Other Reformed writers followed his example when contending against the Anabaptists. We will have more to say about this idea in the body of this work.

One other matter calls for attention in this preface, the difficulties connected with this discussion. They are of two types: first, those that arise from the NCT movement; second, those that arise from the phrase "the New Covenant." Richard Barcellos has stated the difficulties with studying NCT:

> It is somewhat difficult to critique New Covenant Theology for at least three reasons. *First*, New Covenant Theology is not a monolithic movement. New Covenant theologians differ on some of the nuances involved with defining New Covenant Theology. *Second*, New Covenant Theology is a relatively new school of thought and has yet to *hit the press*. Though there is much in print on New Covenant Theology, there is no definitive work, as of yet. *Third*, one major adherent of New Covenant Theology has recently acknowledged that he will have to modify his understanding of the Old Covenant and revise some of his published works.[6]

Stepchildren (Grand Rapids: Eerdmans, 1964), 38.

[5] Jack Cottrell, "Baptism in the Reformed Tradition," in David W. Fletcher, ed., *Baptism and the Remission of Sins* (Joplin, Missouri: College Press, 1990), 50. Cottrell's chapter is based on his Princeton Seminary doctoral dissertation, *Covenant and Baptism in the Theology of Huldreich Zwingli* (1971).

[6] Barcellos, op. cit., [in preface.] Barcellos does not identify the person he mentions in the third point. But given the other two points he has made, this kind of "modification" will be going on for

This analysis is right on target. It is too soon to know how these difficulties will be reconciled, but if NCT proves to be a viable understanding of the Scriptures, the work could well extend into the period beyond our lifetimes.

The other set of difficulties are connected directly with the subject, the New Covenant. In a perceptive article, the late Carl Hoch listed nine such difficulties that bear on all sides in this discussion, making self-satisfaction by any of us a dangerous attitude indeed.[7] Among those he mentions are the lack of a fully systematic treatment of the New Covenant in the pages of Scripture, no agreed upon definition for the word "new" in the phrase "New Covenant," and the shortage of texts on the New Covenant in the NT.

Let us mention some others. The word "covenant" itself has been subject to shifts in understanding over the centuries. Some have taken it to mean a contract between God and man; others have vigorously denied this, claiming that God has nothing to do with conditions that man must fulfill. Still others, on firmer grounds, we believe, have described it in the following way:

> What then is a covenant? How do you define the covenantal relation of God to his people?
> A covenant is a *bond in blood sovereignly administered.* When God enters into a covenantal relationship with men, he sovereignly institutes a life-and-death bond. A covenant is a bond in blood, or a bond of life and death, sovereignly administered.[8]

---

a long time to come.

[7] Carl B. Hoch, Jr., "The New Covenant: Its Problems, Certainties and Some Proposals" in *Reformation and Revival Journal* 6, no. 3 (summer 1997): 55-60.

[8] O. Palmer Robertson, *The Christ of the Covenants* (Phillipsburg, NJ: Presbyterian and Reformed, 1980), 4.

Preface

At first glance this may look like a contract definition, but it is not. It avoids both the contract and the unilateral ideas by the words *sovereignly administered*. The point is that a covenant given by God is *imposed* on men. It is entirely from God. Men have no part in any negotiation over it, but it contains stipulations about their conduct and it may also include penalties for disobedience. We may illustrate this by a situation that often arose in ancient warfare. A king would invade another country and completely defeat its armies. This created a situation where negotiating was out of the question, but a covenant was not. The victorious king would determine on his own to protect and defend the conquered people, on the condition that they remained faithful to him. In making this covenant demand he did not ask what they thought of it. He imposed it on them, and that was that!

Still another difficulty arises from a difficulty in theological English. The question of the relations between the Old and New Covenants is a question of continuity and discontinuity, that is, a question of degrees. But theology has no agreed upon way of describing degrees of continuity and discontinuity, nor do we have any proposal to make. The effect of this has been irritation all around. A reader has to guess what degree is meant when a writer says, "I want to emphasize continuity," or "I want to underscore discontinuity." These words have become so contentious that the reader may easily let his own prejudices, rather than context, decide the issue. All of this is further complicated by hyperbole, as when someone exclaims, "The New Covenant has *infinitely higher standards* than the Old." (Just to put the reader at ease, this is not a quotation from anyone! It simply displays the problem.)

Finally, these relations have been complicated by the many meanings the word *law* may have in Scripture. Each time men have written on this subject they have hoped and presumably believed that they have avoided this pitfall. If memory serves us correctly, Richard Barcellos has navigated around this peril pretty well. We would like to think that we have done the same.

CHAPTER 1

The Christian Appeal of a New Covenant Theology

Tom Wells

In the preface we listed five reasons why a discussion of NCT seems appropriate. I want to explore these, one by one, so that the reader will be clear as to what we mean.

The NT as the Apex of God's Revelation

Few Christians, I think, will question the fact that in the NT we have the latest (and, indeed, the final) essential revelation of God for the church age, the age in which we live.[9] This would seem to be common property among us, even for those Charismatics who contend for present revelation in some subsidiary sense. Like all convictions, this one has practical ramifications that must be faced. The critical point here is this: NT revelation, due to its finality, must be allowed to speak first on every issue that it addresses. This point, of course, is a logical

---

[9] This statement assumes that there is such a thing as *progressive revelation*, not simply in the sense that some revelation is earlier in time than other revelation. That is, of course, a truism. No one argues that Genesis and Romans were written at the same time. The assumption here is that *there is advance in revelation* as well as an accumulation of sources. To think otherwise would be to treat the Bible as a systematic theology book, with each part equally valid at all times. Again, virtually all Christians agree to this.

point. No one sins by starting his or her Bible education by reading Genesis, Exodus, etc. first. Nevertheless, the NT holds logical priority over the rest in determining theological questions upon which it speaks.

We may see how that works out in practice by a number of illustrations. First, it has been traditional among churches descended from Anabaptism to be *peace churches*. They have opposed war on various grounds and have acted on their convictions. It is patent, however, that if they had read the OT first, that is, given it logical priority, they could have never arrived at their pacifist convictions. Why? Because the Lord clearly commanded Israel to fight. More than that, those fights were not mere defensive battles. God commanded Israel to virtually destroy the Canaanites completely. The exceptions authorized by God, like Rahab and her family, are so few that they are statistically insignificant. I use this illustration because I am not at all sure that the Anabaptist conclusion is correct, and therefore I have no axe to grind in the matter. My stance against Anabaptism here, however, allows me to make two vital points. First, the Anabaptists were absolutely right in settling this question on NT grounds. Second, if I disagree, as I do, my disagreement has also to be on NT grounds. I must conclude that they have not taken into consideration everything that the NT says on this subject. Only if they opposed warfare *absolutely and at all times* could I call in the OT. In that case I could show their basic principle to be wrong, but I could not say that their conclusion was unsound without NT evidence, if in fact the NT spoke on the subject.

As radical and as dismissive of the OT as all this sounds, all Christians must see at once that it is correct. Why? Because all Christians recognize that the Lord Jesus could have commanded his people, if he had wanted to, to abstain from all warfare. As long as he did not ground his demand in the position that all warfare *at any time in history* has been and is wrong, the full inspiration of the OT would remain intact. The logical priority of the NT, however, would settle the question for us. We must read the NT first.

Let us take another illustration. What will happen if we start at Genesis and build our doctrine of the people of God from consecutive reading of the OT? Among other things, we will have a pretty thorough and extensive idea of who the people of God are, long before we come to the NT. The people of God is Israel, the physical descendants of Jacob and, before him, Abraham. Even if our eyes were more open to spiritual realities than were the eyes of the Jews in Jesus' day, I suspect we would show little more comprehension of the breadth of the phrase "children of Abraham" than the disciples did, not only before Pentecost but even afterward. We very likely would have shared the astonishment of the disciples, who as late as chapter eleven of Acts say, "So then, God has granted even the Gentiles repentance unto life" (11:18).

What would be the consequences of this reading? Let me mention some. We might easily assume that since there is one people of God, God would only have one covenant with them and one sign of that covenant, circumcision. When we arrived at the Major Prophets, if we were particularly perceptive, we might make some small adjustments. Of course the NT, when we came to it, would change our convictions on these matters, but we would have a predisposition to find as little change as possible. After all, we know there is one people, one covenant and one covenant sign.

Some of you will recognize that while the above illustration is necessarily simplified, it represents the point of view usually called "Covenant Theology." Try to look at it sympathetically for a moment, even if it does not represent your own convictions. If you do not do so, the following discussion will seem to be a parody, and I do not intend it that way, at all. What would you do with the truth you felt you had learned from the OT? Here is one possible scenario. First, though the people of God is clearly Israel, you would have to make room for Gentiles within that people. There is, indeed, much in the

NT that might seem to support your view.[10] Second, you would have to wrestle with the one-covenant idea in the face of your previous conviction. You could take one of two options: you could rename your one covenant by calling it something else, or you could rename the two covenants so prominent in the NT. You might call these covenants mentioned in the NT *administrations* of the one covenant. This would tend to keep the changes forced on you by the NT to a minimum.

Finally, you would have to deal with the covenant sign you learned from the OT. Clearly circumcision must go. That is one thing that is explicit in the NT. What could you do under these circumstances? One possibility would be to insist that circumcision and baptism are virtually the same thing. In these ways you would preserve the understanding you received by reading the OT.

Now let me repeat something I have already said: the above explanation is not intended to be a parody. More than that, I do not even mean to disapprove of it and reject it at this point. It was not given for that purpose, but rather to show how someone who read the Bible and gave the OT logical priority might reason. Given the premise that the OT must be given logical priority, the steps I have outlined are not in themselves unreasonable. Perhaps that is the reason the *Geneva Study Bible* has its major article on baptism at Genesis 17.

Suppose, however, you read the NT first, that is, giving it logical priority. In that case you might draw very different conclusions. For instance, you might conclude that there is not, in fact, only one covenant, but two that are particularly

---

[10] I mean the sentence I have just written quite seriously. I do want to mention, however, that Romans 9:6b is not such a verse. Many have read in the KJV, "For they are not all Israel, which are of Israel," and thought they heard an assertion that Israel takes in more than Jews. The NIV has correctly caught the meaning, "For not all who are descended from Israel are Israel." In this verse Paul is excluding some Jews from Israel, not including some Gentiles.

prominent, the Old and the New. You might also conclude that there are two groups called the people of God, Israel and the church. You might decide further that they stand in typical relation to one another. In that way you would account for the large number of names and images that they share in common. Finally, you might decide that since there are two covenants, they have distinct signs.

We can make the same point in discussing the vexing question of whether Sabbath law still applies to Christians. Let us suppose again that we start our investigation of this question in Genesis. Almost immediately we meet Sabbath-like language in Genesis 2:2,3 where we read, "[O]n the seventh day he rested from all his work. And God blessed the seventh day and made it holy." In Exodus we will see the Sabbath laid on Israel and included in the Ten Commandments. Beyond that, we will find that the entire OT bears witness to the necessity of Sabbath observance, often by recording Israel's failure to obey God. There can be no doubt that God is serious about Sabbath observance. By the time, then, that we come to the NT we may very well have a predisposition toward Sabbath observance, and who could blame us?

What will happen if we come to the NT first on this subject? (Remember that by *first* I mean "giving it logical priority.") For many of us who have done this, a hypothetical reconstruction of our observations runs along the following lines.[11] We have seen that Jesus, as a Jew living under the full Mosaic law, kept the Sabbath. In addition we have seen his claim to be "Lord of the Sabbath," a claim that would allow him to introduce some kind of change in it or even to abolish it. We simply could not say, at this point, what he might do. In

---

[11] I use the phrase "hypothetical reconstruction" for two reasons. First, when a position has arisen in our minds from extensive and complex evidence, it is impossible to trace how all the details fell into place. Second, what we can be sure of, however, is that the process was not as neat and tidy as these reconstructions are!

finishing the Gospels, we notice Christ meeting with his disciples on the first day of the week. In Acts, we observe that the seventh day is again prominent (13:14, 44; 16:13; 17:2; 18:4), though the disciples once met on the first day (20:7). None of this gives us a solid foundation for a decision. We obtained a hint about practice, but hardly about theory from 1 Corinthians 16:2 and Revelation 1:10. Hebrews 4:1-11 looked more promising but more difficult.

Then we came to Paul's direct teaching about the keeping of days (Rom. 14:5-6; Gal. 4:10; Col 2:16-17). Here we felt we were on firm ground. Listen to him as he makes two points to the Roman Christians. Here is the first: "One man considers one day more sacred than another; another man considers every day alike. Each one should be fully convinced in his own mind." What does Paul mean? It seemed to us he was saying that the question of keeping days is a matter of indifference. Indeed there was no other way to take his words. We agreed with John Murray long before we read his comment:

> The person who esteems every day alike, that is, does not regard particular days as having peculiar religious significance, is recognized by the apostle as rightfully entertaining this position. This could not be the case if the distinction of days were a matter of divine obligation. Hence it is the person esteeming one day above another who is weak in faith: *he has not yet understood the implications of the transition from the old economy to the new* (Rom. 14:5).[12]

---

[12] John Murray, *NIC: The Epistle to the Romans* (Grand Rapids, Eerdmans, 1965), 2:178 (emphasis added). In an appendix, pp. 257ff., Murray maintains that this has nothing to do with the Jewish or Seventh-Day Sabbath, but Sam Waldron has shown that Murray is mistaken in that matter. It is a pleasure to commend Waldron's book, *The Lord's Day* (Grand Rapids, Time for Eternity, n.d.) for an even-handed treatment of the subject, a good grasp on the literature, and the cautious way he finally draws his conclusion. It will

The second point Paul makes is this: "He who regards one day as special, does so to the Lord." (Rom. 14:6). We concluded that Paul's concern for Christians was not "days" but motivation. This conviction grew as we heard him criticize the Galatians in still stronger terms: "You are observing special days and months and seasons and years! I fear for you, that somehow I have wasted my efforts on you" (Gal. 4:10-11). We decided to accept Paul's advice (command?) in Colossians 2:16, "Do not let anyone judge you by what you eat or drink, or with regard to a religious festival, a New Moon or a Sabbath day." We accepted his apparent reason: "These are a shadow of the things that were to come; the reality, however, is found in Christ" (Col. 2:17). Again, the point is not that you accept this reconstruction as your own.[13] As with the other reconstructions in this chapter, the point is to show that it is not unreasonable in itself.

While it will not be hard for you to decide which of these scenarios I prefer, that is *not* the focus of this discussion. Rather it is this: the large amount of baggage (presuppositions) that any of us bring to the Scriptures depends in large measure on which part of Scripture we, subconsciously no doubt, read first, or treat as logically prior. And here, it seems to me, is the danger. If the process really has been subconscious, it may very well be controlled by the systematic theologies that we admire or by the creeds and confessions to which we adhere, or by other sources of prejudice on our part, *without our ever realizing what is happening*. That might be all right, if we genuinely have a predisposition to let the NT control our thinking, though even then it would be better to discern what we are doing. But

---

be clear, of course, that we do not agree. He finally comes down on the "Christian Sabbatarian" side. His discussion of Murray is on p. 58.

[13] The Sabbath question is treated by Fred Zaspel at length in chapter 13 and by myself in chapter 14.

if we are working from the premise of the priority of the OT, we are certain to go astray. That is why I think we must certainly read the rest of Scripture in the light of the apex of revelation, which is the NT. Read it all we must! But which testament controls our thinking and which we use for fine-tuning is the all-important consideration.

The Far-reaching Implications of our Slavery to Jesus Christ.

One of the common titles given to Christians in the Greek NT is the title "slaves."[14] It had its roots in the ancient world where captives of war became chattel and monarchs were absolute rulers with everyone else fully subject to them. Such subjection might be a token of honor when a man was singled out for high responsibilities in the kingdom. Nevertheless the idea of utter subjection remained. This is nicely illustrated in the case of Haman in the book of Esther. One minute he held "a seat of honor higher than that of all the other nobles" (3:1) in Xerxes' kingdom. The next minute he was on the way to the gallows (7:1-10). No trial intervened. None was necessary. He was Xerxes' slave to do with as Xerxes pleased.

---

[14] Many English versions translate the Greek word for slave(s) as "servant(s)." I cannot account for this, except out of fear of overemphasizing the baseness and contempt connected with slavery in the Roman empire, or, perhaps, of contradicting the Lord Jesus in John 15:15, "I no longer call you [slaves]. . . . Instead, I have called you friends, . . ." If that is its source, it is reductionistic, treating a complex relationship as if it were simple. In the same context Jesus said, "You are my friends if you do what I command" (15:14)! That would be a strange basis for simple friendship. In any case, the word means *slave*. "The meaning is so unequivocal and self-contained that it is superfluous . . . to trace the history of the group" (*TDNT*, s.v. "slave.").

The counterpart to the slave was the *master*. In the Bible, various words indicate this position in society including master, lord or king. These words are applied both to God and to the Lord Jesus in relation to mankind. God and Christ are looked upon as slave-holders or slave-masters, demanding submission from their subjects. Both have the power of life and death, including eternal death, over all persons without exception. There is no higher court of appeal from their decisions. In the words of Paul, "One of you will say to me: 'Then why does God still blame us? For who resists his will?' But who are you, O man, to talk back to God?" (Rom. 9:19-20a). Every attempt to "go over" God's head must fail! These facts are the common property of Christians.

Beyond this we see, first, with reference to the Lord Jesus, the special claim which he has on Christians by virtue of his death on their behalf. It is true that Christ has become the Lord of all men, but that is not Paul's point in Romans 14. In Paul's words, "For this very reason, Christ died and returned to life so that he might be the Lord of both the living and the dead" (Rom. 14:9). The "living and the dead" here are Christians, as the previous context (14:5-8) shows, especially in the description of men's motives in v.6 and by the assurance that his servants will stand (i.e., in judgment) in v.4. Of course this does not mean that God the Father's claim to lordship over believers is in any way compromised. In keeping with the Lord Jesus acting as his agent, God exercises his authority through him.

Second, Paul teaches that Christ's dying and rising were for the purpose of establishing a *master/slave relation* between him and his people. If we feel inclined to judge fellow believers, Paul has a word for us: "Who are you to judge someone else's servant? To his own master he stands or falls" (v.4). The word "servant" here was the common word for "household slave" in the Roman world of Paul's day. But this slave has a *Lord* who died to purchase him (v.9). As the NIV says, "For this very reason" (v.9) Christ died.[15]

Third, without supposing that a figure must dictate every detail of the object it signifies, it is clear that taking orders from Christ is a major component in the frequent use of master/slave language in discussing the relation of Christ to his people. In Paul, for instance, we meet the exhortation as free men to think of ourselves as Christ's slaves (1 Cor. 7:22-23). Literal slaves were to remember that they are serving Christ as *his* slaves first of all (Eph. 6:5-8; Col. 3:22-24). Paul, though an apostle, reminded his readers that he and his associates were nothing less than slaves to Jesus Christ (Rom. 1:1; Gal. 1:10; Phil. 1:1; Col. 4:12; 2 Tim. 2:24; Tit. 1:1). English translations often obscure the force of these texts by translating this slave-language as though it spoke only of service and servants.[16] But that is not

---

[15] Commentators have debated who the master is in verse 4, whether God or Christ. See C.E.B. Cranfield, *ICC: The Epistle to the Romans* (Edinburgh, T. & T. Clark, repr. 1981), 2: 702. I have taken it as Christ because (1) Christ's death is said to be for the purpose of establishing such a lordship, (2) Paul normally has Christ in mind when he uses the word "Lord" as he does in vv. 6-9, (3) there seems to be a studied comparison between God and Christ in v.6, and (4) we meet the idea of the master/slave relation between Christ and the Christian again in v.18.

[16] *BAGD*, after translating "doulos" as "slave," makes a note of this phenomenon: " 'servant' for 'slave' is largely confined to Biblical trans[lation] and early American times." *BAGD*, s.v. "doulos." *TDNT* says of "doulos" and its cognates, "All the words in this group serve either to describe the status of a slave or an attitude corresponding to that of a slave. . . . The meaning is so unequivocal and self-contained that it is superfluous to give examples . . ." *TDNT* s.v. "slave." In the NT, however, the idea of contempt of slaves and slavery is absent.

the case. As Rengstorf has written,

> Hence we have a service which is not a matter of choice for the one who renders it, which he has to perform whether he likes it or not, because he is subject to an alien will, to the will of his owner.[17]

While Jesus Christ removes the harshness of this subjection, the central point remains: a Christian is subject to the will of his owner, the Lord Jesus Christ.

This, of course, is what constitutes the Lord Jesus as a law-giver to his people. The slave owner in the Roman Empire was the sole individual law-giver to his slaves. We see this idea reflected as the NT develops Christ's lordship in various ways. Let's look at one example.

In the account of the transfiguration, we find Peter, James, and John with Jesus on the mount when Moses and Elijah appear to speak with him (Mark. 9:2-8). Peter, apparently wanting to allot the luster of the occasion equally among the three major figures, suggests the erection of three tents in their honor. But he is rebuked by God himself with the words, "This is my Son, whom I love. Listen to him!" (v.7). Peter must do what Jesus says. He was already, as he would later acknowledge, a slave of Jesus Christ (2 Pet. 1:1; cf. 1 Pet 2:16). The two Greek words translated "Listen to him!" make this point to all Israel. They reflect the LXX translation of Deuteronomy 18:15, where Moses says, "The Lord your God will raise up for you a prophet like me from among your brothers. *You must listen to him.*" What will Jesus say? The story contains no further word from the Lord Jesus on the Mount. That was not the point. Instead, the Father's statement was all-encompassing; from now on, listen to my Son. Even Moses and the Prophets must stand mute in his presence.

---

[17] *TDNT*, s.v. "slave."

Following the Highest Revelation of the Moral Character of God

In the preface we posed a question: Which is the higher revelation of the character of God, the Ten Commandments or the person, work and teaching of Jesus Christ? The question assumes two things, that the Ten Commandments do, in fact, reveal the character of God, and that it should not be hard for the Christian to make up his mind what to answer. The Lord Jesus, after all, gives us the answer in the enormous claim of John 14. In response to Philip's challenge, "Lord, show us the Father and that will be enough for us," Jesus said, "Don't you know me, Philip, even after I have been among you such a long time? *Anyone who has seen me has seen the Father*" (14:8-9).

In addition, due to continued exposure to Jesus, Philip himself betrays a slight understanding of the answer even before he receives it. He takes the Lord Jesus as one who *could* show them the Father. Think how ridiculous this request would be if it were addressed to me! Yet Philip feels no hesitation in addressing it to Jesus. It does not occur to him to ask what portion of Scripture he should look in to find the Father (though the OT is filled with him). Nor does it occur to Jesus to answer in that way. "Look at me!", he says. "That's where you will see the Father!"

As plain as this is, we have to ask a further question. In speaking as he did, was Jesus thinking primarily of the revelation of God's moral character? The statement might well mean, " if you look at me you will see everything about the Father." A moment's thought, however, will show that if that is what he meant, we will have to include his works and his teaching along with his person. Looking at Jesus would not teach the Father's omnipresence, for instance, nor his infinite power. When one looked at Jesus, he would see preeminently the moral character of God in a way that not even the Ten Commandments could convey. This does not denigrate the OT in any way. It simply recognizes that the Lord Jesus is the embodiment of God's character at the pinnacle of revelatory history.

Second, did his work and his teaching, as well as his person, present moral revelation from God? It did. To take his work first, we find in the sacrificial death of the Lord Jesus the highest possible revelation of the love of God. Look at the following words of Christ: "Greater love has no one than this, that he lay down his life for his friends" (John 15:13). Here, then, we are at the height of love as Jesus intimates what he is about to do for his followers. But is this love *his* love alone? Hardly! It is his Father's love that he shows to his disciples. It was God[18] who so loved the world that he gave his Son. It follows, then, that the work of Christ on the cross teaches by demonstration that the highest revelation of the love of God is the sacrificial death of Jesus Christ. Among God's attributes is a depth of love that has never before been seen in the world. When Christians are not thinking controversially they recognize this immediately.

Is it also a fact that the teaching of the Lord Jesus reveals more of the moral character of God than the teaching of Moses did, including the Ten Commandments? Once more, there can be no doubt about the answer. Is the greatest fact in the world the glory of God? Yes, it is. But what is God's glory? It is just himself in all his attributes, including his moral character. How can we account for the extensive teaching of the Lord Jesus, both in person and through his disciples? Here is Jesus' own explanation for his earthly ministry: "I have revealed you[19] to

---

[18] The contrast between *God* and *Son* in John 3:16 suggests that the Father is in view. If, however, God there means the Trinity, we reach the same conclusion since the Trinity includes all three persons. John 3:34-35 favors the view that *God* refers to the Father.

[19] Literally "your name." *Name* in this case stands for how God may be properly characterized. We might translate either, "I have revealed your character," or "I have revealed what you are like."

those whom you gave me out of the world" (John 17:6). Of his later teaching through his disciples he said, "As the Father has sent me, I am sending you" (John 20:21). What does that mean? Among other things it means that the disciples continued his teaching. Paul writes of his own commandment, "If anybody thinks he is a prophet or spiritually gifted, let him acknowledge that what I am writing to you is the Lord's command" (1 Cor. 14:37). And what was Paul's gospel ministry? It was the revelation, in part, of the glory of God in the face of Jesus Christ (2 Cor. 4:1-6). The glory of God in the face of Christ was his moral glory above all else, the same glory in fact that Jesus himself revealed in his public ministry, now expanded by additional moral and spiritual revelation. It is no longer fashionable to pit Paul against the historical Jesus. Instead we see the writing disciples as penmen who reflected the glory of Christ that came to them in person and by revelation. They did this, not only by descriptions of his person and work, but also by the commands they issued in his name.

The Impact of Biblical Theology[20]

When we speak of biblical theology, what do we mean? Robert Yarbrough has offered this brief definition: Biblical theology is the study "of the Bible that seeks to discover what the biblical writers, under divine guidance, believed, described, and taught in the context of their own times."[21]

---

[20] A large number of ideas and movements have gone under the name "Biblical Theology." For a brief, slightly older survey, see *A Dictionary of Christian Theology*, s.v. "Biblical Theology." Fuller, more recent discussions are in *Evangelical Dictionary of Biblical Theology*, s.v. "Biblical Theology" and *Dictionary of the Later New Testament and Its Developments*, s.v. "New Testament Theology."

[21] *Evangelical Dictionary of Biblical Theology*, s.v. "Biblical

The definition includes the following assumptions. First, it makes clear that such study deals with the inspired biblical texts.[22] Second, it assumes that the biblical author has his own presuppositions—theology even—that he brings to the text. Third, it assumes that his work may include either description or teaching in the more formal sense, or both. (Description of course is a mode of teaching.) Finally, it assumes that the time in which the writer lives will affect the way he says what he says. For our purpose this definition is broad enough, though other things could be included.

The important thing for us to understand is that this kind of study seeks to meet a text on its own terms, *before* the necessary work of informing it by other parts of Scripture. In the hands of negative critics this has led to disaster. For example, it has set Jesus against Paul and Paul against James in ways that evacuate "inspiration" of all of its historical meaning. The problem, however, is not the method but the presuppositions of the practitioners.

The advantage of biblical theology is that, in theory at least, it holds in abeyance the impulse to systematize the Scripture. Moses did not write in Paul's time; his horizon was different. A distance is kept between them for the purpose of examining each on his own terms, much the way we like to be listened to within our own frame of reference. Biblical theology insists on the logical priority of the text in the formation of systematic theology. Texts do not exist to vindicate theologies formed without them. On the other hand, the discipline of systematizing texts is not only respectable but a necessary goal of all biblical study. In no sense must an exegete renounce systematics; he must simply avoid the impulse to *hasty*

Theology."

[22] By "texts" I refer to segments of biblical books, however large or small. In other words, I do not confine texts to single verses of Scripture.

harmonization.

How does all this bear on NCT? NCT is a fresh attempt to put the text first. This in no way implies that others do not make the same effort. Not at all! In fact, most of the positions adopted by NCT were not originated within its ranks. It does not exist because it alone holds these positions. It is made up of men who have been part of a subgroup that does not, in our opinion, take the priority of the text as seriously as it might. We harbor no malice toward those in that subgroup. They are our brothers and, in many cases, our personal friends. As sinners we also share the very failings which we cry out against. (The illusion of utter objectivity has been put to rest in this century and we are glad to mark its grave.)

We do have a decided goal, however. It is to join together three things: the logical priority of the NT over the Old, the logical priority of Lord Jesus over his godly predecessors, and the logical priority of the theology of the text over our own theologies and those of others. In theory almost all Christians share this goal. May God make all of us its practitioners!

NCT and Church History

In one of the ironies of our age, those who espouse NCT find themselves joining a chorus that extends through two millennia. In opposition to the idea of a single covenant that runs through history, most Christians have seen the history of redemption centering around two major covenants: the Old and the New. Consider the following from a "hostile" witness:

> In Christian theology generally the new covenant has been identified with the Christian dispensation, the religiohistorical economy introduced by Christ and the apostles. Accordingly, it is the fulfillment of the promises of the old covenant and is better by degrees than that former covenant . . . . A better solution is to forsake altogether the religiohistorical

identifications of the two covenants. Jeremiah's prophecy of a new covenant is a prophecy of the ultimate consummation of the kingdom of God, and in Paul and Hebrews the contrast between the old covenant and the new covenant has to do not with relative distinctions between the two dispensations of God's covenant of grace succeeding one another in time but with the radical antithesis of two subjective situations: the formalism, legalism, unbelief, and death of ancient Israel on the one hand and genuine experience of salvation by all believers on the other.[23]

The quotation shows the novelty of thorough-going Covenant Theology in the broad perspective of church history.[24] It implies that even among those who have followed it many have not applied their own doctrine correctly.

Early church history bears out Rayburn's contention that the contrast between the Old and New Covenants as consecutive dispensations has been the center of attention. Some illustrations follow, the first from Irenaeus of Lyons (c.130-c.202).

[Jesus] means by those things which are brought forth from the treasure new and old, the two covenants; the old, that giving of the

---

[23] *Evangelical Dictionary of Theology*, s.v. "Covenant, The New." I included the first part of the quotation to make my central point. The rest of it shows why I called Rayburn a "hostile" witness. He strongly disagrees with what he admits has been a majority opinion historically.

[24] This is not to deny that some elements of Covenant Theology are quite old and biblical. For instance, it was early recognized that all who would ever be saved would have to be saved by the blood (sacrificial death) shed under the New Covenant. Augustine takes the New Covenant to be the subject of Galatians 3:17 (*Two Letters against Pelagius*, 3.7-8). At least in this passage he does not recognize the fact of an Abrahamic covenant and, so, blends the Abrahamic and New covenants into one. The same confusion appears in many of the Fathers, and there is no question that those two covenants stand in close connection to one another.

law which took place formerly; and He points out as the new, that manner of life required by the Gospel. . . . And Jeremiah says: "Behold I will make a new covenant, not as I made with your fathers" in Mount Horeb. But one and the same householder produced both covenants, the Word of God, our Lord Jesus Christ, who spake with both Abraham and Moses, and who has restored us anew to liberty. . . .[25]

Note in the next quotation how two covenants are assumed even though Abraham is mentioned.

[Abraham] was made the chief and the forerunner of our faith (who did also receive the covenant of circumcision, after that justification by faith which had pertained to him, when he was yet in uncircumcision, so that in him both covenants might be prefigured, that he might be the father of all who follow the Word of God, and who sustain a life of pilgrimage in this world, that is, of those who from among the circumcision and of those from among the uncircumcision are faithful, even as also "Christ is the chief cornerstone" sustaining all things); and He gathered into the one faith of Abraham those who, from either covenant, are eligible for God's building.[26]

Two things stand out here. First, the presence of only two covenants of importance, and second, the fact that both covenants supply living stones to Christ.

---

[25] Irenaeus *Against Heresies* 4.9.1. Note how Abraham and Moses are apparently both treated as members of the Old Covenant and how the last sentence illustrates the temporal succession of the covenants.

[26] Ibid., 25.1. Note the assumption throughout that everything turns on two covenants. In the mind of the writer the covenant of circumcision blended with the Mosaic Covenant so that he could speak of "both covenants" and "either covenant" meaning the Old and the New. He later writes, "For although Abraham was one, he did in himself prefigure the two covenants . . ." (25.3).

Irenaeus also writes of Samson's destruction of the Philistine temple, "Moreover, the two pillars are the two covenants. The fact, then, of Samson leaning himself upon the two pillars, [indicates] this, that the people, when instructed, recognized the mystery of Christ."[27] Here again we see illustrated the idea of two and only two covenants that play a prominent role in history. We, of course, recognize other covenants, but the point remains: in early church history redemption is chiefly organized around the Mosaic and New Covenants in the eyes of exegetes.

Origen (c.185-c.254) alludes to Ephesians 2:12 which speaks of those who were "excluded from the citizenship in Israel and foreigners to the covenants of the promise." He describes these people as "strangers to the covenants of God given by Moses and by our Savior Jesus, and who have no part in the promises which He has made through them." In saying this, he seems to limit the covenants referred to in the Ephesians verse to two, the Mosaic and the New Covenants.[28] He may well have known of other covenants, but he is silent about them.

Augustine (354-430) recognizes that there are additional covenants in Scripture besides the Old and New. Yet he distinguishes the two in this way: "Now there are many things called God's covenants besides *those two great ones, the old and the new*, which any one who pleases may read and know."[29] His emphasis here is clearly apparent. The Old and the New Covenants must get our attention.

One more quotation from Augustine makes the same point. Referring apparently to Romans 9:4, he says, "And why are the covenants said to belong especially to the Israelites, but because not only was the Old Testament given to them, but also the

---

[27] Irenaeus *Fragments from the Lost Writings* number 27.

[28] Origen *Against Celsus* 8.5.

[29] Aurelius Augustine *City of God* 16.27.

New was prefigured in the Old?"[30] Here again Augustine confines the chief covenants of the Scripture to the Old and New Covenants by apparently exhausting the reference to the covenants that belong to the Israelites by citing these two.

Terminology changes with the passage of centuries. When we come to the medieval period we find frequent reference to the *Old* and *New Law* rather than the Old and New Covenants, and that continued in the Roman Catholic church into this century. Thomas Aquinas (c.1227-1274) illustrates this usage in the following:

> [I]t was fitting that the perfect law of the New Testament should be given immediately [i.e. by God himself]; but that the Old Law should be given to men by the ministers of God, *i.e.*, by the angels. It is thus that the Apostle at the beginning of his epistle to the *Hebrews* (i.2) proves the excellence of the New Law over the Old; because in the New Testament *God hath spoken to us by His Son*, whereas in the Old Testament *the word* was *spoken by angels* (ii. 2).[31]

Here we see Aquinas using various terms to convey the point that the Old or Mosaic Covenant has passed away and the New Covenant has come. He expresses this contrast by contrasting the New Law to the Old, that is, as he shows us in the last sentence, the more recent word of Christ in the New Covenant to the words spoken by angels, a reference to the

---

[30] Aurelius Augustine *Reply to Faustus the Manichaean* 12.3 (italics added). Here the word *Testament* stands instead of *Covenant*. This reminds us that the two segments of the Bible have their names from the presumed importance of the two covenants.

[31] Thomas Aquinas *Summa Theologica*, first part of the second part, 13, ques. 98, art. 3.

Mosaic Covenant.[32]

The Catholic Encyclopedia (1910 edition) illustrates how this language to distinguish the covenants has lasted for almost one thousand years.

> Divine law is that which is enacted by God and made known to man through revelation. We distinguish between the Old Law, contained in the Pentateuch, and the New Law, which was revealed by Jesus Christ and is contained in the New Testament. . . . Christ is the author of the New Law. He claimed and exercised supreme legislative authority in spiritual matters from the beginning of His public life until His Ascension into heaven. In Him the Old Law had its fulfilment and attained its chief purpose. . . . By the death of Christ on the Cross the New Testament was sealed and the Old was abrogated. . . .[33]

When we come to the Reformation period the Spiritualists and the Anabaptists[34] show the same interest in focusing on the distinction between the Old and New Covenants. Here is Spiritualist Sebastian Franck (1499-1543) bringing a charge against both the church fathers and "their descendants," that is, the Catholics and the Reformers!

---

[32] Aquinas does not say that the word spoken by Christ *is* the New Covenant, but that certainly is the intention of the author of Hebrews and, so presumably, of Aquinas as well.

[33] *The Catholic Encyclopedia*, 1910 ed., s.v. "Law, Divine, Moral Aspect of." In the same article, "The Divine Law of the Old Testament" is identified as "the Mosaic Law."

[34] Twentieth century scholarship has made important distinctions between these two groups (along with the Rationalist group). The Anabaptist churches, with two notable exceptions, had no political ambitions beyond freedom for themselves and all others to worship as each group pleased.

They mix the New Testament with the Old, as also today their descendants do. And when they have nothing with which to defend their purposes, they run at once to the empty quiver, that is, to the Old Testament, and from it prove [the legitimacy of] war, oath, government, power of magistracy, tithes, priesthood; and praise everything and ascribe this all forcibly to Christ without his will.[35]

Here it is clear that in the mind of the Spiritualist Franck, the burning issue of the day was the fact that the New Covenant had replaced the Old and neither of the major sides seemed to have noticed!

The Anabaptist, Pilgram Marpeck (?-1556) showed his sentiments on the centrality of the distinction between the Old and New Covenants in a debate with the Spiritualist, Caspar Schwenkfeld (1489-1561). George Williams has described the controversy which centered on baptism in the following words:

> For the exponent of baptismal theology [i.e., Marpeck], with its stress upon the new covenant in Christ, the Old and the New Testaments could not be taken as equally authoritative.[36] For the exponent of Eucharistic theology, Schwenkfeld, the celestial Christ was present to the worthies ("fathers") of the Old Covenant no less than to the saints of the New Covenant. . . . Schwenkfeld asserted that Abraham was "a Christian" before he was circumcised a Jew.

---

[35] Sebastian Franck, *A Letter to John Campanus*, quoted in *Spiritual and Anabaptist Writers*, ed. George H. Williams and Angel M. Mergal., (Phila., Westminster, 1957), 151. By the time Franck wrote this in 1531 [1541?] he had abandoned all churches.

[36] Williams does not represent Marpeck as not believing that the OT was the word of God, but as holding that the NT was *the* governing authority for the Christian. The Anabaptists held to the same canon as the Reformers, though they understood its bearing on Christians differently.

> For Marpeck, Abraham and the Old Testament worthies had only the promise of Christ, and hence even circumcision had only a promissory meaning. Marpeck held that there was a considerable difference between the promissory (*zukünftig*) faith of yesterday of the Old Testament worthies and the present (*heutig*) faith of today of the Christian.[37]

If the idea of Abraham as "a Jew" seems strange, it no doubt shows again how the Abrahamic and Mosaic Covenants were lumped together in the mind of the Spiritualist Schwenkfeld, as they were elsewhere. Marpeck probably held the same view, but he is concerned to identify himself with the other Anabaptists who, "while holding to the Bible as the Word of God, made the New Testament alone normative for the Christian life."[38]

> Marpeck's interpretation of the Bible, like that of the Swiss Brethren, The [sic] Hutterites, and the Mennonites, was Christocentric. Revelation was viewed as progressive and partial before Christ. Only in Christ is the revelation of God complete. Thus, the New Testament alone became the rule of faith and practice for the Anabaptists. Marpeck saw all sorts of dire consequences for Christendom in the failure to interpret the Old Testament properly. The Münsterites as well as Calvin were to be blamed in this regard. They had mistaken the foundation of the house for the house itself. They had based their theocracies on a revelation which was only preparatory and never intended to be final. Marpeck was followed by a host of Anabaptists in this, his most creative

---

[37] George H. Williams, *The Radical Reformation* (Phila.: Westminster, 1962), 472.

[38] William R. Estep, *The Anabaptist Story* (Grand Rapids: Eerdmans, rev. 1975), 142.

contribution to Anabaptist theology.[39]

In reviewing the Anabaptist thought on Scripture, we see its kinship with what has come to be called "biblical theology." That does not mean that they were fully successful in understanding the relations between the Old and New Covenants, but they appear to have headed themselves in the right direction. Not only that, they tried to steer their adversaries into the same stream. There they failed. Whether anyone noticed or not, they adopted the Reformation slogan *sola scriptura* and took it more seriously than their opponents, but traditional ways of doing theology won the day. Precisely for this reason, the preoccupation with the differences between the Old and New Covenants that we have seen prior to the Reformation failed to bear fruit. Instead, a theology that minimized this distinction was developed and cast a shadow over the priority of the NT and New Covenant that has lasted to our day.

Luther laid the groundwork for this misunderstanding by his definitions of law and gospel as demand and promise respectively. If law equals demand and gospel equals promise, then all ideas of sequence or succession between the law covenant and the gospel covenant are ruled out a priori.[40] In the words of Gerhard Ebeling,

> For surely, when we turn from the Reformers' doctrine of law and Gospel to Paul, the most striking difference is, that the successive elements in a unique transition which can never

---

[39] Ibid., 143. Estep's entire discussion of the Anabaptists and Scripture on pages 140-144 is well worth reading.

[40] An interesting sidelight on this misunderstanding shows how the Lord uses all things for his glory. See Appendix One, Law and Evangelism, pp. 271-274, where I discuss the appropriateness of law preaching to the unconverted.

again be reversed are turned by the Reformers' schema into a peculiarly simultaneous conjunction, so to speak a permanently occurring transition which is suspect of not being a transition at all . . . .[41]

For Paul and the rest of the NT, *the law* is, generally speaking, the legislation and covenant that characterized the age in which God dealt primarily with Israel. The law began within history (Rom. 5:13, 20; Gal. 3:17, 19), and the law ended within history (Rom. 7:4, 6; 10:4; Gal. 3:23-25), though its "end" was a thorough transformation. That lies on the face of the NT. *The gospel of the grace of God*, on the other hand, has both succeeded and replaced the law as good news to all men everywhere. The new has come and the old has passed away.[42] Paul looks on the gospel as "promised beforehand through his prophets in the Holy Scriptures" (Rom. 1:2), plainly implying that it had not yet come in OT times. When Paul elsewhere speaks of the gospel being preached to Abraham "beforehand" (Gal. 3:8, NASB), he does not mean that what we now call *the gospel* was announced to Abraham. What Abraham received was *good news* indeed. It was the promise that was fulfilled when the age of the gospel arrived two-thousand years later. The promise described the result of gospel preaching, that is, that all nations (the Gentiles in addition to Abraham's physical descendants) "will be blessed through you" (Gal. 3:8). That was an important promise in itself. But what we now call *the gospel* or *the good news* is the means by which the good news Abraham received was finally and fully brought about.[43] "The promise to Abraham

---

[41] Gerhard Ebeling, *Word and Faith* (Phila.: Fortress, 1963), 260.

[42] See chapters 3 and 4 for the use of new/old language.

[43] John Brown of Edinburgh exactly catches this point on page 120 of *An Exposition of the Epistle to the Galatians* (Marshallton,

was an *anticipation of the Gospel*...."[44]

Since the Reformation, the Scripture text has kept pressing these facts on us, but its sharp edge has been dulled by a theology that blends law and gospel into a single "covenant of grace." Thoroughgoing Covenant Theology has held its own in paedobaptist circles, but Baptists have been torn in two directions. Having committed themselves to covenant-of-grace theology, they nevertheless have insisted that the church is made up only of believers. This looks to paedobaptists like an abandonment of covenantal truth. To other Baptists it looks like a fatal hesitation between two stools.

At this point NCT offers a return to the central concern with Old/New Covenants that we have seen in much of church history and a way out of the dead end that seems to largely ignore the discontinuity that characterizes the transition from Moses to Christ.[45]

DE: Sovereign Grace Publishers, repr. 1970) : "The phrase, 'preached the gospel beforehand,' in consequence of the very definite idea we generally attach to the word '*gospel*,' . . . does not, I am persuaded, convey distinctly the apostle's idea to most English readers. It is just equivalent to, 'made known these good tidings to Abraham long before the period when they were to be realised.'" Two things converged to mislead readers here. First was the common notion held by many prior to the twentieth century that the Bible was filled with technical terms not used as ordinary Greek speakers used them and that *gospel* was one of them. Second was the assumption that *the gospel* as we know it from the NT existed from the time of the Fall, the idea promoted by Luther and the Reformers when they made *law* and *gospel* into panhistorical ideas.

[44] J. B. Lightfoot, *The Epistle of St. Paul to the Galatians* (Grand Rapids: Zondervan, repr. 1966), 137.

[45] See Appendix Two, The Relations of the Covenants, pp. 275-280.

CHAPTER 2

A Brief History of Divine Revelation

Fred G. Zaspel

The propositions which were set forth in the previous chapter rest on the reality of a revelation from God which has been given to us with progressive clarity throughout human history and which reaches its fullest and highest point in the NT Scriptures. Let us see how this is so.

"General revelation," God's self-disclosure in creation and in providence, offers us much. We can learn from it of God's great power and Godhood, his glory, his goodness, his wisdom, his patience, even his righteous requirements of us. Since the very beginning, men and women created in the image of God have heard God speak. Although God's self-disclosure has been universally suppressed and denied in varying degrees, it has remained constant and evident and sufficient to render all of humanity guilty of conscious rebellion against its creator (Ps. 19:1-3; Rom. 1:18-21).

But as marvelous as God's general revelation is, it lacks specificity, and it lacks detail. We need something more. We are ignorant and rebellious; and so we must have more knowledge of him than is available generally through the created order and in our conscience. We desperately need to know what his law requires, and how that law can be kept. And we need desperately to know how we can find remedy for our transgressions of that law. We want to know if God will have us back. We want to know *how* he can take us back and under what terms. For all this and so much more, God's highest earthly creatures require more revelation, a further self-disclosure of God.

Graciously, he has condescended to our need. God has spoken to us "at many times and in various ways" (Heb. 1:1). The ancient prophets, his commissioned spokesmen, relayed God's word received through visions, dreams, and other methods of direct communication. "Thus says the Lord," they would announce. "The word of the Lord came to me, saying . . . ." "The spirit of the LORD spoke through me, his word was on my tongue" (2 Sam. 23:2). These men were God's own mouthpiece, and through them he made himself known to the world. Through them we hear him. The OT Scriptures have God's own imprimatur. More, they are themselves *his* word.

But God was not done—he had more to say. Esteemed though the ancient prophets were, God's fullest self-disclosure would require a still greater ambassador. Climactic revelation requires a special, unique spokesman. It requires one who is thoroughly and intimately familiar with God. Such a task can go to "no one less than God's very own Son" (Heb. 1:2[46]). He is "the brightness of his glory and the express image of his person" (Heb. 1:3) and thus is uniquely qualified for the task. Jesus Christ, the only begotten, the unique Son, is the supreme revelation of the Father (John 1:18).

It is not surprising that the Lord Jesus fulfills the prophetic office. He is uniquely qualified, and as Moses himself prophesied (Deut. 18:15-19), his word is final. "Hear him!" was the Father's own command (Matt. 17:5). It is a matter of the utmost importance that the words of God's Son be heard and heeded. He is God's final, climactic self-disclosure.

In fact, Jesus himself said that his word was the word of the

---

[46] The writer to the Hebrews expresses this thought graphically. "God has spoken to us *in his Son*." "Son" (*huiō*) here lacks the article and emphasizes the character or quality of the noun. Hence, the expanded translation given above. The sense of the statement is that in contrast to "the prophets," the one who is the very Son of God— indeed, the one who is "greater" and "more excellent" (v.4)—speaks with climactic and eclipsing significance.

Father. "My teaching is not mine but his who sent me" (John 7:16). "The word that you hear is not mine, but is from the Father who sent me" (John 14:24). "The words that you gave to me I have given to them" (John 17:8). Jesus understood himself to be God's special ambassador to the world. Accordingly, his teaching was marked by a unique authority (Matt. 7:28-29). His "You have heard that it was said . . . but I say to you" is either unthinkable blasphemy, or it is unique, divine self-disclosure. All this is to say that God has spoken climactically and most fully in his Son. We have in Jesus Christ God's fullest—indeed, his final—revelation. God's chief ambassador to the world is no less than his own Son.

But if God's climactic and final revelation was in and through his Son, how does that benefit us? What good is it to us that God spoke fully and finally two thousand years ago in another world, another culture, another language? Living at this late date, have we missed out? After all, we cannot hear him speak— he has returned to glory.

This is precisely the question which Jesus was entertaining and answering in his "Upper Room Discourse" (John 14-16). It was the night before his death, and Jesus had informed his disciples of his imminent departure. They were bothered by the announcement, of course. But interestingly, Jesus' instruction to them focused on the uniqueness of the person and ministry—the role—of the Holy Spirit. Of primary interest is his unique designation of the Third Person: he is "another helper" (*allon paraklēton*, 14:16)—a replacement, if you will, another Jesus. He will come to be for the disciples the helper Jesus had been to them. His is the continuation of the ministry of the Lord Jesus. This "replacement" idea is emphasized in the following verses. Jesus promised, "I will not leave you orphaned; I am coming to you" (14:18). This statement has been variously interpreted to refer to Jesus' resurrection or his second coming. As true as both of these interpretations are, however, they do not exhaust the significance of our Lord's promise. In context, his point seems clearly to be that he will return to them *via the Holy Spirit,* the "other helper." The Holy Spirit is the continuation of the ministry of Jesus. To date, he is the climax of our Lord's work.

These words are often taken in reference to the Holy Spirit's ministry to all the people of Christ. There is of course a great sense in which that is true. By his Spirit, we all are taught and led in the truth and in the ways of God (1 Thess. 4:9; 1 John 2:27). But Jesus' point here is much more specific than that. He is not speaking broadly of provision to all believers. He is speaking narrowly of his specific provision to his apostles, his specially commissioned ambassadors. He is providing for the continuation of his teaching ministry.

> He who does not love Me does not keep My words; and the word which you hear is not Mine but the Father's who sent Me. These things I have spoken to you while being present with you. But the Helper, the Holy Spirit, whom the Father will send in My name, He will teach you all things, and bring to your remembrance all things that I said to you. (John 14:24-26)

> I still have many things to say to you, but you cannot bear them now. However, when He, the Spirit of truth, has come, He will guide you into all truth; for He will not speak on His own authority, but whatever He hears He will speak; and He will tell you things to come. He will glorify Me, for He will take of what is Mine and declare it to you. All things that the Father has are Mine. Therefore I said that He will take of Mine and declare it to you.(John 16:12-15)

Simply put, Jesus' teaching ministry to his apostles would not end with his departure. Rather, his teaching ministry to them will continue via his replacement, the Holy Spirit, the "other helper." He is not at all saying that the Spirit will "teach every believer everything" or cause every believer to "remember everything which he said" or "guide every believer into all truth." That was not what he said, and that is not what has happened. His promise is to his apostles. This is the task for which he had called them. *They* will be taught "everything." The Holy Spirit will remind *them* of "everything" which Jesus had spoken. The Spirit will guide *them* into "all truth." This is the Spirit's role. Jesus' teaching ministry to his disciples was not complete when he died, but through his replacement, the Holy Spirit, he had provided for its continuation and completion.

There is something of a parallel here. Just as the Son had come to speak for the Father, so also the Spirit would come to speak for the Son. "He will not speak on his own"; he will speak for and of Christ. This is his great role in the history of revelation. He is commissioned to ensure that these chosen men will recall all that the Lord had taught them when he was with them, to guide them into a fuller understanding of it, and to continue that teaching until it is complete. He will give them illumination, fuller revelation, and new revelation. This "other helper" will bring the climactic revelation of the Son to its culmination.

Jesus, then, is emphasizing not only the uniqueness of the Holy Spirit, he is also stressing the uniqueness of the apostles. They are the repositories of God's full and final revelation. God has spoken fully and finally in no less than his Son. God's climactic word "was declared at first through the Lord, and it was confirmed to us by those who heard him" (Heb. 2:3).

Notice this strand of thought in Jesus's high priestly prayer:

> For I gave them the words you gave me and they have received them. As You sent Me into the world, I also have sent them into the world. I do not pray for these alone, but also for those who will believe in Me through their word. (John 17:8, 18, 20)

In other words, a very real power of attorney was given to the apostles. Equipped by the teaching of our Lord himself and via his Spirit, they were our Lord's commissioned spokesmen, his personal representatives.

It is in this sense they are referred to as the "foundation" of the church (Eph. 2:20; cf. Rev. 21:14). Perhaps if it were not for Protestant fear over the Roman Catholic abuse of Matthew 16:18, this would be the unanimous understanding of our Lord's designation of Peter as "the rock" on which he will build his church. It is truly a marvelous promise and provision. As far as the apostles were concerned, they were as weak as any other men. They were uneducated, very ordinary men. Yet they are given this privileged position: *they* will deliver the Word of God through the Son to the world. From God the Father, through the Son, through the Spirit, and through the apostles to the world. In this sense, the apostles are "foundational" to the church.

We evangelicals are instinctively suspicious of tradition. Tradition—ideas and customs and beliefs "handed down" from previous generations—can be enslaving, misleading, and even very wrong. But here is tradition of ultimate value: Divine truth handed down from the Father, the Son, and the Spirit through the apostles to us. "Stand fast and hold the traditions which you were taught, whether by word or our epistle" (2 Thess. 2:15). Indeed, this tradition is the very basis of our fellowship.

> But we command you, brethren, in the name of our Lord Jesus Christ, that you withdraw from every brother who walks disorderly and not according to the tradition which he received from us. (2 Thess. 3:6)

Theological and ethical instruction from the apostles is universally binding. Indeed, it is "from God to us."

So we have advanced yet another step. We have the uniqueness of Christ, the uniqueness of the Holy Spirit, the uniqueness of the apostles, and therefore the uniqueness of the NT Scriptures. How and where did the Holy Spirit lead these men into "all truth"? How and where did he remind them of and explore the significance of our Lord's teaching? In John 21:24, the apostle John identifies his "witness" to the Lord Jesus with his own writing. It is perhaps significant that the provisions which Jesus specified form an apt description of the NT. The Spirit will "remind" the apostles of what Jesus did and said; we have that in the NT Gospels. He will "lead them into all truth" and show them the fuller significance of what Jesus had said and done; this is what is proclaimed in the Acts and expounded in the Epistles. And he will "show them things to come"; we have this in the prophecies of the Epistles and in the book of Revelation. God's word to us climaxed in his Son; we have this word reduced to writing in the pages of our NT. It is not the "red letters" only. The whole of it taken together is God's fullest word to us.

This is a most significant promise so far as we are concerned today. A very important line of questions asked at some time by most Christians is, "How can we know the NT is the word of God? How can we be sure? How can we know it is truth? How can we know it is accurate? Must we rely on an inner witness? Must we rely on the 'self-attesting' nature of it?" No, as helpful as these are, we have something much better. We have Christ's own word on it. He chose and commissioned these men for exactly this purpose. He invested them with his own authority and sent them his Spirit to teach and guide them infallibly. The apostles' witness to Christ and his teaching and work will not be their own invention nor even mere reliance on their own memory. No. It is the very word of the Son himself. Such is our Lord's promise.

Accordingly, when we read of the NT Scriptures coming to us by the inspiration of the Spirit, we should not think of the Holy Spirit acting on his own. He came to further the teaching of Christ. This also is how we should think when we read of "the law of Christ"—it is not the red letters only, but the entire body of writings given by the Spirit of Christ through the apostles.

This is the repeated claim of the apostles themselves. They do not merely preach the gospel; they do so "by the Holy Spirit sent from heaven" (1 Pet. 1:12). Their word was in fact the word of God (1 Thess. 2:13). More specifically, the apostles' words are to be regarded as the very word of Christ. "If anyone thinks himself to be a prophet or spiritual, let him acknowledge that the things which I write to you are the commandments of the Lord" (1 Cor. 14:37). Paul's doctrine came by the revelation of Christ (Gal. 1:14ff, *et al*). His detailed exhortations are "in the Lord Jesus" and "through the Lord Jesus" (1 Thess. 4:1-2ff). His commands are "in the name of the Lord Jesus" (2 Thess. 3:6; cf. 3:12). Indeed, the apostles' words are themselves "the words of our Lord Jesus Christ" (1 Tim. 6:3).

This is perhaps most graphically illustrated in the book of Revelation, written by the apostle John. Over and again he reminds us that what he writes to us, the church, he writes from the Lord Jesus. The Lord Jesus appears and tells him, "What you see, write in a book" (Rev. 1:11). "To the angel of the church at Ephesus, write . . ." (2:1 etc.). "I heard a voice from heaven saying to me, 'Write . . .' " (14:13). "Then he said to me, 'Write . . .' " (19:9). "He who sat on the throne . . . said to me, 'Write . . .' " (21:5). The words of the apostles bear a unique authority. They form the basis of fellowship and the standard of truth (2 Thess. 2:15; 3:14) precisely because they speak for Christ; they carry on and deliver to us God's final word through his Son.

In his comments on Ephesians 2:20 ("The foundation of the apostles and [NT] prophets") John Stott sums up our point well: "In practical terms this means that the church is built on the New Testament Scriptures. They are the church's foundation documents."[47]

How is all this important for the point at hand? It demonstrates the priority of the NT Scriptures. Only now, with our NT canon, do we have "all truth" (John 16:13). The era of

---

[47] John R. W. Stott, *The Message of Ephesians* (Downers Grove, IL: Intervarsity Press, 1979), 107.

Christ and his apostles marked a quantum leap forward in redemptive history. It brought about both a qualitative and a quantitative advance.

CHAPTER 3

Description of the New Covenant (Part One)

Tom Wells

To understand the subject of the New Covenant we will need to grasp two things. First, we will have to have a clear idea of what the phrase "New Covenant" refers to.[48] Following that we will want to see, in a rough way, the points at which a "New Covenant Theology" comes into tension with other understandings of the same phrase along with a brief defense of each of these points. Later chapters will take closer looks at some of these points and offer more extensive exegetical underpinnings.

One thing that all parties in the discussion agree upon is this essential element: there is something called "the New Covenant" spoken of in both the OT and the NT (e.g., Jer. 31:31ff.; 2 Cor. 3:6; Heb. 8:8). What it is and when it prevails has been a point of endless controversy.

This century has witnessed the following variations among serious scholars.

First, some dispensationalists formerly held that there is not one, but two New Covenants in Scripture, one for the Jews and the other for the NT church. This understanding, however, has

---

[48] For definitions of "covenant" see the standard lexical authorities. Also, Robertson, *The Christ of the Covenants*, chap. 1; Leon Morris, *The Apostolic Preaching of the Cross* (Grand Rapids: Eerdmans, 1955), chap. 2.

been almost completely abandoned in recent years so we will not need to pursue it.[49] Other dispensationalists have held that the New Covenant is still future. This position is also eroding among dispensationalists although some still hold it.[50]

More pertinent to today's discussion is the view that the New Covenant is simply an extension of an earlier covenant. In Reformed circles one often hears of "one covenant with two administrations," language that reflects the Westminster Confession (chap. 7, sec. 5) that says, "This covenant was differently administered in the time of the law, and in the time of the gospel . . . ." Behind this language lies the idea that in redeeming fallen man, God has made a single covenant, "the Covenant of Grace." Arrangements between God and man that come later than the Fall must be thought of as phases ("administrations") of this single covenant. In the words of the Confession (chap. 7, sec. 6), "There are not, therefore, two covenants of grace differing in substance, but one and the same under various dispensations."

This language underscores an important truth: God has a single purpose of redemption running throughout history. History proceeds toward a single goal of a redeemed world populated by a redeemed people. More than that, this goal comes to fruition by a single Redeemer, which means that in some important sense all Scripture is about him and his work (Luke 24:27; John 5:46). These truths are of paramount importance and we must never lose our grasp on them.

---

[49] See Bruce A. Ware, "The New Covenant and the People(s) of God," in *Dispensationalism, Israel and the Church*, by Craig A. Blaising and Darrell L. Bock, 91-92, for the grounds of this abandonment.

[50] A vigorous defense of this position was given at the 1995 annual meeting of the Evangelical Theological Society in Philadelphia by Ronald N. Glass.

Nevertheless, it now seems clear that a mistake has been made in speaking of this purpose as "the Covenant of Grace." We may agree in asserting the unity of God's purpose through the ages, but the selection of the word "covenant" to describe this unity has lent itself to important misunderstandings.

The reason for this is simple: in the NT the word *covenant* is almost always used to assert discontinuity. The evidence for this is overwhelming, as well over ninety per-cent of the occurrences of *covenant* in the NT are demonstrably used to assert discontinuity. They do so by naming or referring to an individual covenant that is distinct from other biblical covenants[51]. The percentage goes up further if implicit instances of covenant are added.[52] Only Hebrews 13:20 cannot be determined with the same certainty.[53] This kind of inductive survey cannot prove, but strongly suggests, that no such

---

[51] The full basis for these calculations can be found in Appendix Three, "Covenant" and its Cognates in the NT, pp. 281-283.

[52] Carl Hoch has done a similar study of the *implicit uses* of "covenant" in Heb. 8:7,13; 9:1,18 and 10:9 in Carl B. Hoch, Jr., *All Things New* (Grand Rapids: Baker, 1995), 122-123.

[53] Hebrews 13:20 that speaks of "the eternal covenant" has often been cited as comprehensive. Something that is eternal certainly might extend backwards into eternity past. But several things militate against this understanding. First, to place any covenant into eternity past ignores the fact that all the other covenants of Scripture are initiated in time. Second, the reference to "the blood" of the covenant ties it immediately to the sacrificial death that establishes the New Covenant (Luke 22:20; 1 Cor. 11:25). Third, we may note that other "eternal" things in the Bible start within time and are eternal by virtue of extending into the future. This is true both of eternal punishment and eternal life (Matt. 25:46). For recent discussion and literature see Richard L. Mayhue, "Covenant of Grace or New Covenant?" *The Master's Seminary Journal* 7, no. 2 (fall 1996): 251-257.

comprehensive covenant is referred to in the NT.

The NT leaves no doubt that there is indeed a *new* covenant. We are not at all shut up to the kind of statistical argument that I have presented above. Other factors that enter the discussion include the following:

First, we must not overlook the fact that the covenant under which Christians now live is called *new*.

Second, the terms in which it is announced in Jeremiah 31 emphasize its newness. No one, it would seem, could doubt that the prima facie impression made by this passage is the prediction of something new in history. But we are not left with mere impressions. Jeremiah says that the Lord's covenant will be "not like the covenant which I made with their fathers" (Jer. 31:32) at the Exodus. Whatever else this covenant may be, it will be unlike the Mosaic covenant. The Mosaic covenant was one thing; this covenant is another.

Third, we need to remind ourselves that newness itself is not usually an absolute category. Many things are called "new" because that is the most accurate way to characterize them without asserting an absolute break with what has gone before. Flowing as it does from the mind and heart of the single, self-consistent God, the New Covenant could not be novel in every respect. But within the constraints imposed by his own inner self-consistency, the Lord declares its substantive dissimilarity to the covenant that proceeded it.

Fourth, the strong contrast between the Lord Jesus Christ, as the central figure in the New Covenant, and his predecessors argues strongly for a newness that recognizes a large measure of discontinuity. Before he takes up the New Covenant directly, the writer of Hebrews signals the stance he will take in the following words:

> In the past God spoke to our forefathers through the prophets at many times and in various ways, but in these last days he has spoken to us by his Son. (Heb. 1:1-2a)

At first glance one might take this to mean no more than that men and women in an earlier day had heard the prophets, but those who were contemporaries of Jesus Christ heard *him*. Such an understanding of these verses, focusing, as it does, only on the passage of time is utterly inadequate. To take the least important fact first, it seems likely that the writer of Hebrews never heard the Lord Jesus speak. That seems implicit in 2:3b where he speaks of Christian salvation "which was first announced by the Lord, [and] was confirmed *to us* [emphasis mine] by those who heard him." The NIV Study Bible comments on this, "The author himself was apparently neither an apostle nor an eyewitness."

What does the writer mean then? He gives us three contrasts, all of which point to one great truth: a new era in the history of revelation has arrived. The first contrast has to do with *time*. In the past God spoke, but in these last days he has spoken once more. The second contrast has to do with *those who received the revelation*. God spoke to "our forefathers," but now he has spoken to "us." The third contrast has to do with *God's instruments*. Once God spoke through prophets, but now he has spoken "by his Son."[54]

There is much more here than the recognition that God has been revealing himself over hundreds of years of time to different people simply because none lived long enough to receive all that he has said. We are here at the turning point of the ages. Earlier history has been marked off by covenants, and it will not come as a surprise if we meet a new one here. But we are not left to conjecture. Though I cannot pursue the subject here, in much of the book the writer reflects on the newness of the New Covenant.

By ignoring the common use of *covenant* in the NT,

---

[54] It is possible to read the last phrase as qualitative: "He has spoken to us by nothing less than a son!" Either translation contains a strong contrast to God's OT instruments.

theologians have tended to subsume all the covenants under the single "covenant of grace" and have in the process largely ironed out the important differences between them. Nothing in the adoption of the phrase, "covenant of grace," demands this kind of leveling process, but it has certainly facilitated it once it was under way. Remove the two-administration language and the expectations of those coming to the biblical text will be changed somewhat. To speak of two covenants instead of two administrations of one covenant leads one to expect greater differentiation between the covenants than the two-administration language suggests.

It may be objected that theologians constantly make use of language in theology that does not exactly correspond to the language of the Bible. This objection overlooks the following:

First, when systematic theology uses language that does not appear in the Bible, it is usually for the reason that no suitable Bible word exists to express the concept. The word "Trinity" springs to mind here. It stands for a teaching of the Bible which cannot be expressed with any single Bible word. But all must agree that the Bible supplies the word "covenant" for what all sometimes call the Old and New Covenants. If this language is suitable for both Scripture and theology, the burden of proof must lie on those who would replace it.

Second, systematic theology has often confined a biblical word to one of its demonstrable meanings for the purpose of having a biblical term to use in talking about a biblical concept. The word "sanctification" is such a word. While it (or its cognates) has a number of uses in the Bible, in systematic theology it usually refers to the process of growth and development in the Christian life. The Bible clearly uses it that way, though that is not its only use. To use *covenant* in the overarching sense in which a single covenant encompasses virtually all of history first requires a demonstration that it is so used in Scripture. This is especially true since other words are readily at hand.

With respect to God's intentions before time, the Scripture designates them comprehensively as "an eternal purpose which he purposed in Christ Jesus our Lord" (Eph. 3:11; see 2 Tim. 1:9). This "purpose" of God is elsewhere called a "decree" (Ps. 2:7), a "determinate counsel" (Acts 2:23; 4:28), and "foreordination" (1 Pet. 1:20). Jesus called it His "Father's business" (Luke 2:49), "the work" given to Him by the Father (John 17:4), and "the will of Him who sent Me" (John 6:38; see Heb. 10:9).[55]

Third, this kind of substitution not only runs the risk of creating confusion but actually invites it. It seems time, then, to replace the language of two administrations in one covenant with the biblical recognition of covenants. Fortunately a growing number of scholars are recognizing this fact as they come to insist upon biblical and exegetical theology.[56] Willem VanGemeren has written: "Reformed Theology has always been interested in continuity, but continuity must reflect the results of exegesis. Hence, it is not desirable that covenant be the overarching motif."[57] Systematic theology, as the crown of biblical investigation, can never come into its own until it is biblically based.

If we grant the "newness" of the New Covenant, we must also ask the question, "Precisely in what way is the New Covenant new? Is there a central point at which the New

---

[55] Jon Zens, "Is There a Covenant of Grace?" *Baptist Reformation Review* (autumn 1977): 44.

[56] O. Palmer Robertson shows sensitivity to this issue, though he retains the use of the word "covenant" to describe God's overarching purpose. See *The Christ of the Covenants*, 53-57.

[57] Willem VanGemeren, "Systems of Continuity," in *Continuity and Discontinuity*, ed. John S. Feinberg (Westchester, IL: Crossway, 1988), 52. In my judgment this seminal book, in which men from both sides of this controversy speak plainly, needs to be reissued, perhaps with some up-to-date revision.

Covenant sets forth a fundamental break with all that went before it?" Hebrews summarizes the way the New Covenant differs from the Old. Barcellos has usefully set out these differences:

> First, unlike the Old Covenant, the New Covenant cannot be broken... [verse 32].
> Second, unlike the Old Covenant, the law of God will be put in the minds and written on the hearts of all covenant citizens (verse 33).
> Third, unlike the Old Covenant, everyone in the New Covenant will know the Lord (verse 34a).
> Fourth, unlike the Old Covenant, everyone in the New Covenant will have their sins forgiven (verse 34b).[58]

These contrasts are striking.

We must not, however, think only in terms of the contrast between the Old and the New Covenants, but between the New Covenant and all that preceded it. The terms of the prophecy contain the materials for taking a further step in our understanding. They point us to the fact that God would form a people, a new nation, under the New Covenant who would not break it, because all of them without exception would know the Lord. The people of the Mosaic covenant were not, for the most part, the kind of people who would keep the covenant, so the Lord could have done one of two things: either change the people or change the covenant. In the event, he chose to do both. He formed a new people and gave them a covenant in keeping with his work in them and the time in redemptive history at which he formed them. The new people, as I hope to show shortly, is the church of Jesus Christ. The time in redemptive history that demanded a new covenant was the time in which "God spoke . . . to us by his Son" (Heb.1:1-2).

But was the church a new thing in history? Many have

---

[58] Barcellos, *Defense*, 22-23.

denied it, finding the church in the OT all the way back to Adam. Covenant Theology has often identified Israel and church, so that they could not exist sequentially. When, then, did the church begin?

The evidence for the NT founding of the church seems ample. In the mind of the Lord Jesus as revealed in Matthew 16 the church could not have preceded his ministry. The evidence here for the newness of the church falls along two lines. First, Jesus uses a future verb tense in speaking of his church, "I *will build* my church" (16:18). In his eyes, the church appears to be yet future and this is almost certainly what he means. In view of the fact that many have held that the church has existed throughout the history of fallen mankind, it is surprising how nearly unanimous commentators are on this point. Ridderbos, on 16:18, in the compass of two pages refers to the "future church" four times as well as speaking of the "future fellowship of believers," the "future community" and the "community that would replace Israel as the people of God."[59] Hendriksen qualifies his endorsement of this future understanding only slightly:

> The expression "my church" refers, of course, to the church universal, here especially to the entire "body of Christ" or "sum-total of all believers" *in its New Testament manifestation* . . . (Emphasis added.)[60]

Something else in Matthew 16:18 also points to the newness of the church: the foundation—"this rock"—which was contemporary with the Lord Jesus. Precisely what or who Jesus had in mind in speaking of "this rock" has been the

---

[59] H.N. Ridderbos, *Matthew* (Grand Rapids: Zondervan, 1987), 303-304.

[60] William Hendriksen, *New Testament Commentary: Matthew* (Grand Rapids: Baker, 1973), 648.

subject of controversy. We need not settle that here, however. We will only look at the two popular alternatives, the confession of Peter or the person of Peter himself. (It is interesting to note in passing that these two understandings each have a long history going back to the early days of the post-apostolic church.)[61]

If the confession of Peter is the rock upon which Jesus built his church, the church could not be earlier than the time when that confession formed in the minds of his followers. The confession is not "the church will be (*or* is) built on Christ." That confession might have been made centuries before Peter's confession, although even that would have had to be predictive. Rather, the church is built on this understanding, on the certainty that "You [i.e., Jesus of Nazareth] are the Christ, the Son of the living God." If that is the church's foundation rock, the beginning of the church awaited men and women who could make that confession.

We get the same result if we understand Peter himself to be the rock. However glorious the old people of God was under the Old Covenant, that people existed without having Peter as its foundation. For Jesus' church to rest in *any* sense on Peter, the church could not be older than Peter himself. Both the future tense of the verb and the words of Jesus describing the foundation he was about to lay demonstrate that the church of Jesus Christ was a product of the age of the New Covenant.

The rest of the NT confirms this understanding. Think first of Ephesians 2:14-22. This passage is, of course, rich in descriptions of the church, "the two one," "one new man," "one body," "fellow citizens," "God's household" and "a holy temple." But the thing that interests us here is the foundation

---

[61] For extensive documentation of this point see the older work by John Peter Lange, *Commentary on the Holy Scriptures: The Gospel according to Matthew* (Grand Rapids: Zondervan, repr. 1960), 296-297. See especially the notes added by the American editor, Philip Schaff.

Description: Part One

of the temple, which includes "apostles and prophets, Christ Jesus himself being the corner stone" (2:20).

The figure of the temple is intended to show the historical process that produced the church.[62] Paul is particularly concerned to describe the earliest layer in its composition, what we might call "the first generation" of "living stones" (cf. 1 Pet. 2:4-5). Since the Lord Jesus is the cornerstone, these "stones" will have to be his contemporaries. There can be no question of this temple existing hundreds of years before he existed as "Jesus." The foundation consists of him and his apostles, all men of the first century. In addition, however, there are prophets. Is there here, in the foundation, at least one group of OT believers? Clearly not. This building has no basement; the apostles and prophets are joined to Christ Jesus, as I have pointed out, as his contemporaries.

We tend to identify prophets with OT times, but we must not forget that prophets also play a major role under the New Covenant, in the pages of the NT. Whenever Paul uses "prophet(s)" to designate OT prophets, he makes the connection with Jewish history (1 Thess. 2:15) and the past indisputably clear (Rom. 1:2; 3:21; 11:2-3). Elsewhere he breathes the atmosphere of the NT situation, an atmosphere strange to us, where "prophets" was an everyday category both among the pagans (Titus 1:12) and within the church (Acts 11:27; 13:1; 15:32; 21:9-10). We who use that word largely for men and women of the OT have a hard time placing ourselves into the social environment in which Paul lived. To look no further than the Ephesian letter itself we see references to these NT prophets in 3:4-5 (note the contrast between

---

[62] Speaking of Paul's emphasis on growth here, Rudolph Schnackenburg, *The Church in the New Testament* (New York: Herder & Herder, 1965), 96, writes, "The edifice is no finished, well-constructed fortress equipped against attacks, but a structure that is still being built, striving towards heaven, led by inner forces towards completion."

"other generations" and the current "apostles and prophets"). Ephesians 4:8-11 describes the same persons as gifts "bestowed on the church by the *ascended* Christ; hence, prophets of the New Testament era...."[63] According to Ephesians 2:20, then, the church is a NT entity.

We find the same truth set forth in a different way in 1 Corinthians 12:12-13:

> For even as the body is one and yet has many members, and all the members of the body, though they are many, are one body, so also is Christ. For by one Spirit we were all baptized into one body, whether Jews or Greeks, whether slaves or free, and we were all made to drink of one Spirit.

In verse 12, Paul reflects on the interdependence of the organs of the human body and compares that body to the body of Christ. In verse 13, he explains how the body of Christ was formed.

Why does Paul speak of baptism in, with or by the Holy Spirit? The answer seems straightforward; he alludes to the repeated and emphatic comparison between John the Baptist and Jesus contained in the Gospels and in Acts. For example, Mark 1:7-8.

> And he [John] was preaching, and saying, "After me One is coming who is mightier than I, and I am not fit to stoop down and untie the thong of His sandals. I baptized you with water; but He will baptize you with the Holy Spirit." (cf. Matt. 3:11; Luke 3:16; John 1:28, 33)

---

[63] The words, including italics, are from William Hendriksen, *New Testament Commentary: Ephesians* (Grand Rapids: Baker, 1967), 142, on 2:20. They are part of a larger argument which concludes: "[R]eference to the prophets of the old dispensation is definitely excluded . . ." Hendriksen represents the consensus among modern commentators, though Lenski is an exception.

Description: Part One 55

Or, again, in Acts 1:5, this time from the lips of the Lord Jesus, "John baptized with water, but you shall be baptized with the Holy Spirit not many days from now." It is in such words as these that we find the antecedents to Paul's language and thought in 1 Corinthians. In Mark 1:8 and parallels, John foretold the striking difference between his ministry and that of Jesus. In 1 Corinthians 12, we have passed the point in salvation history where the prophecy of John has become reality and Paul refers to that fact.

This immediately clarifies one point. When Paul says, "we were all baptized," he does not specify the agent, but we see that the Lord Jesus is the one who does the baptizing. Why does he do it? To put us, as Paul says, "into one body," the body that he calls "Christ's body" in verse 27 and simply "Christ" in verse 12. We are looking here at Paul's account of the origin of the church from a different vantage point than he selected in Ephesians 2. There he was concerned with the corporate relation of believers to God as his temple. Here he has another focus. He is concerned here with the corporate relation of believers to one another within the new thing called "the body of Christ," and "to explain how they, though many, are one body."[64]

One point remains: how did Christ do this? How did Christ create one body? The answer to that question depends very much on how we translate the Greek behind the NASB's word "by" in the first phrase of verse 13. The options are either "by," "with," or "in," but, in my judgment, only the translation "in" does justice to the idea Paul is setting forth. NASB's "by" seems to suggest that while Christ did the baptizing, he did it by the agency of the Holy Spirit. But the truth set forth in the references in the Gospels and Acts is that the Holy Spirit, like the water in John's baptism, is the medium into which we are

---

[64] Gordon D. Fee, *The First Epistle to the Corinthians* (Grand Rapids: Eerdmans, 1987), 603, on 12:13. His entire discussion of this verse on pp. 603-606 will well repay careful study.

baptized; Christ baptizes us *in* the Spirit as John baptized his converts *in* water. The image at the end of the verse, "and we were all made to drink of one Spirit," confirms this by introducing a complementary idea we find elsewhere in the NT, the idea that God is in his people and that they are also in him. As the agent of Christ, the Spirit surrounds and occupies God's people. We are immersed in the Spirit and yet, by our "drinking him," he is also within us. John bears witness to the same truth in 1 John 4:13: "We know that we live in him [God] and he in us, because he has given us of his Spirit."[65]

As a result we may paraphrase 1 Corinthians 12:13 as follows:

> Christ has baptized all of his people in the Holy Spirit for the purpose of forming them into one body, the body of Christ. This body includes both Jews and Greeks, both slaves and free men and women. We also have had the Spirit put within us, so that the promise that God would be in us and we in God has been fulfilled.

1 Corinthians 12:12-13 then, confirms what we have previously seen in Ephesians 2, that is, that the church is a NT entity. In the Gospels and in Acts 1, the baptism in the Spirit is still a future prospect, though fully certain; by the time Paul wrote to the Corinthians he could treat it as a thing past for every believer. "We were baptized," Paul says, and as a result we are part of the church which is Christ's body.

We may pause for a moment to review where we have been in trying to establish the character of the New Covenant. After glancing at several contemporary views regarding when the New Covenant prevails, we observed that its very name *covenant* points to discontinuity with what has gone before. This discontinuity is not absolute, but real, prominent in the

---

[65] This is a repeated emphasis of the Johannine writings. See also John 6:56; 14:20; 15:5; 1 Jn. 2:24 and 3:24.

NT, and a feature that is ignored at the peril of the church. Finally, we asked of what that newness consists and concluded that its essential feature was a new people of God, called in the NT "the church" and "the body of Christ." *The New Covenant, then, is the bond between God and man, established by the blood (i.e. sacrificial death) of Christ, under which the church of Jesus Christ has come into being.* Many would agree to this definition, but others raise questions that we must address next. They concern Israel (the OT people of God), the church's relation to her, and the "law" that prevails in this new people.

CHAPTER 4

Description of the New Covenant (Part Two)

Tom Wells

Historically there has been no consensus on the relation of Israel to the church of Jesus Christ. On one extreme, classical dispensationalists have tended to deny all connection between the two,[66] while on the other extreme, classical covenant theologians have tended toward an identification of the two as one body. In each case I have used the words "tended to" because both systems have sometimes recognized typological connections between the two while not varying much from their basic positions.

Both sides, in my judgment, have therefore touched on the truth but emphasized an understanding that is basically false. Though few dispensationalists today would defend the classical view of "no connections," they remain leery of anything that suggests too close a relationship. In particular they continue to deny that the church is in any sense either old or "new" Israel. Covenant theologians also remain close to their classical moorings. The evidence of both Testaments, however, points to the typological connection as more nearly basic. It will be possible here only to outline this evidence.

---

[66] One thinks of L. S. Chafer's rejection of the word "parenthesis" to describe the church age on the grounds that a parenthesis is connected to what proceeds and follows. He spoke instead of the church age as an "intercalation." See his *Systematic Theology* (Dallas, TX: Dallas Seminary Press, 1948), 4:41.

First, it is evident that the writers of Scripture read the terms of the Abrahamic covenant in two different ways.[67] Old Testament writers often see the promises as fulfilled to the literal nation of Israel while NT writers find their fulfillment in the church. A simple survey of those promises in Genesis 12-17 with their fulfillments noted in both Testaments would illustrate what I mean.[68] While we cannot pursue that in detail here, we will look at two biblical statements that draw attention to this contrast.[69] In Joshua 21:43-45, Joshua tells Israel,

> So the Lord gave Israel all the land which He had sworn to give to their fathers, and they possessed it and lived in it. . . . Not one of the good promises which the Lord had made to the house of Israel failed; all came to pass.

God had promised the land and other things to the patriarchs. Joshua records the fulfillment of the Lord's promises to Israel. Here, without doubt, the physical nation is in view. In Joshua's judgment, speaking by the Spirit of God, the promises were

---

[67] Typology is, in one sense, a part of the larger promise/fulfillment motif. In the following discussion the Abrahamic Covenant contains the promise side of this motif, both with respect to ancient Israel and to the body of Christ.

[68] In speaking of the promises of the Abrahamic Covenant I include the promises of Genesis 12 which precede the formal establishment of the covenant in chapter 15. This is accepted by many scholars on the ground that they "have viewed the covenant as a vehicle by which the promise of God is formalized" (John Walton, *Covenant: God's Purpose, God's Plan* [Grand Rapids: Zondervan, 1994], 15).

[69] For fuller discussion of this point see Appendix Four, The Promises of the Abrahamic Covenant, pp. 285-287.

given to ethnic Israel. We must read the Abrahamic covenant in that way.[70]

But here another biblical writer, this time from the NT, reflects on the Abrahamic promises. In Hebrews 11:39-40 we read,

> And all these, having gained approval through their faith, did not receive what was promised, because God had provided something better for us, so that apart from us they should not be made perfect.

Here is a quite distinct view of the promises of God, which calls for several observations. While it is possible that Joshua and the writer to the Hebrews did not have precisely the same promises in view, they nevertheless are looking at the promises connected with the Abrahamic covenant and seeing them in quite different ways. Everything is fulfilled in Joshua; nothing is fulfilled in Hebrews. Clearly they are reading the evidence from differing perspectives. What is the basic difference? Earlier in chapter 11 the writer of Hebrews tells us that Abraham went "to a place he was to receive for an inheritance" (11:8). This place was "the land of promise" and the promise extended to Isaac and Jacob who were "fellow heirs of the same promise" (11:9).

So far the writer of Hebrews might well be laying the foundation for Joshua's statements on fulfillment. But the following verses show a very different understanding. We are told that Abraham had his eye on a different land altogether.[71]

---

[70] Joshua is not alone in the OT in this reading of God's promises. Cf. Jehoshaphat's prayer in 2 Chron. 20:7, "O our God, did you not drive out the inhabitants of this land before your people Israel and give it forever to the descendants of Abraham your friend?"

[71] Though the text uses the word "city" in v.10, vv.13-16 show that another country (with other cities?) is in view.

And he was not alone. All his faithful descendants died "without receiving the promises," and confessing "that they were strangers and exiles" on the very earth that contained the land of Canaan (11:13).

How can we make sense of this? By seeing the typological nature of the land of Canaan. It pictured the larger "country" which therefore was also contained in the promises. That will explain how they can be said not to have received the promises that took in "the land of promise."

Another evidence of this type/antitype connection between Israel and the church is found in the common names given them in the NT. A fair number of these exist and this fact is probably one of the things which led covenant theologians to identify Israel and the church. If that identity is impossible, as it must be if the church is founded in the NT era, then to understand Israel as a type or picture of the church seems the most likely way to grasp their relationship. For example, the phrase "My people" (approximately one hundred twenty-five times in OT, of Israel) is either applied directly to the church (Rom. 9:24-25; 2 Cor. 6:14-18) or plainly adapted to it (1 Pet. 2:9-10). This last reference falls in a group of OT phrases, "a chosen race, a royal priesthood, a holy nation, a people for God's own possession," all of which are taken directly from the OT and made descriptive of the church. The easiest explanation for this is the typological one. I may illustrate this by referring to a picture of my wife. If I showed you her picture I would say, "This is my wife, Luann." But if I had the privilege of introducing her to you in person I would say the same thing, "This is my wife, Luann." And that is what the NT writers do.[72]

Further evidence of this typical connection is found in the rites, ceremonies and ordinances of the two covenants. Such things as circumcision, the Passover, and the sacrifices on the

---

[72] See this extensively illustrated in Paul S. Minear, *Images of the Church* (Phila.: Westminster, 1960).

one hand, and baptism, the Lord's table and the NT "sacrifices" (Heb. 13:15; 1 Pet. 2:5) along with the sacrifice of Christ are obviously both distinct and related. Typology explains this relationship.

Finally, we may think of the parallels between the Lord Jesus in his relation to his church, and various officers of ancient Israel. As Moses, Aaron, David, Solomon and others stood at the head of Israel in various capacities, so the Lord Jesus stands at the head of his church as one "greater than" any and all of these (Matt. 12:42; John 8:53ff. Cf. Matt 12:6, 41). (Compare the summary of the offices of Christ as prophet, priest and king, popularized by John Calvin but reaching back as far as Eusebius.)[73] The ancient nation was "baptized into Moses" at the decisive moment in its history (1 Cor. 10:1-2), i.e., they came under his leadership. But the new nation is baptized into Christ (Rom. 6:3; Gal. 3:27; 1 Cor. 12:12-13) and so has come under his direction.

Typology, however, does not quite exhaust the relation of Israel to the church. Covenant theologians have often insisted on an "organic" relation as well, and in one sense they are right. From the standpoint of eternity future, looking back, the church will prove to have been God's elect individuals from every era. We may illustrate this point by Paul's discussion of Israel and the olive tree in Romans 11 and, at the same time, see how it fits with the NT establishment of the church.

Paul starts the chapter by recognizing that Israel, God's ancient people, is made up of both believers and unbelievers. A godly remnant has always existed (vv. 1-6), but the masses stumbled and fell (vv. 7-11). So much is this the case that the nation itself is spoken of as stumbling, transgressing and suffering rejection by God (vv. 11-15). Paul proceeds:

> For if their rejection be the reconciliation of the world, what will their acceptance be but life from the dead? And if the first piece

---

[73] See *New Dictionary of Theology*, s.v. "Offices of Christ."

of dough be holy, the lump is also; and if the root be holy, the branches are too. But if some of the branches are broken off, and you, being a wild olive, were grafted in among them and became partaker with them of the rich root of the olive tree, do not be arrogant toward the branches; but if you are arrogant, remember that it is not you who supports the root, but the root supports you.

In order to grasp Paul's extended figure we must ask two questions: first, what is the olive tree, and second, when does Paul think that some of the branches were broken off?

The critical point in answering "what is the olive tree?" is to reflect on the unity of root and branches. The branches are obviously human beings; the root must be of the same kind, a person or persons. This conclusion is confirmed by the other analogy in v. 16, the comparison of the firstfruits of dough and the rest of the batch. Clearly whatever the firstfruits is, the batch must be as well. The root, then, as most commentators have held, is either Abraham or the Patriarchs. "Nothing is more natural than to call the ancestors the root, and their descendants the branches."[74] The olive tree stands as a whole for Israel, as that nation has been derived from Abraham (cf. Jer. 11:16). This is in keeping with Paul's interest throughout Romans 9-11 to trace the history of salvation as it bears on the Jewish nation.

When does Paul think of the natural branches as being cut off? Is this, in Paul's mind, an ongoing process in Israel's history or is there some definite point in their history where this "breaking off" occurred? Though few older commentators directly address this issue, implicit in their discussions is the idea that there came a time in history when this happened. The reason lies close at hand: for Paul, Israel's "rejection" (v. 15) comes at the time in salvation history in which God turned to the Gentiles. Their trespass and rejection "trigger the stage in

---

[74] Charles Hodge, *Commentary on the Epistle to the Romans* (Grand Rapids: Eerdmans, 1965), 366-367.

salvation history in which Paul (and we) are located, a stage in which God is specially blessing Gentiles . . ."[75] (cf. Matt. 21:43). With these points before us, we are now prepared to look at the relation of ancient Israel to the church.

Paul's figure of the olive tree reminds us that throughout her history ancient Israel was a mixture of believers and unbelievers. This has led some to call the tree "the visible church in the OT." With Gentiles grafted in, it would presently stand for "the visible church as it now exists." This understanding, however, is not consistent with the figure itself, since there has been no time in history when unbelievers have been cut off from this assumed visible church. To the extent that the visible church idea is true, it is still an amalgam of believers and unbelievers. That "cutting off" awaits the final judgment. Instead, the olive tree is the church of God's effectually called elect, formed after the death of the Lord Jesus, out of the true believers of the Jewish nation (past and present) and believing Gentiles.

Paul describes here the process by which the true church was formed. First, God stripped all Jewish unbelievers from the ancient nation, leaving only the spiritual children of Abraham. Then he added to them (starting at Pentecost) both Jews and Gentiles, as they were born again, to continually augment his new community, the church of Jesus Christ (cf. Acts 2:47b). Certain things follow from this. First, ancient Israel with her unbelieving branches was never the church of Jesus Christ. Second, Paul does not contemplate unbelievers being added to the olive tree. If God had intended that, he would have had no reason to strip off the unbelieving branches to begin with. Third, there is nevertheless an organic relation between the church and God's individually elect people from ancient Israel. We who are believers in Jesus Christ are now part, with them,

---

[75] Douglas Moo, *NIC: The Epistle to the Romans* (Grand Rapids: Eerdmans, 1996), 696.

of the olive tree as it exists today, i.e., the "invisible" or "universal" church of God.[76]

Finally, we must ask the question, "What law now governs the New Covenant community, the church of Jesus Christ?" This is the other major point of tension with some understandings of the church. The answer to this question is not only difficult, but has suffered, perhaps more than any other related question, from severe misunderstandings among the parties. Let us see if we can clarify the subject. Two or three points will be in order.[77]

First, we must be absolutely clear that the category "law" is indispensable to the church. Much confusion has existed over what is intended by it, but the category itself is basic to the relation between God and man.

Second, we must recognize that the NT speaks of "the law of Christ" as the rule of the Christian (1 Cor. 9:21; Gal. 6:2), whatever is intended by this phrase.

Third, we must also acknowledge that the NT offers us little exposition that directly explains what this law is. Nevertheless,

---

[76] I do not have space to discuss the question of who the individual is who is threatened with being yet "cut off" in 11:21-22. If the reference is to God's elect, it seems to me best to take the representative view of this individual as seen in the commentaries of John Calvin, Charles Hodge and Everett Harrison, among others, on these verses. In the words of Hodge, "Paul is not speaking of the connection of individual believers with Christ . . . but of the relation of communities . . . . There is no covenant or promise on the part of God, securing to Gentiles the enjoyment of these blessings through all generations, any more than there was any such promise to protect the Jews from the consequences of their unbelief" (Hodge, *Romans*, 370). For another view, however, that is consistent with my contention that only believers are being discussed, see Thomas R. Schreiner, *ECNT: Romans* (Grand Rapids: Baker, 1998), 607-609.

[77] Fred Zaspel and I discuss the subject of law in much greater depth in chapters 9 and 10 below.

Description: Part Two

we have the materials for determining the question in what I have earlier called *the logical priority of the Lord Jesus*. Let me explain what I mean.

The Christian church has a long tradition going back at least to the Epistle of Barnabas (ca.70-100) of treating Christ as a lawgiver to his people.[78] Among the Puritans this was a very popular idea, and rightly so.[79] To accept a law from someone means to accept that person as the authority within some limited sphere of life. Such authority, however, is never absolute except in a single case, that of God. There is no appeal from his authority either by judicial trial, by the use of force, or by any other means. Of such misguided efforts the psalmist says, "The One enthroned in heaven laughs; the Lord scoffs at them" (Ps. 2:4). All Christians agree to this fact, so it requires no argument.

Under the New Covenant, however, it undergoes a subtle variation in that Christ sets himself forward as the comprehensive Lord, a position that we understand can only be accorded to God himself. The justification for this remarkable claim by Christ is twofold: first, by very nature he was God and, second, his person as the God-man was awarded the full title "Lord" (i.e. Yahweh) upon the completion of his mission in this world (Phil. 2:9-11). We should not be surprised, then, to hear him say, "All authority in heaven and on earth has been given to me" (Matt. 28:18). While we understand that even such

---

[78] *ANC Vol. 1, The Epistle of Barnabas*, 138: "[God] has therefore abolished these things [i.e., incense, new moons, etc.], that the new law of our Lord Jesus Christ, which is without the yoke of necessity, might have a human oblation."

[79] Ernest F. Kevan marshals the evidence in *The Grace of Law* (Grand Rapids: Baker, 1976), 184-185. They did not, however, think of this law as a new law, but as the "Moral Law of God," which they identified with the Decalogue.

"absolute" authority has a single limitation (1 Cor. 15:27), there can be no appeal for us from the rule of Jesus Christ.[80]

Certain things follow from this.

First, for us, there is no competing authority in matters that pertain to God. There is nothing logically prior to Jesus Christ to which we must look for the regulation of our lives. (The word *"logically"* is very important here, signifying the necessity of coming to the Lord Jesus first for instruction, even if he quotes from law that comes from a time earlier than the time of his public ministry.) The authority of Jesus is such that this is true for all men since the ascension of Christ.

Second, what is true of all men is especially true for Christians who have consciously owned the lordship of Christ as the organizing fact around which their lives must revolve. That means they have no moral and ethical allegiance to anything, including the OT and its laws, *that is logically prior to Jesus Christ*. That is what absolute authority claims and that is what allegiance to absolute authority concedes. Whatever other authorities may exist in this world (and there are many others) each must be submitted to only out of the understanding that Jesus Christ lays such submission upon believers in him. Any other acceptance of a prior claim is illegitimate. This is to say no more and no less than what is implicit in the confession, "Jesus Christ is Lord."

As radical as all this sounds, it is not new. It has played an important (though, sadly, often subsidiary) role in the consciousness of Christians from the very beginning. We may illustrate this point from the English Puritans:

> Because of easily-recognizable differences between the relation of men to the Law before and after faith, it became

---

[80] For more on the slave/master relation between believers and the Lord Jesus see chapter one, pp. 14-17.

customary to speak of the believer as related to the Law "in the hands of Christ."[81]

This is, of course, an assertion of the logical priority of the Lord Jesus in the direction of his people. More than a thousand years earlier, the church father Origen illustrated the same point:

> We who belong to the catholic church do not reject the law of Moses, but we welcome it, provided it is Jesus who reads it to us, so that as He reads we may lay hold of His understanding and interpretation.[82]

Once more, we see here the logical priority of the Lord Jesus in the moral and ethical instruction of his people, even where there is no rejection of "the law of Moses." It is this priority of Jesus that the NT is concerned to maintain against all competitors. It is the sense of this, which virtually every Christian feels when he first comes to the NT, that occasions the apparent devaluation of the OT that many complain of. But most Christians recognize that the OT remains the inspired word of God while at the same time acknowledging that the great mass of its legislation is no longer directly applicable to the *practice* of believers today.

It is this priority of the Lord Jesus that is so evident in the Sermon on the Mount. There is no consensus among scholars on the precise aim of the Lord Jesus in Matthew 5:21-47 where he quotes OT law (or in one case, what apparently purported to be OT law, 5:43b) and proceeds to comment on it. Clearly he is not abolishing this law (5:17-19), but is he modifying it, explaining it more fully and/or delivering it from the perversions of the traditions to which the Pharisees were heirs? As interesting and important as this question is, however, it

---

[81] Kevan, *Grace*, 184.

[82] Origen *In Josuam* 9.8, quoted in Alec R. Vidler, *Christ's Strange Work* (London: Longmans and Green, 1944), 50.

does not yet come to the central issue. Whatever Jesus is doing he is doing as the final authority on the subject, and he is doing what no other contemporary Jew would dare to do. His repeated "But I tell you" (5:22, 28, 32, 34, 39, 44) reveals the consciousness of an authority that transcends the work of all other interpreters. Ned Stonehouse has captured the two points made above in the following paragraph:

> That Jesus' fulfillment of the Old Testament law involved far more than an affirmation of the validity of the law appears unmistakably in the illustrations of his interpretation of the law provided by the antitheses of the sermon on the mount. The accent on the authoritative new utterances of Christ in truth is so powerful that in certain instances an apparent impingement upon the abiding authority of the law is disclosed. Six times Jesus, completely on his own authority, and without any attempt to vindicate his categorical declarations, seems to set his own pronouncements in antithesis to "that which had been spoken," the deliverances consisting of, or at least including, in every instance a quotation from the law of Moses (Mt. 5:21ff., 27ff., 31ff., 33ff., 38ff., 43ff.). It was the absoluteness with which Jesus spoke, as possessing authority in his own right, and not deriving the authority of his utterances from Scripture or revered traditions like the scribes, that caused the crowds to express amazement at this teaching (Mt. 7:28). There had appeared on the scene a new self-confident voice, the voice of one who assumed an authority in no sense inferior to that of the commandments of God given through Moses.
>
> The sovereignty with which Jesus speaks is so absolute that his fulfillment of the law seems to carry with it the invalidation of the law of Moses.[83]

Here Stonehouse repeatedly sets forth the *impression* left on the reader: "apparent impingement upon the abiding authority of the law," "seems to set his own pronouncements in antithesis

---

[83] Ned B. Stonehouse, *The Witness of Matthew and Mark to Christ* (Phila.: Presbyterian Guardian, 1944), 198-199.

to . . . the law of Moses," "not deriving the authority of his utterances from Scripture," and an authority which "seems to carry with it the invalidation of the law of Moses."

From what do these impressions arise? Not from a desire to destroy Mosaic law! They arise from the priority that Jesus demands for himself, even in handling the undoubted word of God.[84]

We come now to the final critical question: how does the priority of Jesus Christ work out in practice?

To answer this question we must first address a number of impressions often held in connection with the Mosaic law. First, when many speak of "the Law" they have in mind only the Decalogue or Ten Commandments. That meaning has an honored history in the church, but as far as I can see the Scripture does not use the phrase in that way. If it does, it is a rare and uncharacteristic use. Second, the idea that "the Law" is the Ten Commandments is often associated with another idea, the conviction that, generally speaking, the NT regulations and rites that parallel those in the OT are simpler under the New Covenant. Since the Decalogue is itself a relatively short statement, when these two ideas are combined they produce a demand that if the Decalogue is to be replaced, some very compact summary must be given for the rule of Christ.

We find a naive answer to this search for compactness in the popular notion that all God asks of us is that "we do as we would be done by," i.e., the "Golden Rule." More sophisticated answers make the presence of the Holy Spirit or a serious effort to love God and our neighbor all we need. This last solution comes to us on the firmest biblical ground, but represents an overly realized eschatology. In eternity future it will be a sufficient rule, but just now it is short on details. All of these solutions founder on the same fact: the NT contains a multitude

---

[84] For more on the Sermon on the Mount, see chapters 5-8, pp. 77-138.

of commands and demands, the very things that we normally call "law."

Can these rules and regulations, at least on their moral side, be reduced to the Ten Commandments? Or to put it another way, is "the law of Christ" identical to the Decalogue? There are important reasons for answering these questions negatively.

First, the highest and best revelation of God is found in the Lord Jesus himself. Yet it is beyond dispute that the display of the excellencies of God found in Jesus Christ is primarily the display of his moral excellencies. Can we really believe that all of this is fully anticipated in the Decalogue? Second, only on the assumption that the Ten Commandments explicitly or implicitly contain all of this same revelation can we think of putting them on the same level as the Lord Jesus himself.

Now it must be said in defense of many older scholars that they did, in fact, make this assumption. They did nôt mean to whittle down morality to ten rules or a hundred, to the neglect of all else. The Puritans, for example, repeatedly show that they believed that the Decalogue implicitly contained all the demands of God as reflected in his moral character. But the evidence for that fact was always wanting, as indeed it would have to be, if there is such a thing as progressive revelation. The only alternatives are to empty the word "implicit" of tangible content or reduce it to mean that whatever else would be revealed would be consistent with what had already been given. Given the fact of the self-consistent Law-giver, that is simply a truism.

Nevertheless, the Puritans tried to hold the "implicit" view. There are a number of ways of confirming this. We find it in the individual Puritan authors[85] as well as in the more authoritative

---

[85] Thomas Vincent, *The Shorter Catechism Explained from Scripture* (Edinburgh: Banner of Truth, repr. 1980), 113, e.g., asks the question, "Is there, then, anything included, as commanded in the moral law, but what is expressed in the ten commandments?" Though he does not answer the question directly, it is clear that he intends a negative answer.

catechisms such as the *Westminster Larger Catechism* in its exposition of the Ten Commandments. John Frame has written:

> The Larger is sometimes thought to be over-detailed, even legalistic, in its exposition of the law. One emerges with an enormous list of duties that are difficult to relate to the simple commands of the Decalogue. There is truth in such criticisms, but those who urge them often fail to realize the importance of applying scriptural principles authoritatively to current ethical questions.[86]

To be fair to Frame we must carefully note his qualification, but the criticism, as he himself says, is just.

But what of the simpler, briefer *Shorter Catechism*? Look at its exposition of the Fifth Commandment, "Honor your father and your mother . . ." The exposition features two questions concerning the meaning of the commandment:

> Q.64. What is required in the fifth commandment?
> A. The fifth commandment requireth the preserving the honor, and performing the duties, belonging to everyone in their several places and relations, as superiors, inferiors, or equals. . . .
> Q.65. What is forbidden in the fifth commandment?
> A. The fifth commandment forbiddeth the neglecting of, or doing anything against, the honor and duty which belongeth to everyone in their several places and relations.[87]

What shall we make of this? Though this is excellent in itself, it is evident that unless someone already came to the

---

[86] *Evangelical Dictionary of Theology*, s.v. "Westminster Catechism."

[87] Of the many sources for the *Shorter Catechism*, I have chosen to quote from James Benjamin Green, *A Harmony of the Westminster Presbyterian Standards* (n.c.: Collins/World, [repr] 1976), 134. This is an outstanding presentation of the *Standards* with commentary by Mr. Green.

commandment with the conviction that *it had to be comprehensive of all human relations*, one would never gather it from the simplicity of the command.[88] As evidence for the wider sweeping conclusion that everything moral is comprehended in one of these ten commands, both the *Larger* and *Smaller Catechism* offer just three verses, Matthew 19:17, 18, 19.[89] This is, surely, much too narrow a base from which to draw such a comprehensive conclusion. Further than that, assuming that Matthew 19 contains the best evidence for this opinion, we must note that it was not available to OT believers at all.

Nor is that all. In the Mosaic law the penalty for breaking the fifth commandment in some cases was death (Exod. 21:15, 17; Lev. 20:9; 21:9; Deut. 21:18-21). It is difficult to see on what grounds this penalty could be avoided among all the other relations that are thought to be in this text. If one argues that the case laws make this distinction, one comes very close, on this assumption, to setting the case laws against the fifth commandment itself.

The Ten Commandments, then, could not have functioned as a compact summary of all moral law. And they never did among the Jews. In a book written for the direct purpose of insisting that Christians must keep the Ten Commandments, we read:

> The Jews did not divide up their Law into moral, judicial and ceremonial precepts. For them it was a whole, covering God's revealed will for all the areas of their common life. The Christians have had to divide it . . . .[90]

---

[88] See a similar criticism of this kind of treatment of the Decalogue in John Brown, *Discourses and Sayings of our Lord Jesus Christ* (London: Banner of Truth, repr. 1967), 1:197ff.

[89] See Green, *Standards*, 117, *Larger Catechism*, Q. 98 and *Shorter Catechism*, Q. 41.

[90] Vidler, *Strange Work*, 54.

As soon as we see that the demand for a compact rule of life is neither implied nor explicitly found in the Scriptures, we are prepared to receive from Christ a total law based on the New Covenant documents. No slogan, even of Scripture, can contain it, but it is clearly there, as it must be if Jesus Christ is Lord.

Let me suggest its parameters.

First, it consists of the commands of the Lord Jesus himself as he gave them in his public ministry and as they are informed by his own example.

Second, it consists of the demands laid upon believers in the NT, the New Covenant document. These two are basic, and both are subject to the further illumination of the Holy Spirit who has been given in greater measure, in part, for this very purpose.

Finally, as a personal and secondary suggestion, I would add the re-examination of the OT with the idea in mind of finding those things that are moral laws in the light of the NT and that are in keeping with the explicit demands of the Lord Jesus Christ in the NT.[91] One field in which this might be pursued is the book of Proverbs. In these, it seems to me, we have *the Law of Christ*.

What is this thing called the New Covenant? We may now sharpen the definition that we gave earlier with our findings on Israel and the law:

The New Covenant is the bond between God and man, established by the sacrificial death of Jesus Christ, under which all who have been effectually called to God in all ages have been formed into the one body of Christ in NT times, in order to come

---

[91] This idea is parallel to the suggestion heard in many places that the explicit types/antitypes of Scripture encourage us to seek out others that are not explicit. For discussion and literature, see Scott A. Swanson, "Can We Reproduce the Exegesis of the New Testament? Why Are We Still Asking?" *Trinity Journal* 17 (spring 1996): 1, 67-76.

under his law during this age and to remain under his authority forever.

CHAPTER 5

Matthew 5:17-20 — The History of the Interpretation

Fred G. Zaspel

For all the centuries of lively discussion concerning the relation of law to gospel, the subject still finds surprisingly little agreement.

Introduction

In his own day, John Wesley complained that "there are few subjects within the whole compass of religion so little understood as this."[92] And even at this late date there appears to be no prevailing consensus.[93]

Of particular concern in this discussion is the status of Mosaic law since the coming of Jesus Christ. In what way(s) did he affect it, if at all? Still more specifically, how did the revelation which Jesus brought relate to that of Moses? Does Moses' law remain the final court of appeal in questions of

---

[92] John Wesley, *Sermons: On Several Occasions*, vol.1 (London: Wesleyan Conference Office, 1876), 482. Cranfield similarly scolds interpreters for their generally careless treatments of the subject; "St. Paul and the Law," *SJT* 17 (1964), 43-44.

[93] Cf. Wayne G. Strickland, ed., *The Law, the Gospel, and the Modern Christian: Five Views* (Grand Rapids: Zondervan Publishing House, 1991).

ethics? What bearing does it have on ethical and behavioral issues which face the New Covenant believer?

Within this discussion, Matthew 5:17-20 looms large. Indeed, the whole NT theology of law grows out of this pivotal statement of Jesus. It is of "primary importance in trying to understand Jesus' attitude to the law"[94] and, consequently, in developing a consistent theology of law and its relation to the Christian.

In this passage, Jesus specifically disclaims any conflict between himself and Moses and enthusiastically affirms his harmonious relationship with the older revelation. But the exact nature of this relationship continues to be a matter of debate.

The question of the interpretation of Matthew 5:17-20 occurs within in the larger question of the interpretation of the Sermon on the Mount (Matt. 5-7).[95] But it is on these verses in

---

[94] D. A. Carson, *From Sabbath to Lord's Day* (Grand Rapids: Zondervan Publishing House, 1982), 79.

[95] For surveys of the various approaches see the following: Warren S. Kissinger, *The Sermon on the Mount: A History of Interpretation and Bibliography* (Metuchen, NJ: The Scarecrow Press, Inc., 1975). Carl F. H. Henry, *Christian Personal Ethics* (Grand Rapids: Wm. B. Eerdmans Publishing Co., 1957), 278-326. Joachim Jeremias, *The Sermon on the Mount*, trans., Norman Perrin, ed. John Reumann, Facet Books: Biblical Series, No. 2 (Philadelphia: Fortress Press, 1963), 1-12. John A. Martin, "Dispensational Approaches to the Sermon on the Mount" in *Essays in Honor of J. Dwight Pentecost*, ed. Stanley D. Toussaint & Charles H. Dyer (Chicago: Moody Press, 1986), 35-48. Harvey K. McArthur, *Understanding the Sermon on the Mount* (1960; reprint, Westport, CT: Greenwood Press, 1978), 11-25.

particular that the discussion turns. From the discussion several views have emerged.[96]

Early Church: Qualitative Advance

Just a glance through the Scripture index of the Ante-Nicene Fathers reveals the significance which they attached to this passage.[97] In fact,

> no portion of the Scriptures was more frequently quoted and referred to by the Ante-Nicene writers than the Sermon of the Mount. The fifth chapter of Matthew appears more often in their works than any other single chapter, and Matthew 5-7 more frequently than any other three chapters in the entire Bible.[98]

Harvey McArthur demonstrates that the early church theologians, while denying any outright abolition or contradiction of Moses, consistently speak of Jesus' teaching in Matthew 5 in terms of a qualitative advance on the older revelation. Phrases such as "fulfilling and extending" Moses (Irenaeus), "supplementary additions by Christ . . . add what was wanting" (Tertullian), "completion" (Origen), "greater commandments" (Chrysostom), "perfecting" (Theophylact), and "greater precepts of righteousness" (Augustine), are

---

[96] The following views are presented in summary fashion only, and it should be recognized that within each view are significant variations among the interpreters. Those views which have bearing on the present discussion will receive further analysis in connection with the exegesis below.

[97] Nearly six full columns of references to Matthew 5-7; thirty-nine references to Matthew 5:17-20. A. Cleveland Coxe, ed., *The Ante-Nicene Fathers*, vol. 9 (1887; reprint, Grand Rapids: Wm. B. Eerdmans Publishing Company, 1990), 237-238.

[98] Kissinger, *The Sermon on the Mount*, 6.

common in their writings.[99] They unanimously understood Jesus' teaching as an addition to Moses' law, an advance whose requirements were significantly higher. The common idea was that Christ's teaching completed the law of Moses—it finished what was begun at Sinai. In this sense there is no destruction or even contradiction of Moses but a growth as from seed to tree (Augustine[100]).

Medieval Church: Evangelical Counsels

The medieval interpretation took final shape in Aquinas who understood Jesus' teaching as "evangelical counsels" which go beyond "precepts" and provide instruction as to how those precepts may be most safely kept. Being merely "counsels" they are not binding, except for monks, whose righteousness was to exceed that of the ordinary Christian. So while refraining from hatred is voluntary, it virtually assures that one will not violate the prohibition of murder. Likewise abstaining from oaths is the safest guard against perjury.[101]

Thus, the "fulfillment" which Christ brought was that of extension. While this view is significantly different from that of the early church, it does preserve the idea of Jesus' law as a qualitative advance.

---

[99] McArthur, *Sermon on the Mount*, 30-33.

[100] Ibid., 35.

[101] Thomas Aquinas *Summa Theologica*, pt. 2.1, ques. 107, art. 1 and 2. See McArthur, *Sermon on the Mount*, 33-36.

Reformed View: True Exposition of Moses

In clear distinction from this Roman Catholic tradition, the Reformers taught that Jesus' teaching in the Sermon on the Mount was but the true exposition of Moses. Luther regarded the antitheses in Matthew 5:21ff as the "correct explanation of several of the Ten Commandments."[102] Calvin's "Exposition of the Moral Law"[103] (the Decalogue) takes pointed aim at the "pestilential ignorance or wickedness of the Schoolmen" and exposes their teaching of "evangelical counsels" as a corruption of the teachings of Christ and an arrogant trifling with God's eternal law. For Calvin, Jesus' teaching was but a restatement of the original intent of Moses. His teaching added nothing new.[104]

Working from the assumption that if the law was perfect and of divine origin then it must remain binding, Puritan and succeeding Reformed interpreters have argued strenuously that the teaching of Christ could make no change or even advance on the older revelation.[105] So, by theological necessity, "the law

---

[102] Martin Luther *The Sermon on the Mount*, cited in McArthur, *Sermon on the Mount*, 37.

[103] *Institutes of the Christian Religion*, vol. 1 (1559; reprint, Grand Rapids: Wm. B. Eerdmans Publishing Co., 1979), 359-361.

[104] John Calvin *A Harmony of the Gospels: Matthew, Mark and Luke*, vol. 1, *Calvin's Commentaries*, trans. A. W. Morrison (1555; reprint, Grand Rapids: Wm. B. Eerdmans Publishing Co., 1972), 183-184.

[105] Samuel Bolton, *The True Bounds of Christian Freedom* (1645; reprint, Carlisle, PA: Banner of Truth, 1964), 62. Ernest F. Kevan, *The Moral Law* (Jenkintown, PA: Sovereign Grace Publishers, 1963), 70-71. Cf. Henry, *Christian Personal Ethics*, 278-326.

of Christ" must be not only consonant with, but identical to the ("moral") law of Moses.[106] Reformed interpreters today do not always follow the Reformers and Puritans in this regard. However, the generally "flat" transition so characteristic of Covenant Theology leaves the moral law of Moses unchanged. Some see Jesus' teaching as a radicalizing of Moses' demands, a deepening and internalizing of his requirements.[107] But still it is merely an articulation and clarification of what the law originally intended, particularly in light of the contemporary rabbinic "defilements" of Moses.[108] Any notion of "advance" would be explained in terms of clarification, not addition. In the Reformed tradition, Christ's "fulfillment" of the law here is understood as confirmation and/or clarification of it, obedience to it, realizing its prophecies, or even accomplishing its demands in the experience of his followers.[109] But—granting the abolition of its civil and ceremonial aspects—the old law remains; Jesus' words "leave no room for the idea of improving" upon it.[110]

---

[106] It should be noted here that Reformed interpreters argue for identity between Moses and Christ only in terms of "moral" law. They do not demand this identification in other aspects of Moses' law.

[107] H. N. Ridderbos, *Matthew* in *The Bible Student's Commentary*, trans. Ray Togtman (Grand Rapids: The Zondervan Corporation, 1987), 99.

[108] Kevan, *The Moral Law*, 70. Patrick Fairbairn, *The Revelation of Law in Scripture* (1869; reprint, Winona Lake, IN: Alpha Publications, 1979), 227-230.

[109] William Hendriksen, *Exposition of the Gospel According to Matthew* in *New Testament Commentary* series (Grand Rapids: Baker Book House, 1979), 289-290.

[110] Geerhardus Vos, *Biblical Theology: Old and New Testaments* (1948; reprint, Grand Rapids: Wm. B. Eerdmans Publishing Co., 1977), 363.

Anabaptist View: Old Law Replaced

Difficult as it is to speak of one interpretation common among the Anabaptists, their view of the law was relatively monolithic (Munsterites excepted). They are widely recognized for their insistence on the newness of the New Covenant. For the Radical Reformers, the law which Christ spoke was no mere reissuing of Sinai. It marked a significant shift in God's program. Harvey McArthur asserts that this is the necessary theological result of their literal and universal application of the Sermon on the Mount,[111] but his assertion goes unsubstantiated. It seems fair enough, instead, to understand their "radical" position in terms of their own distinctive theological emphases. But in either case, they emphatically taught that the distinction between the OT and the NT is absolute, and it is the NT alone that is normative in questions of Christian ethics.[112] Christ's fulfillment of Moses' law is precisely what rendered it "old." It is not merely part of the old law that is abolished; it is the whole of it that is fulfilled and so displaced by the new. The idea here is not so much that of "advance" as it is *change*.

---

[111] McArthur, *Sermon on the Mount*, 39-40.

[112] Cf. Estep, *The Anabaptist Story*, 142-144.

Theonomic Reformed View: Binding Civil Law

Perhaps no one has written at greater length on Matthew 5 than theonomist Greg Bahnsen. For him, Matthew 5:17-19 is "the decisive word" which settles the question of the status of Mosaic law in the New Covenant age,[113] "the *locus classicus* pertaining to Jesus and the law."[114] Agreed. But Bahnsen understands the saying with a distinctive slant. In it Jesus is declaring "the abiding validity of the law [of Moses] in exhaustive detail."[115] It is Jesus' affirmation of the on-going validity of Moses. For Bahnsen, "fulfill" (*plēroō*) has less an eschatological than a confirmatory sense: the meaning is that of *ratification*. Jesus is asserting that virtually all of Moses' law, excepting only its ceremonial aspects, remains binding and must remain binding until the end of the age. Moreover, the principles derived from the case laws are designed as models which all human governments are obliged to follow in the minutest detail.[116] Jesus' mission in this regard was not to advance or heighten the law in any way, but to "rectify the fallen standard of the law" and to "restore a proper conception of kingdom righteousness"[117] by clarifying the law's original but lost intent. This view agrees with the traditional Reformed view in its categorical denial of any addition to the law of Moses by Jesus. But it goes a step further and affirms that, (1) it is the

---

[113] Greg L. Bahnsen, "The Theonomic Reformed Approach to Law and Gospel" in *The Law, the Gospel, and the Modern Christian*, 113.

[114] Greg L. Bahnsen, *Theonomy in Christian Ethics* (Nutley, NJ: The Craig Press, 1979), 3

[115] Ibid.

[116] Bahnsen, "Theonomic Reformed Approach," 110-115, 122-141.

[117] Bahnsen, *Theonomy in Christian Ethics*, 86.

Prominent Interpretations

case laws as well as the moral aspects of Moses that remain obligatory; and (2) these laws are given not only to men in general but to human governments also, in order to be applied in legislation and penology and all judicial proceedings.

Dispensational View: Law Set Aside

Similar to the older Anabaptists, dispensationalists have traditionally argued that with the coming of Christ, the law of Moses was set aside. In regard to this passage, the older dispensationalists taught that Jesus' demands in the Sermon on the Mount are primarily a "Kingdom ethic" to be in force during the millennium, although many of its principles apply today also.[118] Martin demonstrates at length that today this is but one of several dispensational views.[119] On this point, however, there is general agreement: with Jesus' fulfillment of it, Moses' law was set aside. To be sure, Moses is still regarded as "profitable" (2 Tim. 3:16), but as a law given to a specific people (Israel) for a specific time (from Moses to Christ) its purpose has now been served, and it has been abolished. The "fulfillment" of the law of which Christ speaks in Matthew 5:17 is understood in terms of observance of the (Mosaic) law as intensified by Christ,[120] or as the accomplishment of what the

---

[118] *The Scofield Reference Bible* (1909; reprint, New York: Oxford University Press, n.d.), 999-1000. L. S. Chafer, *Systematic Theology* (1948; reprint, Dallas, TX: Dallas Seminary Press, 1978), 5:97. Charles Caldwell Ryrie, *Dispensationalism Today* (1965; reprint, Chicago: Moody Press, 1977), 107-109.

[119] Martin, "Dispensatioal Approaches", 35-48.

[120] L. S. Chafer, *Grace: The Glorious Theme* (1922; reprint, Grand Rapids: Zondervan Publishing House, 1978), 171.

Law prophesied.[121] But the fulfillment does not leave a continuing application of the law in this age.

It is difficult for dispensationalists to speak of *law* for the New Covenant believer in this age of *grace*. But whatever law there is, and whatever its specific function(s), and whatever overlap it may have with the older legislation, it is not to be identified with the law of Moses. The hermeneutic, by definition, is one of discontinuity. The idea is that of change.

Eschatological Continuity: Law Completed

Another view, rooted firmly in a keen attentiveness to redemptive history, resembles the Reformed view in that it emphasizes a strong sense of continuity between Moses' law and the teaching of Christ. But the resemblance goes scarcely further. It holds more in common with the early church views in that it sees the teaching of Christ as surpassing Moses both in the depth and breadth of its requirements and in the authority which it assumes. And it holds much in common with the Anabaptist and Dispensational views in that it renders the Mosaic law as only indirectly binding on the Christian. Moses, in effect, is set aside, but that older law is seen as having an anticipatory sense which "expected" the advancement which Jesus brought. In this view, Moses is not so much abolished as he is "fulfilled" and so reinterpreted in light of the epochal events associated with Christ's first coming.

In different varieties this view is represented by Banks,[122]

---

[121] Strickland, "The Inauguration of the Law of Christ with the Gospel" in *The Law, the Gospel, and the Modern Christian*, 258.

[122] Robert Banks, *Jesus and the Law in Synoptic Tradition* (Cambridge: Cambridge University Press, 1975); and "Matthew's Understanding of the Law: Authenticity and Interpretation in Matthew 5:17-20," *JBL* 93 (1974), 226-242.

France,[123] Moo,[124] and Carson.[125] Strikingly similar is the treatment given to Matthew 5:17-20 by Reformed theologian Vern Poythress.[126] For Banks, "these commandments" (Matt. 5:19) are not Moses' commands but Christ's. His law has fulfilled and thus superseded Moses' law, and it is this that he insists must be followed in detail. While differing with Banks in this detail, Moo and Carson emphasize also that the law of Christ is what Moses' law anticipated. It is not that Moses is set aside so much as he is "fulfilled" by the advance Jesus gave him. Jesus gives Moses' law its new form.

Critical Views: Law Repudiated

In a way that resembled the earlier Marcionites, the Manichaeans taught that Jesus effectively repudiated the older law. To support the claim, Faustus argued with Augustine that since Matthew himself was not present on the Mount when Jesus supposedly spoke these words, the saying of Matthew

---

[123] R. T. France, *Matthew: Evangelist and Teacher* (Grand Rapids: Zondervan Publishing House, 1989), 191-197. *The Gospel According to Matthew* in *TNTC* (1985; reprint, Grand Rapids: Wm. B. Eerdmans Publishing Co., 1990), 113-130.

[124] Douglas Moo, "The Law of Moses or the Law of Christ" in *Continuity and Discontinuity*, 203-218; "Jesus and the Authority of the Mosaic Law," *JSNT* 20 (1984), 3-49. "The Law of Christ as the Fulfillment of the Law of Moses" in *The Law, the Gospel, and the Modern Christian*, 319-382.

[125] D. A. Carson, *Matthew* in *The Expositor's Bible Commentary*, vol. 8, ed. Frank E. Gaebelein (Grand Rapids: Zondervan Publishing House, 1984), 140-147.

[126] Poythress, *The Shadow of Christ in the Law of Moses* (Brentwood, TN: Wolgemuth & Hyatt, Publishers, Inc., 1991), 263-269.

5:17 is spurious.[127] Similarly, some modern critical scholars understand the passage as contradictory to Jesus' own words in 5:21-48 and his radical treatment of the law elsewhere.[128] Others see in the saying a redactional compromise between two conflicting parties within the church: "Matthew" chooses middle ground by clarifying that he is neither bound to rabbinic Judaism nor antagonistic to Moses.[129] Still others see the saying as a creation of the early church in defense of a more conservative view of the law. For these, the passage reflects a disagreement between Matthew (and perhaps James) and Paul.[130] Matthew, the Jewish conservative, labors to preserve the law of Moses and protect it from the more liberal tendencies of the Pauline faction. For others, the saying "seems to indicate that an earlier re-shaping of the Jesus-tradition took place in a conservative direction vis-a-vis the law and Israel"[131] and reflects the Judaistic pressures in the Palestinian church.

It is entirely possible that this saying was preserved by the early (Jewish) church precisely because of its direct bearing on the pressing question of the continuing relevance of Moses' law. But there is no good reason to understand it as other than

---

[127] McArthur, *Sermon on the Mount*, 27-28.

[128] Sherman E. Johnson, *Matthew* in *The Interpreters Bible*, vol. 7 (New York: Abingdon Press, 1951), 291. Cf. Gerald Friedlander, *Jewish Sources of the Sermon on the Mount* (New York: KTAV Publishing House, Inc., 1969), 32. Joachim Jeremias, *New Testament Theology. Part One: The Proclamation of Jesus* (New York: Charles Scribner's Sons, 1971), 253.

[129] Gerard S. Sloyan, *Is Christ the End of the Law?* (Philadelphia: The Westminster Press, 1978), 50.

[130] Stephen G. Wilson, *Luke and The Law* (Cambridge: Cambridge University Press, 1983), 110.

[131] James D. G. Dunn, *Jesus, Paul, and the Law* (Louisville: Westminster/John Knox Press, 1990), 134.

Jesus' own words. It has been argued that the absence of any parallel in the other Synoptics is evidence that the saying is a later creation.[132] But the observation does not prove the conclusion. In fact, there is a very close parallel to Matthew 5:18 in Luke 16:17.[133] Moreover, as will be demonstrated, it is not necessary to assume that there is any conflict at all between the teaching of Paul and that of Jesus in this pericope. The critical views rest on their own presuppositions, and further consideration would lead too far afield of the discussion here. At any rate, the passage should be considered as it stands.

The Contemporary Discussion

Present-day interpreters face essentially the same issues that have been discussed for centuries. Namely, 1) how does Jesus' teaching relate to the law of Moses? Was it a mere reissuing of the Sinaitic legislation? Or did it constitute an advance? If so, in what sense(s)? And, 2) if Jesus' teaching went beyond Moses, what effect did this have on the older law? Was Moses' law abolished after all?

These issues bristle with various intricate exegetical, theological, and hermeneutical difficulties. But the pursuit of the discussion is well worth our while, for at stake, among other things, are one's view of the relationship of the Testaments and of law and grace, the nature of the New Covenant, the interpretation of many other NT passages which

---

[132] R. G. Hamerton-Kelly, "Attitudes to the Law in Matthew's Gospel," *Biblical Research* 17 (1972), 19-32. B. H. Streeter, *The Four Gospels* (London: Macmillan, 1924), 254-25; noted in Richard N. Longenecker, *Paul, Apostle of Liberty* (1964; reprint, Grand Rapids: Baker Book House, 1980), 138.

[133] For further discussion of literary parallels, see Banks, *Jesus and the Law in Synoptic Tradition*, 204ff.

speak of the law's abrogation and/or continuing relevance, the basic framework of biblical hermeneutics, and the whole approach to Christian ethics. In all this Matthew 5:17-20 is pivotal. A right understanding of this passage is a necessary first step.

CHAPTER 6

Matthew 5:17-20 — Contextual Observations on Matthew's Gospel

Fred G. Zaspel

Matthew's Emphasis on Jesus and Moses

One prominent feature of Matthew's Gospel is his close—although often subtle—association of Jesus with Moses and the Torah. One early tradition held that Matthew's Gospel was composed of five books of teaching[134] thought to be parallel to the five books of Moses. This was a literary device not at all unknown in the biblical world.[135] This view was popularized in 1928 by B. W. Bacon[136] and gained considerable attention, but in recent years it has largely been discounted,[137] at least insofar

---

[134] Chapters 1-2, Prologue; chapters 3-7, Book 1; chapters 8-10, Book 2; chapters 11-13, Book 3; chapters 14-18, Book 4; chapters 19-25, Book 5; chapters 26-28, Epilogue. Each section is preceded by a narrative and concludes with a closing formula *kai egeneto hote etelesen ho Iēsous* ("and it came to pass when Jesus said ....").

[135] Cf. the Psalms, the Megilloth, Pirke Aboth.

[136] B.W. Bacon, "Jesus and the Law: A Study of the First 'Book' of Matthew," *JBL* 47 (1928): 203ff. Later in *Studies in Matthew* (1930); cited in Banks, *Jesus and the Law in Synoptic Tradition*, 230.

[137] Cf. France, *Matthew: Evangelist and Teacher*, 142-145.

as the divisions are directly reflective of the Pentateuch. Whether or not this observation is strictly accurate, what does seem clear is that allusions to Moses abound throughout Matthew's Gospel, however subtle or even insignificant some of them may at first appear. Poythress observes that "The first narrative block [of Matthew] (chapters 1-4) has a remarkable number of parallels with the narratives of Mosaic times. The first teaching block (chapters 5-7) has parallels with the teaching of Moses."[138] Joseph Grassi finds in Matthew's unique expression "*this gospel* of the kingdom" a parallel to Deuteronomy's "*this book* of the law."[139] Dale Allison briefly collates impressive exegetical parallels evidencing that in 5:1-2, Matthew intentionally associates the Sermon on the Mount with the giving of the law on Mount Sinai.[140] As evident in the works just noted, this proposition has been well demonstrated from virtually all quarters of biblical scholarship. There is good reason for this. The infancy narrative with the narrow escape of the child (Matt. 2) is strikingly reminiscent of that of Moses (Exod. 2). The noted details of Jesus' ascent from Egypt along with King Herod's fear and the slaughter of the children are significant. Later in Matthew's Gospel, he is careful to present Jesus as the new—and greater—Moses (cf. giving the law from a mountain, ten miracles, giving bread in a desert place, etc.), and it seems this is one subtle introduction to the theme. In

---

[138] Poythress, *The Shadow of Christ in the Law of Moses*, 275.

[139] Joseph A. Grassi, "Matthew as a Second Testament Deuteronomy," *Biblical Theology Bulletin* 19 (1989), 23-29.

[140] Dale C. Allison, "Jesus and Moses (Mt 5:1-2)," *The Expository Times* 98 (1987), 203-205. For further discussions of this theme see the following: France, *Matthew*, 186-189. John Goldingay, "The Old Testament and Christian Faith: Jesus and the Old Testament in Matthew 1-5," Parts 1 and 2, *Themelios* 8 (1982, 1983): No.1, 4-10; No. 2, pp. 5-12. Frank H. Gorman, "When Law Becomes Gospel: Matthew's Transformed Torah," *Listening* (1989), 227-240.

fact, the wording of 2:20 ("for they are dead which sought the young child's life") is strikingly reminiscent of Exodus 4:19. This is the one "like Moses" whom Moses said would come.

The evidence continues.

Jesus' responses to Satan in the wilderness temptation are all from "Israel in the wilderness passages" (Matt. 4:4, 7, 10; cf. Deut. 8:3; 6:16; 10:20). The wilderness event itself follows the baptism in water and lasts *forty* days and precedes the giving of the law. The whole narrative in both cases (Exodus and Matthew) proceeds in the same direction: childhood, exodus through the Red Sea/baptism in the Jordan, wilderness temptation, mountain, law. The temptations also are common to both: the temptations to hunger and idolatry.

Both Moses and Jesus fasted forty days on the mountain (4:2; cf. Exod. 24:18 and Deut. 9:9). As an ethical teacher, Jesus resembles Moses more in Matthew than in any of the other Gospels. In fact, the language of the mountain scene, in which Jesus ascends and descends (5:1, *anabainō + eis to horos*; 8:1, *katabainō + de autou apo tou horous*) is virtually identical to the Septuagint description of Moses at Sinai (Exod. 19:3, 12, 13, 14; 24:12, 13, 18, etc.; 34:29). Moses' law at the outset promised blessing for those who followed it; Jesus does the same, only the blessings he promises are greater (Matt. 5:3-10).

The Moses/Sinai motif is extensive and quite beyond coincidence. Matthew labors to present Jesus Christ in close association with Moses.[141]

---

[141] See my *The Theology of Fulfillment* (Hatfield, PA: The Interdisciplinary Biblical Research Institute, 1993) for a brief exploration of this theme throughout Scripture.

His Emphasis on Jesus as Greater than Other OT Figures

Moses is by no means the only historical point of reference for Matthew. There is also Abraham (1:1), David (1:1; 12:3-4), Joshua (1:21), the priests and the temple (12:5-6), Jonah (12:39-41), Solomon (12:42), and Elijah (17:1-9).

What is striking in all of these is not just the typological reference but the nature of the type's realization. In each case there is no mere parallel being drawn: there is eschatological transcendence. That is, Jesus, for example, is not merely another great Solomon: he is "greater than Solomon" (12:42). Likewise, he is "greater than the temple" (12:6), "greater than Jonah" (12:41). In the midst of all this, the clear implication is that he is also David's *greater* son (12:3-4); in fact, this is precisely Jesus' point in 22:45. Further, he is "Lord even of the Sabbath" (12:8). Similarly, Jesus is not merely a son of Abraham, privileged as that is. He is the son of Abraham par excellence, the one in whom the patriarchal promises reach their goal (1:1). He is not simply a representative of Israel—he is the true Israel (2:15, 16-18). His name is "Joshua," but he is greater than his forebear and brings a greater deliverance: "for He shall save His people *from their sins*" (1:21).[142] Moreover, it would have been very wrong to erect booths for Moses, Elijah, and Jesus: these two other men, great as they were, deserve no equal place with Jesus. "Hear him" was the word from Heaven (17:5). He is greater than Elijah and greater than Moses — greater than the prophets and even the law itself.

---

[142] Given Matthew's pattern of comparison to historical figures and his rather loose typology (as 2:15 and Hosea 11:1), some have suggested that a further parallel with Joshua is possible: when the older Joshua is at the Jordan the waters are opened, but when Jesus is at the Jordan it is the heavens that are opened (3:16).

His Emphasis on Jesus' Authority

In close connection with this is Matthew's emphasis on Jesus' personal authority. This is implied in the references to David, Solomon, Moses, Joshua, etc., mentioned above. Whatever authority these men had, Jesus' is greater.

But there is more. With the clear Sinai motif throughout, the reader may see, in Jesus, God himself speaking from the mountain. Indeed, Jesus' opening statement, "I came to fulfill," and his emphatic and much repeated "But I say unto you"[143] are unmistakable claims of authority. This is precisely the effect it had on the original hearers (7:28-29), and it is a theme which Matthew goes on to stress and to illustrate at considerable length (chapters 8-10). At the conclusion of the Sermon, it is "these sayings *of mine*" that constitute the standard by which men are judged (7:24-27), and it is disobedience to *his* word that constitutes "lawlessness" (*anomia*, 7:23). It would seem evident that Jesus is stressing his personal right to articulate what is the law of God and how it must be kept.

His great authority is precisely the point in 12:8: "The Son of man is lord even of the Sabbath." That is, he has authority over even the law itself. In fact, Jesus (and so Matthew) turns the entire Sabbath controversy in chapter 12 into a Christological manifesto intended to stress this very issue: his authority surpasses even that of the law.

This same point is emphasized again on the Mount of Transfiguration (17:1-10). The allusions to Moses again are evident: the six days (cf. Exod. 24:16), the mountain, the Divine presence and voice, the cloud, the shining face, the divine revelation, etc. But the climactic event is the voice from Heaven demanding that this Jesus, by virtue of his very person, must be heard and obeyed (*akouō*): "This is my beloved Son,

---

[143] 5:22, 28, 32, 34, 39, 44. Note the emphatic *egō* ("I") in each.

in whom I am well pleased; hear Him." The incident appears to be designed to stress again the fact of Jesus' unique authority.

Finally, in his missionary manifesto of Matthew 28:18-20, Jesus lays claim to universal authority (v.18). And in this global discipling enterprise it is "all" of *Jesus*' "commandments" that are to be taught and kept faithfully (v.20).

All this ("But I say to you," "hear and do these sayings of mine," "Hear Him") is unmistakably reminiscent of Deuteronomy 18:15-19. There Moses himself prophesied of one like him, but greater, who would come and, like him, give the law of God. It was this one whose law would be brought to bear in judgment. His authority is supreme, and his law is obligatory.

Conclusion on Matthew's Emphases

Matthew presents Jesus as the new Moses and as a new lawgiver. But he is much greater than Moses, even greater than Moses' law. He bears a supreme authority that is his by inherent right.

It is within this Christological context that Jesus is presented as the "fulfiller" of the law.

The "Antitheses" — Matthew 5:21-48

Continuing to narrow the focus, one clue to what Jesus means to imply when he claims to "fulfill" the law (Matt. 5:17) may be found in the following passage (vv. 21-48), in which he himself handles the law. Indeed, this is one of the very most important factors in making a determination of the meaning of Jesus' claim in 5:17-20. If the meaning of the former passage is not immediately clear, it would seem that this one was intended to follow up on it and clarify. For the purposes of this study, then, it will be considered first.

It is agreed by all sides that Jesus here is commenting on the law of Moses *in some sense*. The question here concerns the nature of these comments. Just how does Jesus treat the law in this sermon? What is his approach to Moses?

Corresponding to the various interpretations outlined in chapter five, several answers have been offered to this question. Generally, commentators understand Jesus here as correcting "abuses and misunderstandings of the law that had arisen in Jesus' day. In particular, Jesus repeatedly stresses the significance of correct motives. His focus on the heart contrasts with the externality and legalism promoted by Pharisaic religion."[145] Carefully guarding against any notion of change or advance in the law, Reformed interpreters in particular see Jesus laboring merely to clear it of rabbinic perversions. With Jesus' emphasis on the inner man (not just murder is forbidden but hatred also, not just adultery but lust also, etc.), he is but expounding the true spiritual meaning of the law, a meaning originally intended by Moses. Bahnsen writes,

> These radical commands (vv. 21-48) do not supercede the Older Testamental law; they illustrate and explain it. The scribes had neglected the radicalism of the law.... In six antitheses between His teaching and the scribal interpretations Christ demonstrates His confirmation of the Older Testamental law.... So, in these antitheses Jesus restores the original demand of the law.[146]

---

[145] Poythress, *Shadow of Christ in the Law of Moses*, 257. However, as mentioned earlier, Poythress does make concessions here that are uncommon among Reformed interpreters. There is a note of "advance" in his view (cf. p.258). Michael Green, *Matthew For Today* (Dallas, TX: Word Publishing, 1988), 74. R. C. H. Lenski, *The Interpretation of St. Matthew's Gospel* (Columbus, OH: The Wartburg Press, 1943), 216ff.

[146] Bahnsen, *Theonomy in Christian Ethics*, 90, 92.

Bahnsen supports his stated position by appealing to his own interpretation of Matthew 5:17-19, which he says, "confirms the law in exhaustive detail."[147] This, of course, begs the question and involves issues to be discussed in the following chapters. But his remarks illustrate well the traditional Reformed position: Jesus is making no advance but is merely expounding ("restoring") the original meaning of Moses' law.[148]

Fairbairn also argued that Jesus was correcting current views of the law held in his day[149] but cautiously admitted that "it is next to impossible for any one to avoid feeling, that an advance was made by our Lord in His own wonderful exposition of the law." But he hastens to add, that this "advance is confined to the clearer light which is thrown on the meaning of [the law's] precepts, and the higher form which is given to their expression."[150] Thus, the advance is not a substantive one.

Near the opposite end of the spectrum, Lewis Sperry Chafer regards the law which Jesus preaches in Matthew 5 as "substituted in place of" the law of Moses.[151] For him and for the older dispensationalists in general, the law of the kingdom is an entirely new law, unconnected with that of Moses.

For others, Jesus' treatment of the law in Matthew 5:21-48 involved a "new applicability;" he is said to have "redefined [the laws] to include more than their original scope. Thus we say that *aspects* rather than simply the laws themselves are renewed from the Old Covenant." This view is a mixing of both sides: the old law is not discarded, but neither is it merely reissued. "It

---

[147] Ibid.

[148] See also Kevan, *The Moral Law*, 70.

[149] Fairbairn, *The Revelation of Law in Scripture*, 227-230.

[150] Ibid., 231.

[151] Chafer, *Grace*, 172. At the farthest extreme would be the critical view mentioned in chapter five; namely, that Jesus is opposing the law in 5:21-48, which in 5:17-19 he says cannot be done.

is only the aspects of those laws that fall directly under the command to love God and neighbor that constitute a continuing obligation for Christians."[152]

Survey / Analysis

It would seem that since Jesus, in Matthew 5:17, claims to "fulfill" the law, his teaching in 5:21-48 should not be completely discontinuous with it. On the other hand, it is not difficult at all to infer this very idea from the "antitheses." "You have heard it said . . . but I say to you" seems at first reading to imply contrast, not continuum. A continuative or even an ascensive sense for *de* ("but") is possible, although unusual. An examination of the passage itself is necessary.

The first question to address, here, concerns Jesus' point of reference. Precisely what "was said" in the "ancient times"? By whom was it spoken? To whom? More specifically, is Jesus here making reference to Scripture or to rabbinical traditions that surrounded it? If Jesus is speaking *in direct reference* to the Law of Moses the implications are considerably more pointed.

"That it was said" (*errethē*) provides the first clue. It is used here in a formulaic manner to introduce various quotations. It seems that these are quotations from Scripture. There can be little question that in the first antithesis (vv. 21-22), the sixth commandment is in view, the prohibition of murder and the prescribed penalty attached to it.

---

[152] Gordon D. Fee & Douglas Stuart, *How To Read the Bible For All It's Worth* (Grand Rapids: Zondervan Publishing House, 1982), 138. Cf. Thomas R. Schreiner, *The Law & Its Fulfillment: A Pauline Theology of Law* (Grand Rapids: Baker Book House, 1993), 145-149. Robin Nixon, "Fulfilling the Law: The Gospels and Acts" in *Law, Morality and the Bible*, ed. Bruce Kaye & Gordon Wenham (Downers Grove, IL: InterVarsity Press, 1978), 56-57.

Likewise, in the second antithesis (vv. 27-28), reference is to the seventh commandment, the prohibition of adultery. In the third antithesis (vv. 31-32), it is Deuteronomy 24 that is in view, the regulation of divorce. In the fourth antithesis (vv. 33-34), a summary of several passages from the Torah concerning breaking oaths is probably in view, but Leviticus 19:12 fits very well as a representative of the others. The fifth antithesis (vv. 38-39) quotes Exodus 21:24 exactly, the law commonly called the *lex talionis*.

Finally, the sixth antithesis (vv. 43-44) differs from all the others in that while it quotes the Torah (Lev. 19:18), it also adds a statement whose origin is difficult to determine: "and hate your enemy."

There are intimations in the OT that the "love your neighbor" command could and should be broadened (Lev. 19:34). However, Deuteronomy 23:3-6 may provide some explanation:

> An Ammonite or Moabite shall not enter into the congregation of the LORD; even to their tenth generation shall they not enter into the congregation of the LORD for ever: Because they met you not with bread and with water in the way, when ye came forth out of Egypt; and because they hired against thee Balaam the son of Beor of Pethor of Mesopotamia, to curse thee. Nevertheless the LORD thy God would not hearken unto Balaam; but the LORD thy God turned the curse into a blessing unto thee, because the LORD thy God loved thee. Thou shalt not seek their peace nor their prosperity all thy days for ever.

Consider also the words of the prophet Jehu to King Jehoshaphat in 2 Chronicles 19:2: "Should you help the ungodly, and love them that hate the Lord?" The psalmist at times speaks similarly: "Do I not hate them, O Lord, who hate you? and am not I grieved with those that rise up against you? I hate them with perfect hatred: I count them my enemies" (139:21-22). An extrapolation of these kinds of statements could provide a point of reference, even though they are not exact parallel statements.[153]

Another possibility is found in the Qumran writings, in which the world was divided into light and darkness. All unbelievers were "sons of darkness" under the control of Belial. Each member of the Qumran sect ("the sons of light") was instructed "to love all the sons of light, each according to his lot in the counsel of God, and to hate all the sons of darkness, each according to his guilt under the vengeance of God."[154] This provides a parallel, although not an exact one. The suggestion that, instead, the saying reflects the teaching of some rabbi(s)[155] is impossible to verify. Allowing for possible variation in number six, all of the antitheses involve a clear reference to Moses. This is to be expected in that Jesus introduces this section with specific reference to "the law and the prophets" (vv. 17-18). This, it would seem, is the first reading of the statements and easiest understanding. "You have heard that it

---

[153] "Therefore it seems perfectly appropriate to see in the phrase "hate your enemies" a legitimate paraphrase of OT attitudes. . . . Only when the NT revelation of Jesus' concept of 'neighbor' is read back into the OT do we conclude that the popular paraphrase is a Pharisaic corruption of the OT." Alan F. Johnson, "Jesus and Moses: Rabbinic Backgrounds and Exegetical Concerns in Matthew 5 as Crucial to the Theological Foundations of Christian Ethics" in *The Living and Active Word of God*, ed. Inch & Youngblood (Winona Lake: Eisenbrauns, 1983), 93-94. Cf. Jeremias, *New Testament Theology: The Proclamation of Jesus*, 252-253.

[154] 1QSI:9-11; cited in John C. Trever, *The Dead Sea Scrolls* (1965; reprint, Grand Rapids: Wm. B. Eerdmans Publishing Co., 1977), 186.

[155] Hendriksen, *Matthew*, 312-313.

was said" cites a quotation from Moses' law; or, as Meier prefers, it is a "divine passive."[156] Bahnsen disagrees.

> 'Ἐρρέθη [*errethē*, "it was said"] is never used elsewhere by Jesus as a discrete formula for introducing quotations from the Older Testament; He commonly uses formulas like "it stands written" instead. The lone instance of a form similar to ἐρρέθη being used by Jesus in this capacity (Luke 4:12) is, in context, conspicuously parallel to "it stands written" (cf. vv. 4, 8; Matt. 4:7). Indeed the New Testament never uses εἶπον [*eipon*] or its derivatives to preface a citation of the Older Testament without explicitly specifying that the source of the quotation is God, Scripture, or an inspired writer (e.g., Matt. 1:22; 4:14; 22:31; Luke 2:24) or at least clearly indicating the same in immediate context (Rom. 4:18; 9:12; Heb. 4:3). . . . [I]f used in Matthew 5 to adduce scripture texts, then it patently fails to fit the pattern discerned elsewhere when derivatives of εἶπον are put to such service.[157]

Ironically, it would be difficult to ask for more contrary evidence than Bahnsen himself provides. His concession in regard to Luke 4:12 is a major one. And his argument concerning the "pattern" of the use of *errethē* with Scripture quotations assumes that fully six references in Matthew 5—as well as the Luke 4 reference—cannot be considered part of the data for establishing the pattern. What he does, in effect, is provide an impressive list of references demonstrating that *errethē* can be and in fact regularly is used to introduce Scripture quotations. It is consistently employed for this

---

[156] Cf. John P. Meier, *The Vision of Matthew* (New York: Paulist Press, 1978), 63-64. Meier notes, "Clear examples of this usage are supplied by the passive verbs in the beatitudes (shall be comforted, shall be satisfied, shall have mercy shown them, shall be called sons—each time with 'by God' understood.

[157] Bahnsen, *Theonomy In Christian Ethics*, 94-95.

purpose by Matthew in the fulfillment formulas.[158] Granted, in Matthew 5, Jesus does not "explicitly specify" that he is quoting Scripture, but it would seem that to proceed with a verbatim quotation of Scripture is indeed "clearly indicating the same in the immediate context," particularly when Jesus himself specifies that he is speaking of "the law and the prophets."

It appears that Bahnsen has unnecessarily restricted the data in order to preserve his argument. To select only the verses desired and define the "pattern" around them is gratuitous. But if this kind of narrowing is justified, there may still be more to observe. So far as Matthew is concerned, while *errethē* never appears outside of chapter 5, its participial forms *hrēthen* and *hrētheis* appear some thirteen times.[159] In *each* case, a Scripture quotation is in view. Judging from this data, a very different "pattern" emerges: in Matthew, the word (*errethē*) is *only* used to cite Scripture.

It must be admitted that this is not Jesus' usual formula for citing Scripture. Generally, he uses *gegraptai* ("it has been written"; e.g., 4:4). But on those occasions his intent, generally, is to cite Scripture as "proof" or to use it to settle some point of doctrine or practice. Here, however, his purpose may be different; and if so, *gegraptai* may be inappropriate. It may carry with it more implications than he wishes in this context, explaining as he is his relationship to the law as its "fulfiller." Again, fuller analysis of the passage is necessary.

It must also be recognized that the sixth antithesis may possibly include a reference to something more than Scripture or to some abuse of Scripture, perhaps even a popular maxim of the day. This, however, is far from certain, and in the previous five antitheses there is no indication from the text that

---

[158] 1:22; 2:15, 17, 23; 4:14; 8:17; 12:17; 13:35; 21:4; 27:9.

[159] 1:22; 2:15, 17, 23; 3:3; 4:14; 8:17; 12:17; 13:35; 21:4; 22:31; 24:15; 27:9.

the quotations are anything but Mosaic commands, however much these commands may have been misapplied.

The next phrase to assess is "to them of old" (*tois archaiois*), which is easiest to understand as a simple dative (indirect object)—"to them of old," or simply "to the ancients." This parallels the "But I say to you" which follows. Moreover, on both occasions in which this phrase is used (vv. 21, 27) there follows a direct quotation from the Decalogue. So then, it is ancient Israel that is in view, "hearing" the law from Moses. The KJV translates the phrase as a dative of agent: "by them of old time." Bahnsen adopts this understanding and uses it in support of his argument that Jesus is not referring to Moses' law at all but to the rabbis. Given the common understanding of law, with its endless tradition of "saying" and "hearing," either translation could possibly serve him as well.

It may be that Jesus is quoting the rabbinic traditions in order then to correctly interpret the law of Moses. But there is little evidence pointing in that direction. Even if similarities to rabbinic teaching could be shown, it would be difficult to overlook the explicit references to Moses.

In either case, the next step is to discern precisely what Jesus does with the law in each antithesis. Does he merely expound Moses and explain meanings latent in the law all along? Or is there some kind of advance? Or is there an abrogation?

In the first antithesis (vv. 21-22), Jesus proceeds from the prohibition of murder to a prohibition of hatred. On close evaluation, it is difficult to agree with those who see this as a mere exposition of the sixth command.[160] But since the assumption in the saying is that the prohibition of murder remains, it is also difficult to work from this point to a strict discontinuity viewpoint. It is likewise difficult to see this as merely a *deepening* of the murder prohibition: it is more an

---

[160] Schreiner, *The Law & Its Fulfillment*, 236. Bahnsen, *Theonomy in Christian Ethics*, 97. Hendriksen, *Matthew*, 295-302.

advance, an extension of it, for no fair exposition of the sixth commandment could arrive at an equally weighty prohibition of hatred. Some sort of advance is involved. However, Moo's suggestion provides one further alternative: "Jesus, with the emphatic 'but *I* say unto you,' enunciates principles neither derived from, nor intended to extend, the meaning of the laws which are quoted."[161] For Moo, Jesus' words constitute an *addition* to Moses. This understanding gives full weight to Jesus' authoritative statement and provides a fair explanation for all the data involved. But the authority could as well be used to extend the teaching of the law as add to it. In either case, there is clearly an advance of some kind: either extension or addition.

There may be a hint of advance also in the punishments which Jesus assigns to these sins. Moses' law called for capital punishment for murderers. Jesus declares "hell fire" to be the end of those who hate (vv. 22-23). The advance here would at least be one of intensification.[162]

The second antithesis (vv. 27-28) proceeds from the prohibition of adultery to a prohibition of lust. The situation here is virtually parallel to the previous case. Again, there is an advance of some sort.

The third antithesis (vv. 31-32) is a bit different, however. In view is Deuteronomy 24:1-4, Moses' permission for and instruction concerning divorce. Jesus neither deepens nor extends this teaching; nor does he give "a proper interpretation" of it.[163] None of these explanations can be derived from the passage in view (Deut. 24). Since the *intent* of Moses' instruction may be considered to restrict (at least hasty) divorce,

---

[161] Moo, "Jesus and the Authority of the Mosaic Law," 19.

[162] Poythress, *Shadow of Christ in the Law of Moses*, 258-259.

[163] Schreiner, *The Law & Its Fulfilment*, 237. Hendriksen, *Matthew*, 304-306.

this may be viewed as another advance: Jesus restricts it even further. Moo suggests that Jesus here goes "beyond the OT in forthrightly labeling remarriage after an improper divorce 'adultery.'"[164] All this is true enough as far as it goes. Still, Moses' instruction involved permission to divorce[165]—and this permission Jesus plainly rescinds. What Moses clearly allowed ("because of the hardness of men's heart," granted; Matthew 19:8), Jesus expressly forbids. Here there is a tightening of the law at least, but it apparently involves an abrogation.

In the fourth antithesis (vv. 33-34), Jesus proceeds from the prohibition of perjury (Lev. 19:12) to a prohibition of oaths generally. Here explanations involving Pharisaic casuistry may be accurate,[166] given the illustrations that follow (vv. 34-36). Allowing this, Jesus still is far from merely expounding the Law of Moses: he expressly forbids what the older law allowed.[167] Since it is generally agreed that Jesus' words involve some hyperbole, the prohibition may not be an abrogation of oaths absolutely. But neither do his words constitute a mere exposition of Moses. Moses' commands which regulated oaths were intended to ensure honesty, and this is what Jesus accomplishes. In doing so, however, he renders the older law obsolete.

In the fifth antithesis (vv. 38-39), Jesus proceeds from the *lex talionis* to non-resistance. Following the lead of Martin

---

[164] Moo, "Jesus and the Authority of the Mosaic Law," 20.

[165] The allowable ground for divorce in Deut. 24:1, "disfavor" and "something indecent," is a broad category, and no precise definition of it is given.

[166] Schreiner, *The Law & Its Fulfillment*, 237. Hendriksen, *Matthew*, 306-309. Carson, *Matthew*, 153.

[167] But not what it commanded, for nowhere did Moses command the taking of oaths.

Contextual Observations 107

Luther, interpreters generally see behind this an abuse of the *lex* for personal revenge, when in fact it was intended for legal/judicial proceedings.[168] But this destroys the parallel: "Do not use the *lex talionis* for personal revenge. Rather, when you are abused, have the authorities exact retribution" is hardly what Jesus has in mind. His point rather concerns a "willingness to suffer personal loss as a characteristic Christian virtue."[169] There is clearly hyperbole involved (again) in the examples which follow (vv. 39-42), and precise definitions are not necessary here. What is important, however, is the observation that while Jesus may not formally repeal the *lex*, he very severely restricts its use.[170]

In the final antithesis (vv. 43-44), Jesus proceeds from loving one's neighbor (Lev. 19:18) to loving one's enemy. The exact origin of "and hate your enemy" is uncertain, as mentioned above. But no matter. However one understands the "hate" clause, it remains that "loving one's enemy" is a principle not immediately evident in any exposition of Moses (particularly in light of Deut. 23:3-6, etc.). This is plainly more than a careful articulation of the love command of Leviticus 19:18. It is an advance. Jesus extends the law's requirement. Simply put, Jesus demands more than Moses.

---

[168] Schreiner, *The Law & Its Fulfillment*, 237-238. Moo, "Jesus and the Authority of the Mosaic Law," 22. Hendriksen, *Matthew*, 310.

[169] Bahnsen, *Theonomy in Christian Ethics*, 118. This is how the apostle Paul seems to interpret this command in 1 Corinthians 6, where he emphasizes that it would be better to be wronged than to take a brother to court.

[170] "In the thinking of the [Westminster] Divines, . . . the *lex talionis* is abrogated by the law of forgiveness." Sinclair B. Ferguson, "An Assembly of Theonomists?" in *Theonomy: A Reformed Critique*, ed. William S. Barker & W. Robert Godfrey, (Grand Rapids: Zondervan Publishing House, 1990), 336.

Conclusion on the Antitheses

The common explanation that Jesus is merely correcting mistaken views of the law's original meaning does not fit the evidence. This is surely involved in some of the cases, but in none of the cases is this explanation sufficient by itself. Rather, it seems that Jesus, 1) claims an authority that is superior to that of Moses;[171] and 2) exercises that authority by taking the law of Moses in whatever direction he sees fit. In some cases, he leaves the particular command intact (#1 & 2). In other cases he extends the teaching of the command as originally given or advances it in some other way (#1, 2, 3?, 6). In still other cases he seems to rescind the original legislation (#3, 4) or at least restrict it (#5). There seem to be elements both of continuity and discontinuity. And there appears to be no simple explanation for this other than that Jesus has claimed and exercised a prerogative that is uniquely his. Indeed, he is greater than Moses, and greater than the law itself.

---

[171] This is in keeping with the Matthean "eschatological transcendence" pattern noted in the previous chapter, as well as the "Christological *egō*" in the antitheses themselves.

CHAPTER 7

Matthew 5:17-20 — The Messianic Mission

Fred G. Zaspel

With this larger theological and exegetical context in mind, we are now positioned for a more careful exegesis of Matthew 5:17-20.

Introduction

Matthew presents Jesus as the new Moses (among other historical figures), yet greater and with superior authority. And when Jesus actually treats the law, he is not hesitant to appear so. What bearing, if any, this has on Matthew 5:17 (Jesus' Sermon text) remains to be shown.

The question that faces the interpreter of Matthew 5:17 concerns Jesus' mission: what is his purpose in coming as it relates to the law of Moses?

Exegesis of Matthew 5:17a

"Do not think" may reflect, as many suggest, a previous charge against Jesus that he was "destroying" the law.[172] If so, the charge may stem from his attitudes toward the Sabbath or the rabbinic traditions. However, the phrase occurs again in 10:34, and both there and here it may be understood merely as a

---

[172] Robert A. Guelich, *The Sermon on the Mount: A Foundation for Understanding* (Waco, TX: Word Books, 1983), 136.

rhetorical device designed to emphasize the positive by negating an alternative. However, given the strong emphasis on Jesus' Messianic credentials in Matthew, "I came" (*ēlthon*) does seem to reflect a sense of Jesus' Messianic consciousness.[173] This word does not occur in Matthew with the frequency that it has in John's Gospel, where Jesus uses it to emphasize his divine/heavenly origin.[174] But following as it does Matthew's "infancy narrative," the voice from Heaven at his baptism, etc., and given the Christological implications associated with the term elsewhere in Matthew, the idea of Messianic authority is likely implied here also. The phrase "the law or the prophets" refers to (OT) Scripture as a whole. The disjunctive "or" (*ē*) connects both divisions, highlighting the fact that Jesus has not come to do violence to either. The verbs "to destroy" (*katalusai*) and "to fulfill" (*plērōsai*) are both telic or purpose infinitives—Jesus is addressing and clarifying the goal of his mission in relation to the Scriptures and thereby emphasizing his centrality to them.

The definitions of *kataluō* ("destroy") offered in the standard lexicons are almost endless, and for this reference (5:17), "abrogate," "abolish," or "annul" are generally offered by lexicographers and commentators alike. "Destroy" stands in contrast to "fulfill," and while the contrast may not be absolute (cf. 10:34), the strong sense of "purpose" is evident. Moreover, the parallel in verse 18 speaks of parts of the law "passing away" (*parelthē*) and likewise reflects the idea of accomplishment of intended goals: the law will not "fall to the ground." *Kataluō* is used five times in Matthew[175] and always by Jesus (or when his words are being quoted).

---

[173] Cf. Matthew 9:13; 10:34; 11:19; 20:28.

[174] Cf. John 1:11; 3:31; 5:43; 6:14; 7:42; 8:14, 42; 9:39; 10:10; 11:27; 12:27, 46, 47; 14:3, 18, 23, 28; 15:22; 16:28; 18:37.

[175] 5:17 (twice); 24:2; 26:61; 27:40.

The other references (outside of chapter 5) refer to "destroying" the temple, and that usage illustrates well the meaning here (as KJV). He has not come to "tear down" or "disassemble" the law in the sense of destroying that for which it was intended. Tasker's idea of "contradicting" does not go far enough;[176] it is only a part of the picture. The purpose of Jesus' "coming" entailed doing something with/to the law of Moses. His affirmation is that he has not come to jettison the law or make it fail its intended design. He will not render it invalid. Liddell and Scott offer several definitions that may fit: cancel, dissolve, dismiss, make useless, cast down. Perhaps "overthrow" fits best. Simply put, Jesus denies that he has come with cross-purposes to the law. He will not invalidate the Scriptures which God has given; he will allow them to stand, and their purpose will continue to be served.

But what is the law's purpose? It has already been shown in vv.21-48 that Jesus will take the law of Moses in whatever direction he sees fit. But in those various directions, what is the cohesive factor? How can his treatment of the law be explained and identified?

The answer to these questions lies in the next infinitive, *plērōsai* ("to fulfill"), the key word to the entire discussion.

"Fulfill" (*plēroō*) in Matthean Usage

With all the press Matthew gives to this word (*plēroō*), the question of definition becomes greatly simplified. A survey of these occurrences follows.

In two instances, *plēroō* is used in a more literal sense. In 13:48, Jesus speaks of "filling up" a fishing net; the meaning is

---

[176] R. V. G. Tasker, *The Gospel According to St. Matthew* in *TNTC* (1961; reprint, Grand Rapids: Wm. B. Eerdmans Publishing Co., 1978), 64.

clear enough. In 23:32, Jesus scolds the Pharisees for their wickedness and describes their sin as "filling up" their fathers' iniquity. In this sense, the sin of Israel's rebellion against God is seen to reach its climax in their rejection of his Son.

Ten of the occurrences of *plēroō* in Matthew are a part of the "fulfillment formulas" or "formula quotations" (1:22; 2:15, 17, 23; 4:14; 8:17; 12:17; 13:35; 21:4; 27:9), and two further uses are virtually identical (26:54, 56).[177] In these twelve instances, Matthew records a narrative of some event associated with Jesus' life, cites a specific passage from the OT, and declares it to be "fulfilled." At first glance, each of these "formulas" makes a clear announcement that God's purposes have reached their culmination in Jesus, and upon closer investigation, the impression is strengthened. In all these, the sense of "fulfillment" is a broad, redemptive-historical one. Often it is the "prediction/verification" sense which is prominent (e.g., 21:4-5). But sometimes the connection is more subtle (2:15, 17-18). "[T]he kind of typology varies considerably. Yet the perception remains constant that the OT was preparing the way for Christ, anticipating him, pointing to him, leading up to him."[178] With his arrival, God's purposes expressed in the Scriptures are reached.

Usage in 3:15 varies but is similar enough. At Jesus' baptism, he claims to embody the practice of righteousness which God requires of all men. The idea is "accomplishment," and "realization of God's purposes" is not far away (although in a different sense than in the formula quotations).

It would appear from the general Matthean use of "fulfill" (*plēroō*) that Jesus' claim is intended to be understood in an eschatological sense. Curiously, the only parallel to this

---

[177] Cf. 2:5, where the formula is the same but condensed and without the use of *plēroō*.

[178] Carson, *Matthew*, 28.

statement found elsewhere in the Gospels is Luke 16:16-18 which points in this same direction:

> The law and the prophets were until John; since that time the kingdom of God is preached, and every man presses into it. And it is easier for heaven and earth to pass, than one tittle of the law to fall. Whoever divorces his wife and marries another commits adultery; and whoever marries her who is divorced from her husband commits adultery.

Again it is Jesus himself who specifies that the law had a prophetic/prospective function; it anticipated Jesus Christ who brought about its expectations; namely, the kingdom. And the coming of the kingdom affected the law—in this instance it meant a rescinding of Moses' divorce allowance. In doing so, the law did not "fall" (*piptō*). The parallel holds even in detail. Christ brought the "full" eschatological intent of the law to final realization. Moses survives, but only as he is taken up into Christ.

It is entirely arguable that Matthew's whole theological motivation in writing his Gospel may be summed up in this one word—"fulfilled" (*plēroō*, seventeen times in Matthew; *teleō*, three times). This is his trademark, his primary thrust emphasized over and again, even without the use of the term. For Matthew, Jesus is the fulfillment of all the expectations regarding David's and Abraham's son, and he is the one who "fills full" all the promises made throughout Israel's history. Speak of Bethlehem, Galilee, the Messiah, the King of Israel/the Jews, the suffering Servant of Jehovah, the Son of Man, or any of a host of other terms pregnant with expectation, and Jesus is the Fulfiller, the answer and goal of them all.

This outlook is evident on virtually every page of Matthew's Gospel. Matthew reveals a keen awareness of redemptive history that causes him to see in the person of Jesus a realization of all of Israel's long hopes (cf. 11:13). He very casually sees in Jesus' ascent from Egypt, for example, a "fulfilling" of the experience of the nation of Israel (2:15; cf. Hos. 11:1). Just as easily, he recognizes in the arrival of Jesus and the accompanying atrocities by Herod at Bethlehem a final answer to Israel's (even Rachel's) sorrows (2:16-18)—this too is labeled a "fulfillment." In neither of these instances is there a specific "prophecy" (prediction) involved, but, for Matthew, the historical events served to foreshadow the "fulfillment" brought about in Jesus Christ. The same is true of the Nazarene "prophecy" of 2:23. For Matthew, Jesus is the culmination of salvation history.

In his significant and influential article "Fulfillment-Words in the NT: Use and Abuse," C. F. D. Moule demonstrates that Matthew's use of *pleroō*, besides its "superficial prediction/ verification" function, is full of implications that are "summed up in the term *Heilsgeschicte*."[179] Observing Matthew's relatively elaborate use of typology, France likewise remarks:

> What may seem to us as an embarrassingly obscure and even irresponsible way of handling Scripture is in fact the outworking of a careful tracing of scriptural themes, which in different ways point to Jesus as the fulfiller not only of specific predictions, but also of the broader pattern of God's Old Testament revelation. . . . This typology is not so much a hermeneutical technique as a theological conviction which expresses itself in various ways in Matthew's presentation of Jesus' life and teaching. Its effect is to show Jesus as the point at which all the rich diversity of God's relations with his people in word and deed converges; that is what 'fulfillment' means for Matthew.[180]

So to say that Jesus is the new Moses, David's greater son, etc., or to say that he holds supreme authority, is entirely right. But it is not enough. He is still more. He is the outworking, the full measure, the goal, and the accomplishment of the Divine

---

[179] Moule, *New Testament Studies* 14 (1967-1968), 293-320.

[180] France, *Matthew: Evangelist and Teacher,* 39-41.

The Messianic Mission

purpose. In short, he is the "fulfillment" of redemptive history. This is precisely the outlook which pervades Matthew's Gospel, and he goes to great lengths to show it.

Within this context, it would be surprising if chapter 5 of Matthew's Gospel would be any different. Indeed, Jesus' Sermon text, the basic proposition which he proceeds to expound, is precisely that: he came "to fulfill" (*plērōsai*).

Contextual Considerations

Contextual matters must be taken into consideration also, and in Matthew 5 itself, the evidence runs along the same lines. First, as pointed out earlier, "to fulfill" (*plērōsai*) stands in contrast[181] to "to destroy" (*katalusai*), which has the sense of invalidating or destroying that for which something was intended. The law will not fall to the ground. So, in this context, "fulfill" should carry the corresponding eschatological significance of "to bring about its intended and ultimate purpose"—*which is precisely its meaning throughout Matthew*. The idea is not that of annihilation/preservation, but overthrowing/fulfilling. It is eschatological actualization that is in view.

> "[I]n some not clearly defined way (the verb *plēroun* [fulfill] has the advantage of positive connotations but not the liability of excessive specificity) the 'true' meaning of the Old Testament scriptures is satisfied, and they reach their intended goal, in Jesus' ministry."[182]

Verse 18 provides three more indicators that point in the same direction. First, the implication of "pass away" (*parelthē*)

---

[181] Note the strong adversative *alla* ("but").

[182] Stephen Westerholm, *Israel's Law and the Church's Faith* (Grand Rapids; Wm. B. Eerdmans Publishing Co., 1988), 204.

is that of failure to achieve an intended goal, "falling to the ground" unfulfilled. There is again an eschatological sense. The same is implied also in *genētai*, translated "fulfilled" in the KJV and "accomplished" in the NASB and NIV. The idea is simply, "happen" or "come about." Jesus is speaking in terms of the law's "prophetic"/ eschatological purposes being achieved (cf. Luke 16:16). This, taken in consideration of the two "until" (*heōs*) clauses, shouts of eschatological fulfillment.

Verse 20 points in the direction of eschatological fulfillment also. More attention will be given to some details in the next chapter, but it could be noted here that the "righteousness" of which Christ speaks and which he demands is presented as the real experience of those in his kingdom (cf. verses 6 and 10). Yet this "righteousness" is presumably the very righteousness expected in the prophets, particularly Isaiah. Here also, then, there is indication of "fulfillment" in an eschatological sense.

Jesus' Point of Reference

Finally, it should be observed that given the way Jesus expounds this proposition in verses 21-48, as well as the specific mention of "commands" (*entolōn*), (the commanding aspects of the law, v.19), it seems clear that it is his *teaching* that is in view.[183] This accords also with the Matthean emphasis on what Jesus "says."[184] The ethical function of the law and prophets anticipated a "fulfilling," which Jesus claims here to give it in the principles he expounds. Largely, the older Reformed view that the "fulfillment"

---

[183] At this point I am in agreement with Greg Bahnsen, although from here we go in opposite directions. Bahnsen, *Theonomy in Christian Ethics*, 50ff.

[184] Cf. the often repeated "Jesus said"; the fifty-five "I say" sayings (significantly more than any other Gospel writer); "my words"; the discourses; etc.

in view is Jesus' active obedience to the Mosaic stipulations has rightly fallen out of vogue.

Strickland continues one dispensational interpretation when he reduces the significance of "fulfill" (*plērōsai*) merely to fulfilling prophecy (in the prediction/verification sense),[185] but this fails to take into account both the immediate context (which is Christ's teaching/law) and the broader significance of "fulfill" in Matthean usage surveyed above. The passage itself (through to the end of the Sermon) focuses, not on Jesus' actions nor on the mere occurrence of what was predicted, but on Jesus' ethical teaching.

Neither does Jesus' teaching here merely clarify the original code. It is more climactic; there is eschatological transcendence. Jesus' teaching brings about the ultimate intention of Moses' law. It expresses fully and ideally the "righteousness" anticipated at Sinai and in the prophets. The old law was not "filled" in itself; it had a forward look. It anticipated a "fulfilling" which, in Christ's teaching, finally came to perfect realization.

Although he comes to different final conclusions than those offered here, Brevard Childs states the point well:

> Jesus' disagreement with the representatives of Judaism regarding the law emerges sharply both in his actions and in his words as is made clear in the series of controversies with the Pharisees (9.1-8, 9-13; 12.1-8; 15.1-20; 19.1-9: cf. Hummel and G. Barth). The depth of the disagreement is underestimated when scholars suggest that Jesus was only opposing the Pharisaic tradition of the law, but leaving the Mosaic law itself intact. Nor is the controversy adequately described by claiming that Jesus sought only to dispense with the Old Testament ceremonial law while retaining the ethical imperatives. *Rather, the issue turned on Jesus' claim to be the new interpreter of the will of God as revealed*

---

[185] Strickland, "The Inauguration of the Law of Christ With the Gospel," 258.

in the law. 'The Son of man is lord of the Sabbath' (12.8).[186]

Conclusion

In the end, therefore, the focus shifts a bit. "[I]t is not the question of Jesus' relation to the Law that is in doubt but rather its relation to him!"[187] How is Moses' law affected, now that its fulfiller/fulfillment has come? In Matthew 5:17, "fulfill" (*plērōsai*) carries precisely the same significance it has throughout Matthew: Jesus came to bring about what Moses' law anticipated. The law pointed forward to him all along; he is its eschatological goal. Only in him does it find its full significance and continuing validity; apart from Jesus' interpretation of it, it has precisely no enduring use.[188] Just as Moses' law advanced the law which God had "written on the heart" of man at creation,[189] so also in Jesus' teaching that advance is brought to full completion. In Jesus, Moses is "fulfilled."

This understanding has several advantages, among which are the following.

1. It does not require a different sense for "fulfill" (*plēroō*) than what is found consistently elsewhere in Matthew.
2. It preserves the contrast with "destroy" (*katalusai*).

---

[186] Brevard S. Childs, *The New Testament as Canon: An Introduction* (Philadelphia: Fortress Press, 1985), 71-72 (emphasis added).

[187] Banks, "Matthew's Understanding of the Law," 242.

[188] Cf. W. D. Davies and Dale C. Allison, *A Critical and Exegetical Commentary on The Gospel According to Saint Matthew* (Edinburgh: T. & T. Clark Limited, 1988), 487. Also Carson, *Matthew*, 144.

[189] Cf. Fred G. Zaspel, *The Continuing Relevance of Divine Law* (Hatfield, PA: 1991), 2-6.

3. It fits very well in the larger Christological context of Matthew.

4. It provides specific explanation for Matthew's repeated presentation of Jesus as greater than Moses.

5. It gives close attention to Matthew's emphasis on redemptive history. Jesus inaugurates a new era which affects even the law of Moses—and, in fact, was anticipated by it.

6. It provides a single explanation for Jesus as the "fulfillment" of the law which applies equally to every detail ("jot and tittle") of it. Jesus' fulfillment of both the ceremonial and the moral aspects of the law is understood in precisely the same sense; namely, type and antitype. Differing explanations in reference to the various aspects of Moses' law, therefore, become unnecessary inasmuch as the "fulfillment" of both is the same.

7. It provides the simplest explanation for Jesus' handling of Moses' law in 5:21-48. He did not merely "intensify" the law. Nor did he merely extend it, add to it, or replace it. All of these explanations are involved at different points, but none is sufficient by itself. His mission was broader than any of those suggestions: he was to bring the law to its intended goal, to bring about its final realization.

8. It allows for the "advance" that is both inherent in Matthew's "fulfill" and evident in the exposition of 5:21-48.

9. It explains the frequent emphasis on Jesus' teaching throughout Matthew's Gospel (e.g., 7:24, 26).[190]

10. It preserves the continuity with Moses that is directly implied in the contrasting phrase "not to destroy but to fulfill"; it is no mere "replacement" theology. Yet it also allows for the dramatic "shift" that is sometimes evident in 5:21-48, and often in Paul, which is required by the "newness" of this age.

---

[190] Cf. 5:22, 26, 28, 32, 34, 39, 44; 11:29; 17:5; 28:20.

11. It rids us of the "tension" between Matthew and Paul; Matthew is not quite the conservative he is often said to be.

Objection

Generally, the more common Reformed understanding has been that Jesus' "fulfillment" of the law was his clarifying its true meaning in some way. Bahnsen argues at length in an even more conservative direction—Jesus here (and in verses 21-48) "confirms" the enduring validity and applicability of every detail of the law.[191] Poythress goes to lengths to show that Bahnsen's evidence for this understanding of *pleroō* (as "confirm") does not support his thesis.[192] He further points out that,

> the language of confirmation could mean either of two things. If "confirm" connotes "confirm as rules binding on all," Mosaic law becomes a rule for our obedience. But if "confirm" connotes "confirm the validity or truthfulness of," Jesus may be simply asserting that the Old Testament law remains the authoritative word of God, as part of the canon. Such an assertion would be compatible with abolishing or radically altering its role as a rule for obedience.[193]

If either of these senses were in view, *histēmi* or *bebaioō* would have better served the purpose.[194] Any notion of a mere reissuing of Moses' law makes 5:17 a misfit within Matthew's "greater

---

[191] Bahnsen, *Theonomy in Christian Ethics*, 39-86.

[192] Poythress, "Does the Greek Word *Pleroō* Sometimes Mean 'Confirm'?" Appendix C, *The Shadow of Christ in the Law of Moses*, 363-377.

[193] Ibid., 394-395, n.13.

[194] Cf. Rom. 3:31.

than Moses" Christology, leaving the whole motif unexplained. And it further reduces "fulfillment" to mere continuance.

Finally, Bahnsen's claim proves too much: if it is "every detail" ("every jot and tittle") of the law that is "confirmed" and declared continually binding, how then can he admit to the abrogation of the dietary and the ceremonial laws? If it is argued (as it is by Reformed interpreters generally) that the ceremonial laws are not abrogated but rather "taken up" in the greater work of Christ, which they anticipated,[195] then it must be asked why a different explanation for the remainder of Moses' law is necessary. This is precisely the position argued here—the entire law had a sense of anticipation about it, an anticipation that was exhausted and realized in Jesus Christ. He is the "new wine" of the New Covenant era, which must not be put into the old wineskins of the Mosaic covenant (9:17); he is the cloth newly woven throughout (9:16).

With regard to parallels between the ages of redemptive history, the question is not so much that of continuity / discontinuity, but of type/antitype. The type gives way to the antitype, which transcends it in some manner. So it is with the law. Not the ceremonial only, but "every jot and tittle," Jesus says, is "fulfilled" in him—swallowed up into its fuller realization.

The whole law, then, was taken up into Christ, and he gave to it its truest significance. What that significance is, is for him to explain;[196] the significance is not—and cannot be—established by a predetermining hermeneutic. Likewise, he determines also what details endure and in what sense. God's law comes to the church through the hands of Christ, the Lord of the law. "The way in which each law is fulfilled in Christ determines the way in which it is to be observed now."[197] Continuity

---

[195] E.g., John Murray, *Principles of Conduct* (1957; reprint, Grand Rapids: Wm. B. Eerdmans Publishing Co., 1981), 150.

[196] By his teaching personally and via the inspired writers of the New Testament; cf. John 16:12-13.

[197] Poythress, *Shadow of Christ in the Law of Moses*, 269.

with Moses there is, but Moses is no longer the center of attention nor the final court of appeal—that prerogative belongs to one greater than Moses.

It is *Jesus* who pronounces with supreme authority what is the will of God, and his teaching forms the ultimate standard of righteousness. He clarifies that righteousness which Moses' law only foreshadowed (cf. Col. 2:17).

CHAPTER 8

The Law of Christ in Matthew 5:18-20 and Related Passages

Fred G. Zaspel

For Matthew, then, what Jesus has to say has an eschatological significance to it. He has not merely reissued Moses. Nor has he abrogated Moses. Nor has he merely replaced, intensified, or expanded him. Jesus "fulfilled" Moses.

Introduction to Matthew 5:18-20

The principles that Jesus enunciates are the "fulfilling" of long centuries of anticipation; Moses has stepped aside and given way to this one whose teaching forms the ultimate standard of righteousness and who pronounces with supreme authority what is the will of God. He clarifies that righteousness which Moses' law only foreshadowed (cf. Colossians 2:17).

Thus, the (Old Testament) Scriptures have not failed their purpose; to the contrary (*alla*), they are fulfilled. Jesus takes up this subject, as indicated by the explanatory *gar* ("for," v.18, KJV), to explain and defend. He continues with the same note of urgency (*amēn*, "truly!" "verily!") and authority ("*I* say"), affirming the necessarily enduring quality ("will by no means pass away") of even the smallest details of the law. The "jot or tittle" (probably the Hebrew letter *yod* and the small distinguishing "hooks" of the Hebrew letters ב and ד) is probably best understood in a hyperbolic sense; even so, it remains that it, along with the repeated "*one* jot" and "*one* tittle" and the emphatic "by no means" (*ou mē*), is intended to stress

Jesus' high view of Scripture (cf. John 10:35). To paraphrase, "By the nature of what the Scriptures are (i.e., the Word of God), their purposes will be carried out to the letter— yes, to every slightest stroke of the inspired pen."

The two "until" (*heōs*) clauses give a time frame for Scripture's fulfillment. The first, "until heaven and earth pass," does not quite say "never"[198] but simply "until the end of this age." Linguistic and contextual similarities in 24:35 show this. The second, "until all comes to pass," as pointed out in the previous chapter, signifies "until everything [which the law anticipates] happens." That is, "so long as this world order continues, the [prophetic aspects of] law will continue to be carried out; not one detail will fail." Jesus has come to give the law its fulfillment, and to the end of this age this will continue.

"One of these least commands"

Jesus next carries the thought a step further (*oun*), "therefore," v. 19: if the law's fulfillment must continue, one implication, at least, is that it must be obeyed and faithfully taught ("do and teach"). To say it another way, it must not be violated by disobedience nor neglect nor misrepresentation ("break and teach men so"). Indeed, that one who does so will "be called least in the kingdom of heaven"—implying, of course, that he actually will *be* the least in the kingdom. The interpretation of the verse turns on the phrase "one of these least commands." To what, precisely, does this refer? Is this an affirmation that every detail of Moses' law "remains binding until the end of the world"?[199] Several options are available. First, it could be taken very literally to mean that throughout this age the church should continue to observe every detail of the Mosaic law. But

---

[198] Contra Bahnsen, *Theonomy in Christian Ethics*, 76.

[199] Ibid., 72.

The Law of Christ

given the teaching that is capsulized in the book of Hebrews, few Christians would want to go this far. Second, it could be taken to mean that the moral law in general and/or the Decalogue in particular should continue to be observed throughout this age.[200] This is the standard Reformed position. But it would be difficult to understand "these *least* commands" as a reference to this "weightier" aspect of the law! Further, it introduces a literary division of the law which is extraneous to, if not inconsistent with, the passage, for it is every last "jot and tittle" that is in view. That which Jesus takes up for example/application (vv. 21-48) fits no such nicely defined category (either moral or civil or ceremonial). Bahnsen's position (that it is the "exhaustive details" of the law, minus the ceremonial aspects) comes closer but suffers the same criticism. What Jesus has to say is in reference to every last single detail ("one jot, one tittle") of the law.

Banks suggests that "these least commands" is a proleptic reference, not to Moses' law, but to Jesus' "*Nova Lex*" ("new law") which has displaced Moses' law.[201] This view has some things to be said in its favor, such as the weight given to Jesus' teaching as the climactic fulfillment of Moses and the emphatic "But I say to you" repeated throughout the following passage. It also finds a possible answer in Jesus' "these words of mine" (7:24, 26). But this all seems exegetically strained. It requires the reader to know beforehand what lies ahead in vv. 21-48. Further, "law" (*nomos*) in verses 17-18 (even in Bank's view) refers to the law of Moses; it would be a surprising shift indeed for "these least commands," stated in the very same breath, to be something different. To understand "these least commands" as a reference to Moses' law is the simpler and more obvious reading.

---

[200] Hendriksen, *Matthew*, 292.

[201] Banks, *Jesus and the Law in the Synoptic Tradition*, 233. "Matthew's Understanding of the Law," 239.

However, Banks is not far off the mark. Jesus has just emphasized that *he* is the fulfiller of the law. He also emphasizes that *every detail* ("jot and tittle") of Moses must continue to be observed — a phrase that is powerfully extensive. The question, then, should be, *in what sense* can every detail of Moses be followed? Answer: every detail of Moses must be followed *as it is "fulfilled" in Jesus*. It was shown in chapter 3 that there is no hermeneutical tool with which the interpreter can predict or sort out the "new" interpretations which Jesus gives to Moses in verses 21-48. It must suffice to say simply that this is how the Lord of the law hands it down. There is no other cohesive factor involved in the various directions in which the law is taken. It is Moses' law, to be sure. But it is Moses' law *as it is given to the church from the hands of Christ*. This is indeed why he emphasizes at the end that "these words of mine" form the basis of eternal judgment (7:24-27). This is why "lawlessness" (*anomia*) is defined as disobedience to *his* words (7:23-24). He did not claim to "rubber stamp" Moses, nor did his exposition (vv. 21-48) resemble a mere reaffirmation of Moses. It resembled, rather, an assignment to the older law of its new and eschatological significance by one "greater than Moses." This is what he claims in verse 17. This is what he does in verses 21-48. This is what he requires in verse 19. Moses' law is not simply displaced; it is fulfilled. But in the process, Moses takes "back seat" to his antitype.

Conclusion

Virtually all Christian interpreters agree that the ceremonial aspects of Moses' law are "set aside" in that they find a new significance in the work of Christ. Having come to this "fulfillment," they are taken up into the new and final realization of that which they anticipated. This is precisely what is argued here in reference to "every detail" (not one aspect only) of the law.

The Law of Christ

Reformed interpreters generally must speak (in so many words) of the fulfillment of the ceremonial law, the cancellation/abrogation of the civil law, and the continuance of the moral law. But all this is confusing and completely unnecessary if the *whole* of the law may be viewed as taken up into Christ and given his new and authoritative interpretation. With this, then, "every detail" of the law (of Moses!) may be observed by the New Covenant believer in precisely the same way: namely, in the way it comes to him from the hands of Christ.

With some details of the law, the "fulfillment" will entail extension or even addition (vv. 21-22, 27-28). With some details, the fulfillment will involve restriction (vv. 38-39) or even abrogation (vv. 31-32, 33-34). Other details may be seen now to have served merely as *illustrations* of something greater (e.g., the sacrifices, the Sabbath). But no matter: the lead is taken by the Lord of the law, he gives the law its eschatological significance. He determines what details remain and in what form, and it is in this form only that the law remains binding in this Messianic age.

For the New Covenant believer, then, every last detail of Moses is "done and taught" in keeping with its fulfillment.

In hermeneutical debate it is often asked whether it is right to assume that all of Moses' law remains unless it is specifically abolished, or if it is right to assume that it is all abolished unless it is specifically stated to remain. In one sense the question is irrelevant, for it is the entire Old Covenant that is abolished (2 Corinthians 3) and not just certain categories of its law. But in another sense the question is wrong, for Christ's claim here is that *all* of Moses is to be *continually* taught and observed—only, in the new form he gives it. It is all of the law that remains, but it is to be obeyed *as interpreted by Jesus*.

Antinomianism?

For many, to reject Moses as the final authority is antinomianism. Yet, "one does not do away with ceremonies, when their reality is kept, and their shadow omitted."[202] This is what is proposed here, only it is applied consistently to all the law and not to ceremonial aspects only.

"These commandments" from Christ do not reflect a substandard, more-easily-attainable righteousness. The law as it is now fulfilled in Christ epitomizes the very highest righteousness, one that surpasses even that of "the scribes and the Pharisees" (v. 20) and one that Moses' law anticipated. These men, who in their day represented the very essence of holiness, had at their best a righteousness which was inferior to that made known by Christ's authoritative interpretation of the law. Indeed, this is the very righteousness of God (v. 48).

In a book designed to popularize the older Puritan view of the law, Walter Chantry admits and affirms the logical implication of his position. His hermeneutic prohibits any advance on Moses, so without qualification he asserts,

> Our Lord Jesus Christ himself *did not give a condensed and definitive code of morality*. In his great sermon on kingdom righteousness (Matt. 5), the greatest Prophet produced no new standard. He merely gave clear exposition of old statutes.[203]

To say anything less is, for Chantry, antinomianism.[204]

A. W. Pink speaks similarly.

---

[202] Calvin, *A Harmony of the Gospels: Matthew, Mark, and Luke*, 181.

[203] Walter J. Chantry, *God's Righteous Kingdom* (Carlisle, PA: Banner of Truth Trust, 1980), 81 (emphasis added).

[204] Ibid., 83.

The Law of Christ 129

> Christ is not here pitting Himself against the Mosaic law, *nor is He inculcating a superior spirituality*. Instead he continues . . . expounding the spirituality of the moral law.[205]

And again,

> Our Lord's design in these verses has been misapprehended, the prevailing but erroneous idea being held that they set forth the vastly superior moral standard of the New Covenant over that which obtained under Judaism.[206]

Dabney spoke in the same terms:

> The whole decalogue is found written out in full, in two places of the Bible; besides a number of other places where one or more of the precepts is cited. These places are Exodus xx:2 to 17, and Deut. v:6 to 21. It is the doctrine of the Catechism, that these "Ten Words" were intended to be a summary of man's whole duty. Why, it may be asked, is so much made of them? Why not make equal account of some few verses taken from the Proverbs, or the Sermon on the Mount? We reply: the manner of their publication plainly showed that *God intended to give them the peculiar importance we assign them.*[207]

This aspect of traditional Covenant Theology has been widely influential, and similar citations could be multiplied. Bahnsen was cited earlier as saying virtually the same thing also. But all this misses Jesus' point entirely. Nowhere here is there

---

[205] Arthur W. Pink, *An Exposition of the Sermon on the Mount* (1950; reprint, Grand Rapids: Baker Book House, 1979), 110 (emphasis added).

[206] Ibid., 127 (emphasis added).

[207] R. L. Dabney, *Lectures in Systematic Theology* (1927; reprint, Grand Rapids: Baker Book House, 1985), 354 (emphasis added).

any implication that Jesus came merely to "clarify" or more fully explain Moses' law. He did nothing of the kind. He came to "fulfill" the law, to give to it its final "filling up." His teaching is a necessary advance, "filling full" that which awaited him for precisely this purpose. In Jesus is found, indeed, a full and complete "definitive code of morality." Apart from him, the old law has no binding relevance whatever, and the "filling" which he gave it reflects and demands a degree of righteousness which Moses' law only anticipated.

So the standard has not been lowered; it has been elevated. The love for neighbor demanded under Moses fades in comparison to the love for enemy demanded by the Lord Jesus. So also Moses' allowances for divorce, made in concession to man's rebelliousness, are rescinded in the law of Christ. Similarly, those old laws forbidding murder are essential, but the law of Christ adds the prohibition of hatred. Did the old law regulate oaths? The fulfilled law forbids them and requires honesty outright and absolutely. Did the old law provide for revenge through legal means? The fulfilled law enjoins patience under God's providential care.

And so on it goes: the righteousness of the old law is brought to its climactic fulfillment in Jesus. Accordingly, the church is not at all obliged to follow the old law in its older form. We are required to follow the law only as it comes to us through the grid of Jesus Christ, the law's Lord and fulfiller. It does not belong to any hermeneutical system to dictate beforehand what part of Moses remains and what does not—which parts are "moral" and which are not. Neither must we displace the law altogether because of another hermeneutic. Nor must we contrive any other device (such as "love") in order to choose what is still required and what is not. It is Christ's prerogative, and his alone, to make such determinations.

The Law of Christ

Summary

Matthew labors to present Christ as greater than Moses. He labors also to show the redemptive-historical eschatological transcendence which Christ brought about. He labors further to emphasize the supreme authority which Christ presents. It would be most surprising if in the midst of all this, Jesus merely reissued the law of Moses.

The generally "flat" transition required by the traditional Reformed hermeneutic does not fit into Matthew's scheme of things.[208] What Matthew presents—what Jesus presents—is not re-ratified Old Covenant law, but fulfilled law for a new era and a New Covenant people. As Douglas Moo has written:

> That this conclusion is in keeping with Jesus' general approach to the OT law is clear from the relatively few number of times he cites the OT as substantiation of his demands . . . , from the clear implications of statements such as "the Son of Man is Lord even of the Sabbath" (Mark 2:28 [and Matt. 12:8]), and from the fact that it is *Jesus'* teaching that his disciples are to convey in their missionary enterprise (Matt. 28:19-20).[209]

It gives explanation also to "these sayings of mine" in 7:24, 26, to *Jesus'* "yoke" in 11:29, and to Matthew's emphasis on Jesus' teaching. Jesus as the fulfiller of the law clarifies the fact that he stands above the law—a stupendous claim which ultimately has no significance at all if the authority implied in it is not exercised. Throughout, the emphasis is off of Moses and on

---

[208] Bahnsen describes Jesus' affirmation to the Pharisees of the "abiding validity of the law in exhaustive detail" as the "boldest feature" of his teaching (*Theonomy in Christian Ethics*, 45). It is very difficult to see how this can be so bold when spoken to men who made their career by saying the same thing!

[209] Moo, "The Law of Moses or the Law of Christ," 205-206.

Christ. It is the law *interpreted through him* that remains binding in all its details.

Exegetical Correlation with Related Biblical Passages

The proposal here is that the law of Moses, while of divine origin and entirely suitable for its purpose in the older economy, has, in Christ, reached its full measure and eschatological climax. He gave to it a final significance that it had anticipated all along. With this "fulfillment" found in Jesus' teaching, the law was finally able to reflect a fuller righteousness in complete conformity to God's own perfections (5:48). He is Lord of the law, and he is its sole authoritative interpreter. The law as it was has served its purpose and remains only in the form in which Christ passes it along to the Church.

In the interests of completeness, an examination of this thesis in light of other related Scripture passages is in order. An exhaustive treatment of these passages is beyond the scope of this work, but a brief survey of some of the more prominent ones will suffice.

Old Testament Passages

The announcement in Deuteronomy 18:15-19 of the prophet like, but greater, than Moses holds significant parallels to Jesus' teaching in Matthew 5. That prophecy lays the foundation for the institution of prophetism in the nation of Israel, but looks forward to one (singular) prophet who will come and announce the will and word of God. The New Testament frequently recognizes Jesus to be the fulfillment of this prophecy (e.g., Matt. 17:5; Luke 24:19; John 4:25; 6:14; 7:40), and Jesus' "But I say unto you" provides allusion to the same. Moreover, Deuteronomy 18:19 warned that it was the words of this prophet to come that would form the standard of judgment.

This fits Jesus' claim in Matthew 5:17-20 exactly, as well as his warning in 7:24-27 concerning *his* words as the basis of judgment. The indication of the prophecy itself is that Moses' law would find a final "fulfillment" in the teaching of the Messiah. Nor is there any indication that "the prophet" will merely clarify what Moses had already taught; rather, he will himself reveal the will and word of God.

Isaiah likewise anticipates a day in which "the law and word of the Lord" will be dispensed to all the nations (2:1-3). Is this a reissuing of Moses' law? Or is more implied? Isaiah 42:4 may provide an answer; there the nations are pictured as awaiting the arrival of the Servant who will establish justice (*mišpāṭ*) and bring "his law" ([*tôrāh*]; cf. 51:4; Mic. 4:2). The Servant of Jehovah will bring the law of God to the nations. What is the exact identity of this law? Isaiah does not elaborate on this, but it is Matthew's burden to present Messiah Jesus as providing exactly this divine instruction for the Church, and the association with Isaiah's prophecy is not difficult to see. Within the context of a canonical process/development approach, at least, Isaiah also anticipates a fuller presentation of the law of God by the Messiah.

Similarly, it is not at all necessary to assume that the law (*tôrāh*) "written on the heart" in the New Covenant prophecy (Jer. 31:33; cf. Ezek. 36:27) is merely a republication or internalization of the unchanged Mosaic law. The prophet himself does not say so; indeed, he states that the New Covenant would "not [be] consistent with" the Old Covenant (*lō' kabbᵉriṯ*; Jer. 31:32; LXX and Heb. 8:9, *ou kata ē diathēkē*). This probably has in view the nature of the covenant, but the difference in covenantal terms and stipulations is at least implicit.

Moreover, Jesus seems to clarify: it is now *his* word, the law of *Christ*, which is to be fulfilled by the New Covenant believer (cf. Gal. 6:2; 1 Cor. 9:20-21).

Gospel Passages

Within the Gospel accounts, Jesus is occasionally seen taking the law of Moses in peculiar directions. It was already observed in Matthew 5:21-48 how he feels free to exercise his Messianic authority as Lord of the law to add, subtract, restrict, or extend the law's teachings as he sees fit. He is the law's new interpreter and fulfiller. Likewise, there is little explanation for his "cleansing all meats" (Mark 7:14-23; Matt. 15:10-20) apart from this very principle; he clearly took a large step beyond the Mosaic boundaries. In fact, it is this very passage that Paul alludes to in his defense of eating meats (Rom. 14:14). Paul viewed Moses through Christ, and his interpretation was established accordingly.

In a similar way, when Jesus' disciples were criticized by the Pharisees for their plucking grain on the Sabbath, Jesus does not defend their actions by accusing their opponents of having too narrow an interpretation of the law (Mark 2:23-28; cf., Matt. 12:1-6). He allows that the disciples' actions constituted a technical violation of the Sabbath, but for defense appeals to his own unique authority as Lord of the Sabbath. His actions here are entirely consistent with his claim in Matthew 5:17 as interpreted above.

Passages in the Pauline Epistles

Modern scholarship commonly speaks of some kind of tension between Matthew and the apostle Paul. Paul's seemingly (at times) reckless abandonment of the Mosaic law is seen as conflicting in some way(s) with Matthew's more conservative approach. However, it has been shown that Matthew's insistence on the continuing validity of every "least" commandment of Moses is in fact *Jesus'* demand that every detail of Moses is to be followed now *according to the way he interprets those details*—which can go in any number of directions. Matthew is not as "conservative" as he is often portrayed; his purpose is to show Jesus' authority over Moses and the fulfillment he gives to the old law. With this understanding of Matthew, the supposed tension or contradiction with Paul dissolves. Indeed, at several points Paul seems to have taken his view from precisely this same teaching presented in Matthew.

Christ the Fulfiller of the Law of Moses

Colossians 2:16-17 provides perhaps the clearest example. "Let no man therefore judge you in meat, or in drink, or in respect of an holy day, or of the new moon, or of the Sabbath days: Which are a shadow of things to come; but the body is of Christ." Here Paul describes the Mosaic law as a *skia*. This may denote "shadow"—having no substance itself but only reflecting the existence of the reality, or it may denote a dim outline or sketch of an object.[210] In either case the point is the same—Paul views the Mosaic law as anticipating a typological fulfillment brought about in Jesus Christ. Interestingly, for Paul this is true of dietary laws and prescribed holy days and even the Sabbath, and not of ceremonial rituals only. The thought is exactly that of Matthew 5:17.

A similar idea is found in Galatians 3:19-28. Paul specifically states that the law of Moses was given, served a purpose, and is no longer needed. More specifically, the law's purpose was to serve as a "tutor unto Christ" (*paidagōgos eis christon*). Not only was its function temporary, but its purpose focused on Christ (here in a soteric sense). To put it another way, it was Paul's view also that the law anticipated Christ. Now that he has come, the law is no longer needed (v. 25) except in the way that he preserves it.

---

[210] See S. Lewis Johnson, "The Paralysis of Legalism," *Bib Sac* 120 (1963), 112.

This very argument finds a parallel in Romans 10:4. Here Israel is faulted for attempting to establish her own righteousness via observance of the Mosaic law. Her zeal is commendable, but persisting in the pursuit of righteousness *apart from Christ* is to miss the purpose of the law entirely. "Christ is the culmination (*telos*) of the law." It is only by viewing the law in light of its Christocentric fulfillment that the law is "established" (*histanomen*, 3:31).[211]

Paul's stern opposition of the Judaizers at Galatia is summed up in the words of Galatians 5:1: "Stand fast therefore in the liberty wherewith Christ hath made us free, and be not entangled again with the yoke of bondage." His whole argument rested on the fact that since Jesus Christ came, the law of Moses has not been left intact; indeed, that old "yoke" should be thrown off. The changes effected by the coming of Christ are significant and wide-sweeping, and as a result the old requirements of Sabbath keeping (4:10) and circumcision (6:12) must be reevaluated in light of him.

The Law of Christ OR the Law of Moses

1 Corinthians 9:19-21 reflects Matthew 5:17 but with a different slant. Paul argues that in any given circumstance he is "free" (*eleutheros*) to choose or refuse to follow Moses; he is not obliged to Mosaic legislation (vv. 19-20) but is "without law" (*nomos*) and has perfect liberty to act accordingly (v. 21a). Not to be misunderstood, he explains that he is not "without law" absolutely. He is not obliged to Moses' law ("as under law, not being under law," *hōs hupo nomon, mē ōn autos hupo nomon*), but rather he is "subject to the law of Christ" (*ennomos Christou*, v. 21b). Just how "the law of Christ" relates to the law of Moses, Paul does not explain here, but he is clear that it is to Christ and not to Moses that his obedience

---

[211] On *telos* as "culmination" see Moo, *Romans*, 636-643.

The Law of Christ

is directed. As in 1 Corinthians 7:19, Paul "sees God's commandments now as the 'law of Christ.'" Obedience to God now "means an obedience to the will of God as disclosed in his Son" and not the old legal code.[212]

This resembles Romans 6:14-15 where Paul emphasizes that for man "under grace" (a term roughly equivalent to his "in Christ"), the demands of Moses are no longer obligatory. Again, in 1 Corinthians 7:19, Paul *contrasts* the law (*entolōn*) of God with Mosaic demands (circumcision). Of course, other Pauline statements of discontinuity and/or the abrogation of Moses fit nicely into this construct also.

Passages from Hebrews

Large sections of the epistle to the Hebrews are taken up with an explanation of the "oldness" of the Mosaic economy, and a survey of them all is unnecessary at this point. In connection with the thesis here, two passages stand out.

First, whatever else is involved in the contrast of Hebrews 3:5-6, what lies on the very surface is the fact that it is Christ and not Moses who stands over his "house." The primary focus of the book of Hebrews may be the ceremonial aspects of the Mosaic law, but the implications of the contrast are more extensive. Here, Moses stands as a type of Christ, as a servant in the house who gives way to Christ as his fulfiller.

Then, in 7:12, the author deals with the change from the old to the new in the broadest terms: "For the priesthood being changed, there is made of necessity a change also of the law." The obvious point has to do with the change of law necessarily implied by Christ's priesthood being that of Melchizedek. With changes so sweeping, there simply must have been a new law brought in. Indeed there has—the law of Christ. Again, while

---

[212] C. K. Barrett, *The First Epistle to the Corinthians* (Peabody, MA: Hendrickson Publishers, 1968), 169.

the relation of the law of Christ to the law of Moses is not explained here, the contrast is nonetheless clearly stated for our help.

Conclusion

That Christ is the eschatological fulfillment of the law of Moses is the unanimous affirmation of the New Testament writers. The nature of the law's teleological relationship to Christ as taught by Jesus in Matthew 5:17 is pivotal; it is the basic, summary statement of the doctrine that is expounded later throughout the New Testament. So far from "tension" or contradiction, there is happy and extensive agreement among all the inspired writers.

CHAPTER 9

The Continuing Relevance of Divine Law[213]

Fred G. Zaspel

Introduction

At least part of what makes the subject of divine law such a rewarding area of study is the wide range of biblical and theological issues which it touches. The study of divine law takes the student from the many passages bristling with exegetical challenges to hermeneutical issues such as redemptive history and typology and on through to theological categories such as ecclesiology, soteriology, even eschatology. But most rewarding of all, as we should expect, the study finds its culmination in the person and work of Christ. It is to this end that our study should always lead us.

Further, as is widely recognized among Christian interpreters, it is a biblical-theological approach that most easily and most accurately facilitates this pursuit. Like so many other teachings of the Scriptures, we should expect to find the doctrine of divine law progressively unfolded throughout the history of redemption. Specific issues of discussion (and dispute!) are best treated in this context.

---

[213] Much of the material from this chapter appeared first in *The Continuing Relevance of Divine Law* (Hatfield, PA: Interdisciplinary Biblical Research Institute, 1991) and "Divine Law: A New Covenant Perspective," *Reformation and Revival* 6, no. 3 (summer 1997).

Survey of Law Before Moses

The subject begins virtually with history itself. "Law came by Moses" (John 1:17), but of course that is not to say that prior to Moses there was no law from God. Indeed, we so take this for granted that when we read in the OT of pre-Mosaic sinners judged for their wickedness we never stop to ask what law code it was that they had violated and to which they were held accountable. We very naturally and very rightly understand that *they knew better*. In fact, if we could ask the question of the apostle Paul, his answer would be the same: *they knew better*. It is this very point he expounds at some length in Romans 1-2. "That which may be known of God is manifest in them, for God has showed it to them" (1:19). The knowledge of God that man possesses is consistently suppressed (1:18ff). That is to say, even before Moses, man's sin took the nature of rebellion. Man does "not approve" of God or his law (*ouk edokimasan,* 1:28). Against this, God's law, man has universally turned away, and that even in the knowledge of the coming judgment (1:32).

Are there exceptions to this rule of universal rebellion? Only in degree. All have transgressed, and even those who "had not the law" instinctively knew and to some degree obeyed the law's requirements (2:14). This law "written in their hearts" (2:15) served both to inform their "conscience" and to direct their lives. Accordingly, when Paul declares "all under sin" (Rom. 3:9), the Gentiles are not condemned for their violation of the terms of Sinai; for the Sinaitic legislation was never given to them (2:14). Rather, they are declared culpable for suppressing the truth that was *in them* (Rom. 1:18-19). These things they knew to be wrong independent of the formal legislation of Sinai.

To say the same from a contrasting standpoint, Paul speaks of Gentiles who "keep the righteousness of the law" (Rom. 2:26; cf. 2:14). This could hardly imply that the Gentiles "who have not the law" of Moses are in fact fulfilling every requirement of it, for the consciences of all men "accuse" as well as "defend" (Rom. 2:15). Clearly, he means only that they observed principles of righteousness that were in keeping with those contained also in the law of Moses. It is in this sense alone that Gentiles can be said to "fulfill the law" (v. 27). Again, it is evident that there is a law—a standard of moral righteousness—that is independent of Mosaic legislation. Divine law is published universally within every man; it is a standard of righteousness that exists independent of any formal codification. To restate the point, those who violated the eternal moral precepts of divine law prior to Moses knew better.

For that matter, we very naturally and very rightly understand the same in reference to those Gentiles of Moses' day who were "far off" (Eph. 2:13) from the law which he mediated to Israel. We are not surprised that the prophets who went to such people did not, in order to establish their guilt, hold before them the tablets of stone.[214] Their sin constituted rebellion against the law of God, yes, the law of God written on their hearts. As men made in God's image, they knew better. And when their "iniquity became full," they were judged accordingly.[215]

---

[214] Eg., Amos 1-2.

[215] Genesis 15:16. Note the various sins for which men were condemned by God in pre-Mosaic times: covetousness (Gen. 3:6), false worship (4:5, whatever the exact nature of it), murder (4:8-11), adultery/sexual profligacy (6:1-7; 19:4ff), evil thinking (6:5), dishonor of parents (9:22-25), pride and selfishness (11:4ff), injustice (16:5ff), incest (19:31ff), lying deceit (ch. 27), false gods and idolatry (Exod. 12:12; Rom. 1:25), etc. Guilt was justly established in all these apart from formal legislation. However subjective, divine law is specific and detailed.

Summary of Law Before Moses

The picture we see of divine law in the OT, both in pre-Mosaic times and in "extra-Mosaic" contexts is one of inner witness, conscience. God's image in man impresses within him an intuitive sense of right and wrong. Formal code or no, it was a sufficiently clear rule of life, which all men, in varying degrees, have both obeyed and suppressed. It is to this that men were and are justly held accountable.

The Occasion of Law Through Moses

Since it is into this context that God gave his law to Israel through Moses, we may be excused for wondering why it was necessary! Why give law to those who already have God's law in them?

The answer, of course, lies in the unique status of the nation of Israel. With them, God was entering into special, covenantal relationship. That relationship carried with it specific privileges and responsibilities, and these responsibilities had to be made plain. Accordingly, a covenant, detailing the terms of the relationship was formally enacted. It is in this covenant that God's law to Israel through Moses is embedded.

The Content of Mosaic Law

Given its unique, covenantal setting, it does not surprise us that this Mosaic law was not identical to that law of God in man. It was far more specific and detailed. Those principles of divine law, which were both eternal and universal, were not only formally codified in the law of Moses but also fleshed out in specific ways. For example, man's obligation to worship God is something recognized intuitively (cf. Rom. 1:18-25). In the Mosaic legislation this requirement was given specific

The Continuing Relevance of Divine Law 143

applications: the Sabbath and other holy days and festivals, the sacrifices, the entire Levitical system. These additions were specific applications and extensions of the principles embedded in the law of God, given now within the framework of a particular covenantal relationship and obligatory as long as that covenant was in force. But they were not essential elements of that divine law itself. To repeat, divine law underlay and formed the basis of the Mosaic legislation, and it was there given a particular codification and many specific applications.[216]

Important also is the recognition that this law of God in men's hearts from creation onward is nearly identical with the Decalogue which came by Moses. Other than the fourth command (Sabbath) virtually all of the "ten words" were in force well before Moses;[217] it would seem, since the beginning of human history. Idolatry, murder, theft, adultery, and the like, did not first become wrong when Israel was at Sinai. The great bulk of the Decalogue is clearly but a formal codification of the law of God that was (and is) in man's heart naturally. These matters are reflective of the very character and holiness of God and are thus eternal principles of righteousness that are binding upon all men regardless of formal codification—Mosaic or otherwise. With or without formal legal codes, all men are judged by this standard. The law of God exists quite independently of Mosaic legislation. There is indeed overlap, but not exact duplication.

The relation between the law of God and the law of Moses, then, is one of foundation–extrapolation. That is, Mosaic

---

[216] This also explains the "Because I told you to do it" nature of so many of the law's requirements (e.g., the dietary regulations).

[217] It is impossible to find clear pre-Mosaic statements regarding the third and fifth commands (the name of the LORD and honor of parents), but these obligations would appear implicit in the actions of the patriarchs toward their parents and in their reverence toward God.

legislation is founded upon the law of God and makes specific applications from it. It formally stated the principles of divine law and also gave specifics as to how those laws were to be carried out in that economy. With Moses, the law of God was formally codified and applied to a people who stood in a distinctive covenantal relation to God.

The two laws, moreover, are neither identical nor altogether different. The one formed the basis of the other, and the second required more than the first. But the two cannot be equated absolutely. Divine law written on the heart informs all men in terms of enduring principles of morality. The Mosaic codification of that law informed Israel of its peculiar responsibilities in its privileged relationship under God.

What exactly was Israel's part in this covenant? A great bulk of the Pentateuch and the writings and the prophets all extrapolate this very issue. In brief, Israel's responsibilities are summarized in the Ten Commandments, "the basic, fundamental law of the [Old] covenant."[218] They are "a concise but comprehensive summary of the duties of the Israelite towards God and man. . . ."[219]

---

[218] Barcellos, *Defense*, 22.

[219] Samuel R. Driver; cited by B. B. Warfield, "The Sabbath in the Word of God" in *Selected Shorter Writings of Benjamin B. Warfield* (1916; reprint, Phillipsburg, NJ: Presbyterian & Reformed Publishing Co., 1970), 1:311. That the Decalogue is the summary statement of the Mosaic law seems to be the implication of Exodus 34:27-28—"And he wrote on the tablets *the words of the covenant, the ten commandments*" (Exod. 34:27-28). Note also that in 2 Corinthians 3:7, Paul speaks of the old covenant as "written and engraved on stones."

The Nature of This Law

This "Old Covenant" further stipulated not only the specific responsibilities of the Israelites, with whom the covenant was made, but also the responsibilities that God, in covenant agreement, took on himself in this relationship. What was God's part? He would bless Israel in every way *if* she would do her part. Leviticus 26 spells this out in detail.[220] Indeed, God made this clear at the very outset: "Now therefore, if ye will obey my voice indeed, and keep my covenant, then ye shall be a peculiar treasure unto me above all people" (Exod. 19:5; see vv. 1-8). If Israel would remain faithful and obedient, she would enjoy God's protection and blessing. "You shall therefore keep my statutes and my judgments, which if a man does, he shall live by them" (Lev. 18:5; cf. Rom. 10:5). But "Cursed is everyone who does not continue in all the things that are written in the book of the law to do them" (Deut. 27:26; cf. Gal. 3:10).

The Old Covenant was, therefore, very much performance oriented. Attempts to characterize the Mosaic covenant as gracious in nature inevitably fail. The agreement was one of conditional blessing, and the obedience it required was absolute and allowed no exception. One must "continue" in obedience to "all" the law's demands (Deut. 27:26; cf. Gal. 3:10). It is for this reason that the apostle refers to the Old Covenant as "the letter that kills" and "the ministry of death" (2 Cor. 3:6-7). In contrast to the New Covenant, which is established upon "better promises" (Heb. 8:6) and offers life to sinners, the Old could only condemn sinners. It held promises of blessing for those who were obedient, but for those who transgressed its demands it held only a curse.

---

[220] Notice throughout the chapter the "If you . . . then I . . ." nature of the covenant.

Mosaic Law and Redemptive History

The law was given formally through Moses because of the unique relationship into which God entered with Israel. But that relationship, we find, had a purpose. It was not an end in itself. It was established for the purpose of demonstrating something essential to the outworking of God's redemptive program.

Here was a law given that demanded obedience for life (Lev. 18:5; Deut. 27:26). This raises yet another question: Did not God promise to Abraham that his blessing would come by grace? How could law, with all its curses, enter where grace had already been promised? Paul takes up this question in Galatians 3. "The law is not of faith, but 'The man who does them shall live by them'" (3:12; citing Lev. 18:5). Moreover, "if the inheritance is of the law, it is no longer of promise" (3:18). That is, law speaks of works, not faith. By very definition and upon threat of condemnation, law demands absolute obedience. "But God gave it to Abraham by promise. What purpose then does the law serve" (vv. 18b-19a)? That is, why did God insert law after he had already made the promise of grace? Surely, the law, coming later, could not annul the promise (v. 17)! Why add law, with its rigorous demands and threats, when grace has already been announced?

Answer: the law was "added because of transgression"[221] (v. 19b). That is, the law's purpose was to objectify sin and thereby demonstrate it as "transgression." This is Paul's statement in Romans 5:13 also: "Sin is not recorded[222] where there is no

---

[221] *Tōn parabaseōn charin* ("because of transgression") here expresses purpose.

[222] *Ellogeō*, "to keep a record of something—'to record, to list.' . . . 'but where there is no law, no account is kept of sins.' . . . 'a sin is not listed as a sin.'" (*Greek-English Lexicon of the New Testament Based on Semantic Domains*, 2nd ed., s.v. "ellogeo.")

law." The idea in both of these passages is that of itemization, objectification, delineation. The purpose of the law was to specify sin with clarity. Once sin is thus objectified, that sin is shown to be transgression.

It is in this sense that the law "was added because of transgression." Paul presents the nation of Israel as a showcase nation, a microcosm of the world. In the experience of Israel, in giving the law, he set out to demonstrate on a national level the fact of human sin and thus the law's inability to justify. Given man's failure, the law could only condemn.

But he did this only "until the seed came" (v. 19), "before faith came" (v. 23). The law functioned as Israel's "tutor unto Christ,[223] that we might be justified by faith" (v. 24). That is to say, by establishing the fact of human sinfulness, men are driven to Christ, the only alternative. This is Paul's gospel. Christ is "the seed" to whom the promise was made (v. 16); and in that he alone has satisfied all of the law's demands, both actively and passively, he is the only means of justification. Righteousness comes, not by personal merit in the eyes of the law, but by faith in the one whose merit is truly sufficient and who died as "a curse for us" (v. 13).

The law, with all its beauty and holiness, was incapable of justifying sinners. In pronouncing condemnation, it pointed away from itself to Christ.[224]

It spoke of sin, but in doing so it spoke of him; for that reason while the law itself is not gracious, it was made to serve a gracious purpose in redemptive history. It did not annul the Abrahamic promise of grace, even while demanding perfection (vv.17, 21). It rather forced men to see the necessity of that promise of grace. In fact it threw them back upon it, and herein lay its purpose in the history of redemption (vv. 21- 24).

---

[223] *Paidogōgos eis Christon.*

[224] Cf. Romans 3:21, "being witnessed by the law."

The Continuing Relevance of Divine Law Under the New Covenant

Moses' law, then, served a very significant purpose in the divine schema. It reaches its "end" (*telos*) in Christ (Rom. 10:4).

So now what remains of law? Plainly, we should not expect that with the passing of the Old Covenant there remains no more law! God's law was well known and well read before its Mosaic codification, and it has been ever since. Nor should it surprise us, after Moses, to find sin defined as "lawlessness" (*anomia*, 1 John 3:4) or to find explicit references to law (Gal. 6:2; James 1:25) or to find duties enjoined upon us as obligatory. Early dispensationalist writers regularly denied the continuing relevance of law in the life of the believer who is "under grace."[225] But the obligations of God upon his creatures have not ceased, and never could these obligations have any less binding force. The Formula of Concord (1576), although confusing the law of God and the law of Moses, is entirely correct in its insistence that the law of God is today a "certain rule after which [regenerate men] may and ought to shape their life."[226] The law of God is an eternal standard; never could it become any less a binding rule of life.

---

[225] Chafer, *Grace,* 87ff, 152ff; M. R. DeHaan, *Law or Grace?* (Grand Rapids: Zondervan, 1965), 140-141; Arno C. Gaebelein, *The Gospel of Matthew* (Neptune, NJ: Loizeaux Brothers, 1961), 232; Clarence Larkin, *Rightly Dividing the Word* (Philadelphia: Rev. Clarence Larkin Est, n.d.), 195-196; McClain, *Law and Grace* Winona Lake, IN: BMH Books, 1973), ch.7; C. I. Scofield, *Law and Grace* (Winona Lake, IN: BMH Books, 1973), ch. 6. For a brief interaction with this view, see my *The Continuing Relevance of Divine Law*, 8-10.

[226] Article 6, "Of the Third Use of the Law" (Philip Schaff, *Creeds of Christendom* [Grand Rapids: Baker Book House, 1983], 3:131).

The Passing Relevance of Moses

But what of the Mosaic formulation/codification of that law? And what of us who are related to God under the terms not of the Old but of the New Covenant? Is there a codification of law for us?

Here we enter a large body of teaching, found primarily in the Pauline literature, which teaches both that Moses' law has "passed away" (*katargeō*) and that we are not "without law" (*anomos*). In some sense, Moses is gone, but law is not. This demands clarification.[227]

Since the relationship between the law of God and the law of Moses is one of obvious overlap and similarity but not exact identity, some differences between the two are of course expected. Specific applications of divine law under Moses—such as ceremonial rites, dietary regulations, and certain civil and personal obligations—were not themselves essential to the law of God which underlay the Mosaic legislation. They were specific applications of that law to those who were related to God under the terms of that Old Covenant; they stipulated how one living under that code was to love and serve God and live with his neighbor. Accordingly, we should not expect the Old Covenant to be the ultimate expression of the believer's rule of life under the New Covenant.

Moreover, when Paul speaks of the law as a rule of life, he insists that we must not allow a man to be judged on Mosaic

---

[227] This passing relevance of Moses is spoken of both in terms of the law's justifying and/or condemning qualities (soteriology) and of the law as a rule of life (the so-called "third use" of the law). As a condemning force it has nothing whatever to say to those who are "in Christ." This was discussed earlier; it forms a large segment of the Pauline soteriology. The law's condemning power is stopped in that it is satisfied in the penal death of our substitute, who provided for us all the righteousness the law requires (Rom. 3:21-26; Phil. 3:8-9; etc.). But it is Moses as a rule of life that is under discussion here.

grounds (e.g., Col. 2:16). In a way that often struck Paul's critics as antinomian, Paul spoke recklessly (or so it would seem) about the passing relevance of the Mosaic code. He repeatedly speaks of it in the past tense. The law *had* its purpose, it served that purpose, and now it is passed away. Indeed, this was both a matter of heated dispute in the early church and of unified pronouncement by the apostolic company (Acts 15). The issue generally centered on the place of circumcision in the New Covenant community and the necessity of law-keeping as a means of justification (Gal.), but the decision rendered was a part of a larger principle; viz., that Moses' law itself had no binding relation to the believer whatsoever (Acts 15:10, 19; 2 Cor. 3; Gal. 3:19-25; 5:1-12). Paul's repeated theme of Christian liberty (Rom. 14; Gal.) argues from the assumption that Moses' law is not binding on the Christian; indeed, it is the weaker brother who insists upon Mosaic demands (Rom. 14:1ff; cf. Gal. 4:9-11; Col. 2:16). Again, the Mosaic code is consistently spoken of in the past tense and so as no longer in effect (Rom. 8:3; 9:31-32; Gal. 3:23, 24; 4:5; Heb. 7:19; etc.), and as fulfilled and replaced in Jesus Christ (Matt. 5:17-20; Heb. 7:12; 10:1-9). Indeed, it was "abolished" (*katargēsas*, Eph. 2:15; cf. 2 Cor. 3:11, 13) and "wiped out" (*exaleipsas*, Col. 2:14). It is in fact the very Mosaic *covenant* that is now annulled and replaced (Heb. 8:6-9:1; 2 Cor. 3), not just a part of it, but the whole of it. With the covenant itself abolished, its law written on tables of stones (2 Cor. 3:7) is likewise no longer in force.

The popular hermeneutical attempt to divide Moses' law into so many parts and then interpret NT statements of the passing of law accordingly is simplistic, and it cannot be maintained exegetically. As Poythress observes, "under close scrutiny this formula reveals insufficiencies.... [N]o simple and easy separation between types of law will do justice to the richness of Mosaic revelation."[228] To argue that not the moral (i.e., Decalogue) but only the civil and/or ceremonial aspects of Moses are passed, when Paul says that it is in fact the Old Covenant itself, "written and engraved in stones," that has passed away, misses Paul's point. It is Moses *en toto* that he says has gone (2 Cor. 3). Moreover, the apostle speaks not only in general, all-encompassing terms, but also in specifics. That which is "written and engraved in stones" (2 Cor. 3:7) and "the handwriting of ordinances which was against us" (Col. 2:14) refer not to civil or ceremonial applications of the Decalogue but to the Decalogue itself. It is the Mosaic legislation in its entirety and the Decalogue specifically that Paul says is "done away" (*katargēsas*, 2 Cor. 3:11, 13; cf. *exaleipsas*, Col. 2:14).

Of significance here also is the identification of the Old Covenant with the Decalogue in Exodus 34:27-28 and 2 Corinthians 3:7 noted earlier. All sides agree that these passages at least indicate that the Decalogue is the summary statement of

---

[228] Vern Poythress, *The Shadow of Christ*, 283. F. F. Bruce remarked similarly—"In the reformed tradition derived from Geneva, it has frequently been said that, while the man in Christ is not under law as a means of salvation, he remains under it as a rule of life. In its own right, this distinction may be cogently maintained as a principle of Christian theology and ethics, but it must not be imagined that it has Pauline authority. . . . Again, it is sometimes said that Christ is the end of the ceremonial law (including not only the sacrificial cultus but circumcision and the observance of the sacred calendar) but not of the moral law. Once more, this is a perfectly valid, and to some extent an obvious, theological and ethical distinction; but it has no place in Pauline exegesis. It has to be read into Paul, for it is not a distinction that Paul himself makes" (*Paul: Apostle of the Heart Set Free* [Grand Rapids: Eerdmans, 1977], 192-193). Briefly stated, however helpful it might be to view given Mosaic laws under various categories, it must be acknowledged that this is not a categorization which either Jesus or the apostles endorse; much less is it used by them *as the hermeneutical tool* for handling the question of the fulfillment or abrogation of Moses.

the Old Covenant. If this is so, then there is no dividing of Moses. The legislation of Sinai is an inseparable unit, and these identifications must inform the apostolic declarations of its abolition. It is the Mosaic code as a whole and in all its parts that has passed away, and the apostolic declarations to that end must therefore be seen to embrace even the Decalogue.[229]

Still further, the three-fold division of Moses fails of its own definitions. If the "ceremonial" law is but an application of the first table of the "moral" law, and if the "civil" law is but an application of the second table of the "moral" law, as is commonly acknowledged,[230] the supposed three divisions of Moses have thereby been reduced to two and then to one. And that one part is the Decalogue. "The whole law" (*holon ton nomon*, James 2:10) stands or falls together as an indivisible unit.

It would be wrong to forget this stated, essential unity of the Old Covenant/Decalogue when reading NT statements of the Covenant's/law's abolition (e.g., 2 Cor. 3). The statements are as broad and inclusive as they appear, and this is to be

---

[229] This is Luther's position exactly. "That Moses does not bind the Gentiles can be proved from Exodus 20[:1], where God himself speaks, 'I am the Lord your God, who brought you out of the land of Egypt, out of the house of bondage.' This text makes it clear that even the Ten Commandments do not pertain to us. For God never led us out of Egypt, but only the Jews. The sectarian spirits want to saddle us with Moses and all the commandments. We will just skip that. We will regard Moses as a teacher, but we will not regard him as our lawgiver—unless he agrees with both the New Testament and the natural law. . . . Paul and the New Testament . . . abolish the Sabbath, to show us that the Sabbath was given to the Jews alone." Luther goes on to explain that to the new covenant believer, every day is equally holy. "How Christians Should Regard Moses," *Luther's Works* 35:165-166. Luther's entire treatise here is worthy of careful attention.

[230] Walter Kaiser, *Toward An Old Testament Theology* (Grand Rapids: Zondervan, 1978), 118.

The Continuing Relevance of Divine Law

expected. The New Covenant believer is not under the Old Covenant, but the New. It would be an odd thing indeed if the summary statement of the Old Covenant remained unchanged as the summary statement of the New Covenant and was made to be the rule of life for the New Covenant believer. We would rather expect that for New Covenant believers, divine law would be codified in the New Covenant.

At this point, Jesus' statements in Matthew 5:17-20, examined earlier, are crucial. There we saw that Jesus claims to make a significant advance on the older, Mosaic legislation. He presents the law of Moses as having a forward look, anticipating a fuller significance to come. It is progress as from caterpillar to butterfly. Moses is not left intact—he is fulfilled, brought to full maturity in Jesus. As stated earlier, Moses has taken back seat. No, he is not now to be ignored; but the law he gave remains relevant only insofar as it is read through Christian lenses. Moses can no longer be read by himself. His fulfiller has come, and it would be wrong to ignore him for Moses' sake. It is no longer Moses, but Jesus who objectively informs our conscience. It is *his* moral instruction that shapes our lives and defines true sanctification.

Paul reasons from this very premise in 1 Corinthians 9:20-21, where he argues that he is not bound by Moses; he is rather "subject to the law of *Christ*."[231] Paul explains that while in a given circumstance he is free to choose either course of action, he is free from Mosaic legislation (v.20); he is "without law" and has perfect liberty to act accordingly (v.21a). However (not to be misunderstood!), he is "not without law" absolutely; he is "subject to the law of Christ." Here Paul is clear on both scores: 1) he is *not* obliged to Moses' law,[232] and 2) he *is* obliged to the law of Christ. Again, Jesus stands above even Moses.

---

[231] *Ennomos Christou*, v. 21b.

[232] *Mē ōn autos hupo nomon.*

Paul spoke like this earlier: "Circumcision is nothing, and uncircumcision is nothing, but what matters is the keeping of the commandments of God" (1 Cor. 7:19, NASB). Any man living under the Old Covenant would object, "But circumcision *is* the commandment of God!" And so it was. But Paul discards it out of hand—it is "nothing." Clearly, Paul's frame of reference was not Mosaic but Christological.

The writer to the Hebrews speaks the same way when he observes that "the priesthood being changed, there is made of necessity a change also of the law" (Heb. 7:12). The Lord Jesus brought with him a new law which has displaced the old.

James uses the curious expression, *nomon basilikon*, "law of the king" or perhaps "kingdom law" (James 2:8), and this may provide insight into James' thinking that is relevant to our discussion here. James was and is well known as an apostle to the Jews and a lover of the law. He was and is also well known for his very heavy dependence upon the teachings of his half brother, Jesus, particularly those found in the Sermon on the Mount. In this verse specifically, James' "law" quotation is, "You shall love your neighbor as yourself" (Lev. 19:18; cf. Matt. 22:39).[233] This he describes as law that belongs to the king and which pertains to the kingdom. For James, the law that guides him is "the sum total of demands that God, through Jesus, imposes on believers."[234] All this is to

---

[233] Curiously, for James, kingdom law is not the Decalogue but the law of love.

[234] Douglas J. Moo, *The Letter of James* (Grand Rapids: Wm. B. Eerdmans Publishing Co., 2000), 112. Peter David's comments are worth noting here: "Would it be possible to read this [*nomon basilikon*] in a Jewish Christian context without thinking of the kingdom of God (2:5) and the kingship of Yahweh that was in

say that his love for the law was not at all stifled by Jesus, but his *view* of the law had very evidently been altered by him. This is the viewpoint offered here exactly—we do not abandon Moses. But neither do we look to Moses directly. We look rather at Moses via Christ.

This aspect of Christology is one that is frequently fleshed out in the NT. As already noted, this is a prominent note in the Matthean Christology. *His* words must be obeyed (Matt. 17:5). It is *his* words that will be brought to bear in the final judgment (7:24-27). And it is *his* words that must form the whole substance of our discipling ministry (Matt. 28:20). The other NT writers build on this idea also. On the eve of his crucifixion, Jesus explained to his disciples that while he had more to tell them and although he was soon to leave, he would nonetheless give "all truth" to them via the Holy Spirit whom he would send in his name (John 16:12-14; cf. 17:8). This, Jesus' word, the disciples would in turn give to us (John 17:8, 18, 20). The full revelation in Christ (Heb. 1:1-2)[235] is the "tradition" that the apostles pass along to the Christian community and that we are responsible faithfully to "hold" (2 Thess. 2:15). For all the NT writers, Jesus has highest priority, even in terms of moral and ethical instruction. We will not go back to

---

Christian thought invested in Jesus? Is it not most natural to see a reference to the whole law as interpreted and handed over to the church in the teaching of Jesus. . . ?" *Commentary on James NIGTC* (Grand Rapids: Wm. B. Eerdmans Publishing Co., 1982), 114. See also Ralph P. Martin, *James WBC* (Waco: Word Books, 1988), 67.

[235] Cf. Jude 3, "the once-for-all-delivered-to-the-saints faith" (*tē hapax paradotheisē tois hagiois pistei*).

Moses, for it is in Jesus that Moses finds "completion."[236]

We have already seen something of the illegitimacy of the three-fold division of Moses (moral, civil, ceremonial) when used as a hermeneutical tool. Here we observe another inconsistency in the way three-fold division is commonly used. Often this division of Moses' law is appealed to as an aid for understanding the NT statements (especially by Paul) regarding the abolition of the Old Covenant law. It is commonly held that Paul means to say that the "ceremonial" and/or "civil" law is abolished but not the "moral" (i.e., the Decalogue). In light of several wide-sweeping statements regarding the law's abolition, this interpretation seems strained. Paul does not speak in such terms; he simply speaks of the law's passing. The understanding of Moses as fulfilled in Christ as offered here has the distinct advantage of showing that *all* of the law is fulfilled *in exactly the same way*. Moral, civil, ceremonial—all the law has the same prophetic function, looking forward to Christ; in his person, work, and teaching he "fulfills" it all as its eschatological realization.

---

[236] John Brown, Discourses and *Sayings of Our Lord* 1:70. Here is the entire quote: "I apprehend the word 'fulfil' is used in the sense of 'complete,' 'fill up,' 'perfect.' This is so common a use of the term, as to make it unnecessary to quote examples of it. It is as if he had said, 'My design is not to invalidate the Old Testament revelation, but to complete it. It is but the first part of a great divine manifestation; I come to give the remaining and the most important part of it.' Our Lord came to complete divine revelation. . . . In these words our Lord sanctions the divine authority of the Old Testament Scriptures, and at the same time holds himself up as the person appointed by God to finish the work which they had left incomplete. . . ." Along with this, in a footnote, Brown cites Luke 7:1, Acts 13:25; 14:26; Col. 1:25; Phil.2:2; 2 Thess. 1:11.

Continuing Relevance of Moses and the Hermeneutical Task

There is some continuing relevance afforded Moses in the NT Scriptures, as even a casual reading of the NT will reveal. On several occasions, NT writers at least seem to quote and apply Moses' law to the NT believer (e.g., Rom. 13:9; 1 Cor. 9:9; Eph. 6:1-3; 1 Tim. 5:18; 1 John 5:21).

It is this observation that has frustrated many interpreters. Some have concluded that all of Moses' law, except the ceremonial aspects, remains binding on the New Covenant believer. Some have concluded that "the moral law" of Moses remains intact while the civil and ceremonial laws have passed away. Some have assumed that *all* of Moses remains binding *unless specifically repealed* by Jesus or the NT writers. Still others have assumed that *nothing* of Moses remains binding *unless specifically restated* by Jesus or the NT writers. In one sense the confusion is entirely understandable, for the NT writers both "abolish" Moses' law and continue to enforce many of its commands. It would seem that the NT writers want to have Moses and not have Moses all at the same time!

But the Gordian knot is easily undone when it is understood that Jesus is to Moses what the butterfly is to the caterpillar. Moses is not struck down. Moses did not "fall" (Luke 16:17). Nor was he "destroyed" (Matt. 5:17). Moses is "fulfilled." In Christ, Moses reaches maturity and emerges in full bloom. Moses' law still has relevance, but only as it comes to us from the hands of the Lord Jesus. Christians today must still read Moses, and for great profit, but when they read him they must be careful to wear their Christian lenses. Moses' law is not simply incorporated into the New Covenant as it was revealed through Moses—it is fulfilled, advanced, and brought to completion.

Plainly stated, Christ does not relegate Moses to the status of a museum showpiece. Neither should we expect to find Moses with the same status today that he enjoyed before the coming of Christ. Having been fulfilled, he is surpassed, and it is our pleasure today to read his law in the shape given it by the Lord Jesus Christ.

So then, how do we understand a given Mosaic command today? The difficulty is simplified considerably if we opt to accept all Mosaic commands as binding unless the NT specifically tells us otherwise. Alternatively, it makes things very easy if we simply rule out *every* Mosaic command unless it is specifically reissued in the NT. But these options are not just simple—they are simplistic, and they overlook our Lord's role as Moses' fulfiller and completer. Perhaps a few examples will help.[237]

First, consider the Mosaic prohibition of bestiality (Exod. 22:19; Lev. 18:23; 20:16; Deut. 27:21). This command is nowhere repeated in the NT. Does that mean that bestiality is now allowed under the terms of the New Covenant? Of course not. But how can we know? Must we depend upon the Mosaic code alone? No, bestiality in the NT is condemned on two grounds. First, in 1 Corinthians 7:2 and Hebrews 13:4, we have explicit prohibition of all sexual activity outside the marriage union. Even more to our point, the NT condemns *porneia* ("sexual immorality"; e.g., 1 Cor. 6:18), and at this point the interpreter must ask what it is that constitutes *porneia*. To answer that question we are forced to recognize that for the NT writers *porneia* is informed by the OT. They had a whole-Bible-hermeneutic, and following their lead so must we.

Or, regard the Mosaic endorsement of capital punishment. Can this be justified on New Covenant grounds? Yes, in two ways. First, in Romans 13:4, Paul speaks of our governmental leaders who do not "bear the sword in vain." Obviously, the sword is not used for correction but for execution, and Paul acknowledges this right. Paul does not bother to provide an extensive list of what crimes are rightly punishable by death, but

---

[237] See chapter 13, "The Sabbath: A Test Case."

the right itself is assumed. Also, there is the pre-Mosaic stipulation that murder is an attack on God's image and, therefore, worthy of death (Gen. 9:6). Murder as a personal attack on God is a notion that is not confined to the Old Covenant alone; it remains a capital offense in every age.

We may also take the Mosaic commands regarding a husband's responsibilities to his wife. Are they sufficient by themselves to guide the Christian husband? According to Moses, a husband must not commit adultery (Exod. 20:14), he must not falsely accuse his wife of unfaithfulness (Deut. 22:13-19), and if he would divorce her he must do so following proper procedure (Deut. 24:1-4; cf. Matt. 5:31). No pastor-counselor would be satisfied with this! He would turn in his NT to Ephesians 5:25-33 or 1 Peter 3:7 and exhort strongly in terms of love and care and respect and consideration and sacrifice and selflessness. Christ has advanced Moses significantly.

Or take the command of Deuteronomy 25:4 — "Do not muzzle the ox while it is treading out the grain." Does this command remain intact? Certainly, the principle of fair treatment of animals is entirely consistent with the law of Christ. But in the New Covenant Scriptures, the command is given a significant advance. According to Paul, this command concerning the ox teaches us to honor and provide generously ("double") for those who lead in the church and teach the Word of God (1 Tim. 5:17-18; cf. 1 Cor. 9:9). Is this simply a fair exegesis of Moses, or is it some sort of advance? The latter seems obvious.

The subjects of murder, adultery, divorce, oaths, and love are all given specific attention in Matthew 5, as we saw in chapter six, and each takes an unpredictable turn according to the sovereign will of Christ. The point is simply this: we may (must!) still use Moses, but we must use Moses acknowledging the priority of Christ.

All this illustrates well that it is much too simplistic to assume either that all of Moses remains except that which is specifically repealed, or that none of Moses remains except that which is specifically restated. This does mean that the interpreter's task is more complex. Informing *porneia* ("immorality") and other such terms with our whole Bible demands study. Finding how a given law from Moses receives treatment by Jesus and/or the NT writers demands attention to detail. But this is the interpreter's task exactly—he must use his entire Bible. He must read his entire Bible as a Christian, from his New Covenant perspective, to be sure, but he must use his entire Bible. The law of Moses finds its fulfillment in the law of Christ, and we must look to see *how* this is so in any given case.[238]

---

[238] "The law of Christ" (1 Cor. 9:20) should not be understood in terms of the teachings of Jesus only but of the NT writers also (see chapter 2). This is evident from the fact that Jesus himself speaks of his teaching as coming to us via the apostles (John 16:12-15). A related expression is found in James 2:8—*nomon basilikon*, "law of the king" (see comments above).

CHAPTER 10

The Meaning and Source of Moral Law

Tom Wells

Whatever else may be said, there is one thing on which all sides agree: questions concerning law are difficult. This is evident from the frequent references to law in this book. It is also evident from the vast amount of literature produced in the last quarter century on that subject. Much of this literature, however, has been devoted to specific codes of law, such as the law of Moses or the law of Christ.

Less discussion, I think, has been focused on *moral law* as a category.

One reason for that is clear: the phrase *moral law* is not a biblical phrase. Nor is the slightly broader phrase, *the moral law*. But as these are used by theologians the intention is to cite them as having biblical *content*, and we will treat them with that in mind.

What do we mean by *moral law*? Discussion and description of moral law are much more common than definition, but here are some quotations on the subject to get us started.

> Moral law is in the last analysis but the reflection or expression of the moral nature of God. God is holy, just and good, and the law which is also holy, just and good is simply the correlate of the holiness and justice and goodness of God. Man is created in the image of God and the demand . . . is that he be conformed in the

inmost fibre of his moral being and in all the conditions and activities of his person to the moral perfection of God.[239]

Here we have both definition and helpful description of moral law.

We will look at a second description of moral law, with an emphasis on the repeated words *intrinsically right*. The author is discussing the list of duties in Titus 2:1-10.

> [N]early every item in this list, when analyzed independently, can be seen as *intrinsically right* and not just in accord with the culture of that day . . . . Certainly the interpersonal qualities asked of slaves (vv.9-10) are *intrinsically right* for any working situation and are asked of the slaves for that reason. . . . Certainly for a wife and mother to love her husband and children and be sensible, pure, and kind (vv.4-5) are *intrinsically right* and not just norms of first-century culture.[240]

These two quotations give us the materials from which to frame a working definition of moral law.

Moral law is the law that has its source in the unchanging moral character of God with the result that it is intrinsically right and therefore binds all men of every era and every land to whom it comes.

There is little, if anything, that most Christians will object to in this definition.

When we come to the question of where this law is found, the situation changes dramatically, as we have seen. The answer, however, seems clear: moral law is found wherever there is a revelation of the moral character of God. *When we see God, we see the standard to which we must conform.* This in turn raises another question: is the revelation of God's character progressive? The

---

[239] John Murray, *Collected Writings of John Murray* (Edinburgh: Banner of Truth, 1976), 1:196.

[240] George W. Knight III, *The Pastoral Epistles: A Commentary on the Greek Text* (Grand Rapids: Eerdmans 1992; reprint, 1996), 317 (emphasis added).

Moral Law

clear answer of Scripture is, yes.[241] There could hardly be another answer for those who read their Bibles.

Certain things follow from this. First, from the moment God appears on the scene to reveal anything of his moral character, we *should be able* to recognize something of what his will for us is. For example, it was his faithfulness to what he says that led him to expel Adam and Eve from the garden. In doing that, he showed us—if we have eyes to see—that faithfulness to our word is demanded of us.

Second, we understand immediately that we cannot pick a point in time at which we now know enough about God to think we have *the* moral law. Suppose we wanted to retain the phrase, "*the* moral law"—what then? At each point in history, all the accumulated revelation of God's moral character would constitute "*the* moral law" for us, only to be modified shortly due to further revelation. For that reason, the category "*the* moral law" is not a useful one. Historically, at least, it has been used statically, not dynamically. In other words, where the phrase has appeared, it has been used to define an entity that did not change by expansion. (We grant that it did not change by retraction.) If we insist on using it today, it would be best to confine it to the two great commandments on love, precisely because they are so short on details that our understanding can

---

[241] John Walton has argued at book-length that the essence of "the covenant" (in which he includes the Abrahamic, Mosaic, Davidic, and New covenants) is the progressive revelation of God. While finding the essence of the covenants is notoriously difficult, he shows that God's self-revelation is a major theme throughout the Scriptures. He says, e.g., "My contention, then, is that while the covenant is characteristically redemptive and ultimately soteric, it is essentially revelatory." Elsewhere he identifies this revelation as God's "self-revelation." See John H. Walton, *Covenant: God's Purpose, God's Plan* (Grand Rapids: Zondervan, 1994), 25, 109.

grow and develop within them. A detailed code, like the Decalogue, does not have this kind of elasticity.[242]

Third, we will never in this life reach the end of this cumulative process. John makes this clear when he writes in a context devoted to moral issues, "Dear friends, now we are children of God, and what we will be has not yet been made known. But we know that when he appears, we shall be like him, for we shall see him as he is" (1 John 3:2). At no point short of his coming will we have all the information necessary to compile *the* moral law. All we have in the meantime are large fragments at best. It will take the perspective of eternity future to see it all.

Fourth, even the concept *moral law* depends on cumulative revelation. It is difficult to say when it first became obvious, because all law from God to mankind came with moral force. The purpose of dividing it into moral, ceremonial, and civil categories was surely never to deny that fact, but to emphasize that one portion of it, the moral, was of transcendent quality.[243] While the distinction between moral and ceremonial law is reasonable, even if not fully exact, it probably does not become

---

[242] If it is argued that all moral law is *implicit* in the Ten Commandments, it is difficult to know what this means due to the ambiguity in the word *implicit*. This might mean that a process of logic properly applied to the Decalogue could reveal all the Law of Christ. I believe that this is simply false. On the other hand, the implicitness might be thought to be the kind of thing represented in the NT by the word "mystery." Mysteries are indeed often based on OT Scripture, and might be said to be implicit in them, but the NT "uses it to mean the secret thoughts, plans, and dispensations of God which are hidden fr[om] the human reason . . . and hence must be revealed to those for whom they are intended" (*BAGD*, s.v. "mystery").

[243] For the history of this division see Jonathan Bayes, "The Threefold Division of the Law," *Reformation Today* 177 (Sept.- Oct. 2000): 3-11.

Moral Law

evident except under one of two conditions. First, it may become a live option when men and women start to ask the question, "Which of these laws is more important than the others?" This question offers a good opportunity to distinguish between laws and types of laws. I think it is fair to say that this kind of question does not arise early in a new period of revelation. It is surely doubtful that the wilderness generation thought in these terms. If they did, they certainly got their priorities wrong! They were faithful in carrying the tabernacle from place to place, as God commanded, but they were not faithful to the God who "inhabited" it (a far more important command!). The other circumstance under which it may become a live option is when one stands outside the system of law being studied. People like us are an example of this. We look at the Mosaic code with a detachment that was not possible for Jews who were threatened with the destruction of their nation or personal death for infractions of it. We have the leisure, as it were, to put it under a microscope and dissect it. Why? Because in large measure it does not apply to us in the same way as it did to them.

That does not mean that no one who lived within the Mosaic system could make such distinctions. Certainly the prophets could and did. Even in their case, however, we need to make important qualifications. First, we must remember that they wrote by inspiration of God. Second, we have no reason to believe that any one of them was ever able to sort all of the Mosaic Law into these divisions. Third, we know that the prophets often had little or no impact on the understanding of the people. For all of these reasons, the idea of moral law was likely to have been a vague idea among God's OT people for many centuries. Law they recognized; moral law was for most of them shadowy at best.

The point of this long discussion is this: it required the advance from promise to fulfillment, from Old Covenant to New Covenant, from shadow to reality, to make the category of moral law stand forth.

Specifically, in the sight of Jesus Christ as the ultimate revelation of the moral character of God, men saw, heard and felt the reality of moral purity, and hence moral law, as never before. Even that, however, took time for the church to understand. As late as Acts 11 we see that Peter had no clear grasp of it. When the sheet filled with all kinds of animals was let down from heaven, he was told, "Get up, Peter. Kill and eat." He was shocked! "I replied," he says, " 'Surely not, Lord! Nothing impure or unclean has ever entered my mouth' " (11:7-8).

What, then, is the basis for recognizing moral law? An absolutely sure basis is the passing away of some law that once was enforced by God. Such a law is clearly *not* moral. It does not transcend the covenant with which it was associated. Beyond that, there is no certainty among God's laws except the clues that we receive from the latest advance in revelation. For all practical purposes for us today, that means the NT, and preeminently, the Lord Jesus in his person, his teaching, and in his authorized agents (Eph. 2:20).

In summary, here are the salient points. First, no law that can be compiled by us in this age can qualify for the title *"the moral law."* Only the perspective of eternity future can provide that. Second, even the category "moral law," while easy to define, is difficult to recognize with certainty. We know it best by finding it repeated by Christ. This identifies it as "transcendent" law. Thus, the evidence of its being transcendent is that it shows up in the law of Christ. Without that clue, however, the category of transcendent law would be much harder to identify. Hence, the revelation of transcendent law comes from him, though the fact of its transcendence is prior to the appearing of Christ.

The safest rule, then, is to obey all that Christ commands, either explicitly or by clear implication. Treat him as the new Torah, for that is part of what he is. To borrow words from John Owen on the passing away of the Mosaic law, "The only securing principle, in all things of this nature, is to preserve our souls in an entire subjection unto the authority of Christ, and unto his alone."[244]

---

[244] John Owen, *An Exposition of the Epistle to the Hebrews* (Marshallton, DE: National Foundation for Christian Education, repr. n.d.), 5:464. This edition reproduces the seven volume Goold edition of 1855, but is bound in four volumes. The more recent Banner of Truth edition appears in seven separate bindings. In the quotation, Owen is discussing Hebrews 7:18-19. He adds, " 'the law' there doth evidently intend the *whole law*, in both the parts of it, moral and ceremonial, as it was given by Moses unto the church of Israel."

CHAPTER 11

Critiquing a Friendly Attack (Part One)

Tom Wells

Early in 2001, a friendly but extensive criticism of NCT appeared in the form of a book by a Reformed Baptist pastor, Richard Barcellos. Its book-length extent makes it a pioneering work. Barcellos recognizes that and fully expects to see those who hold NCT change some of their positions, demanding in return some changes in his criticisms. For the most part, Barcellos does not find much to commend in NCT.[1] Unless we who hold NCT make a fairly extensive response it will appear that we have little to say. For that reason I turn now to the book, *In Defense of the Decalogue*.

Barcellos' book has proved stimulating in several ways. At first, I found it difficult to read because I expected it to defend traditional Reformed views. The title and sub-title of Barcellos' book is *In Defense of the Decalogue: A Critique of New Covenant Theology*. Nearly every word in that title raises associations in the minds of Reformed and Calvinistic Baptists, such as I am. I was surprised to learn, however, that the critique would approach the question of continuity in a non-traditional way.

---

[1] He does have a commendatory paragraph in his introduction (pp. 12-13). In a book sub-titled *A Critique of New Covenant Theology*, he naturally enough focuses upon disagreements, and I will do so as well.

This fact led to a second stimulus. In reading Barcellos, I have come to better understand my own position. There could hardly be a nicer surprise!

The Central Challenge

After the introduction, the book opens by coming immediately to the main issue, whether the law written on the hearts of New Covenant believers is the Decalogue.[246] "The issue under consideration is what Jeremiah meant when he said in Jeremiah 31:31-34 that 'I will put *My law* [emphasis added by Barcellos] in their minds, and write it on their hearts'" (p. 15). He adds, "Most New Covenant theologians would *not* identify the law written on the heart in Jeremiah 31:33 as the Decalogue" (p. 16). These two sentences not only set the stage for the central discussion, they also contain assertions that at first made Barcellos difficult to understand. In terms of the traditional debate between those who hold to the perpetuity of the Decalogue and those who do not, his sentences seem straightforward. He apparently contends that the Decalogue as it appears in Exodus 20 is still literally applicable to Christians. His opponents say, "No, when the New Covenant comes, a *new law* comes with it." This is the way the traditional discussion has been conducted, and the author's two sentences seem to repeat the long-time disagreement in the same terms. *This conclusion, however, will keep us from understanding the issue as he frames it.*

---

[246] Barcellos argues at length that the law in Jeremiah 31:33 is the Decalogue (pp. 16-24). I suspect that this is too constricting and that the law there is the full Mosaic law. But at this point I will accept the equation since it will make little difference to my arguement. What I say about the decalogue will be equally true of the whole Mosaic system and OT. They all undergo the same transformation in the Bible as I understand it.

To show you what I mean, let me tell you a short parable that I will later apply to various parts of this discussion.

Steve and Ken were good friends who had a common interest in the outdoors, so whenever they had a few free hours they would roam the woods and meadows near where they lived. One day Steve spotted a caterpillar on the leaf of a tree and pointed it out to Ken. There was a good deal about the caterpillar that caught their attention. It had three pairs of legs and feet with hooks that helped it to grasp the foliage. But the thing that interested them most was the fact that it was secreting something like silk as it rested on the leaf. They studied it for a while, enjoyed pointing out other characteristics of the insect to one another, and then returned to their homes.

Not long after that they had another opportunity for a walk together. Ken suggested that they see if they could find the caterpillar again. Shortly they found the tree and looked at the general area where they had left the caterpillar secreting its silk-like threads. Almost immediately they both spotted a beautiful butterfly.

"There's our caterpillar!" Steve sang out with glee.

"Where?" said Ken.

"Right here," Steve replied, putting his finger almost on top of the butterfly.

"That's not our insect!"

"It is!"

"It is not!"

Later, when Steve got home he said to his wife, "The trouble with Ken is, he needs to study a little biology. If he did that, he'd discover that the caterpillar goes through a marvelous transformation to become a butterfly." At the same time Ken was saying to *his* wife, "I'm really worried about Steve. I'm afraid he's going blind. Today we saw a beautiful butterfly, and he insisted it was a caterpillar! He thought it was something we saw the other day, but this insect was brand new."

In the parable, everything turns on the knowledge that in its life cycle, the butterfly goes through an enormous transformation. If Ken had known that, he would have understood what Steve was saying. Without that understanding, he was left in the dark.

The darkness in the parable is the kind of darkness that has often fallen over the debate about the Ten Commandments and the law written in the hearts of believers in this age. For much of church history there was no recognition of the great extent of the transformation that was promised between the Old and New Covenants. As a consequence, scholars did not think in terms of a transformation of the Decalogue. If one looked at both Testaments, he appeared to have two choices. He could contend that the Decalogue was the law written on the heart under the New Covenant, or he could argue that the law of the New Covenant was new law. The third option was unlikely to occur to him: the Decalogue was the law, but under the condition of its fulfillment in Christ.[247]

In recent years a large number of scholars have concluded that this third option best describes the relation between the Old or Mosaic Covenant and the New Covenant. The argument is generally carried on from the fulfillment language of the NT. I need not describe the process in detail here. Fred Zaspel has done so in his discussion of Matthew 5:17ff.[248] Briefly put, it amounts to this: all of the OT, including the Old Covenant, is prophetic of Christ. In this view, the Lord Jesus in his person, his work, his teaching and his body (i.e., the church) provides the fulfillment of the entire history of redemption as contained in the OT. The Old Covenant is the caterpillar and the New Covenant of the Lord Jesus is the butterfly. Alternately we may

---

[247] Some of the Puritans, as I have shown on p. 69, did have an inkling of this, as reflected in the phrase "receiving the law from the hands of Christ." So far as I am aware, however, this idea was never fully developed. In my own experience of more than a quarter of a century debating these things, almost all my own debating has been carried on without due reflection on these facts.

[248] See chapters 5-8.

say that the various parts of the Old Covenant are caterpillars (plural) and various facets of the New Covenant are butterflies. This is the typological approach. It can be seen, for example, in giving the Lord Jesus the names *prophet, priest* and *king*. The OT prophet played caterpillar to the Lord Jesus' butterfly! So too did the OT priest, and king.

The previous paragraph calls for certain observations.

First, in this understanding, people may use the language adopted by each of the opposing sides as the discussion was formerly carried on. Has the Old Covenant passed away or is it still with us? The answer is: it depends. In one sense it is gone, but in another it is still very much with us in Jesus Christ. Has the OT high priest passed away or does he still function? Is the Passover a thing of the past? Is there a king like Solomon? These questions, and many others that you yourself could frame, all have the same answer: it depends on how you view them. If one side prefers to speak what we might call "caterpillar language" using *perpetuity* and *God's law revealed to Israel as his Old Covenant nation* (both descriptions lifted from Barcellos in describing his own position), they are free to do so. The other side, however, must be free to use "butterfly language," and speak of Christ as *new lawgiver* and a *higher and more spiritual law than the law of Moses* (all descriptions lifted from Barcellos in describing NCT).[249] If this sounds radical, it is not. It is supported by two salient facts: first, the Bible uses both kinds

---

[249] Phrases describing Barcellos' position are taken from pp. 13 and 21 respectively. Those describing NCT are from p. 11.

of language in discussing the law;[250] second, Barcellos himself finds it desirable at some points to adopt the very type of terminology he at other times opposes.[251]

Second, this raises the question, where does Barcellos come down on these distinctions? Is he like Steve in my parable, or is he the naive Ken? If I understand him, after reading him repeatedly, he sees both truths. He is like Steve. That is why he adopts language that normally reflects the newer understanding, phrases like "redemptive-historical" (p. 64), in the following sentences. After citing the OT statement, "Out of Egypt I called my Son," as quoted by Matthew, he writes:

> Here the concept of fulfillment refers to the eschatological realization and application of an Old Testament text. Although no ethical dimension is involved in this case, the principle is illustrated nonetheless. What Christ does to the Law and the Prophets, the whole Old Testament, is to bring them to redemptive-historical maturity. Christ came to bring the Old Testament to an advanced stage of eschatological realization and application. Christ is fulfilling the law and will do so until heaven and earth pass away when He comes again and ushers in the age to come in its fulness and glory. . . . What Jesus is saying [in Matthew 5:17] is that the Old Testament is still binding on His people, *but not in the same way it used to be*. The Old Testament is still authoritative as far as our sanctification goes, *but the coming*

---

[250] For newness language in the the NT generally see Hoch, "The New Covenant and Its Problems." Specific verses relevant to this discussion include "Christ is the end of the law" (Rom. 10:4), and [Christ] has destroyed the barrier, the dividing wall of hostility, by abolishing in his flesh the law with its commandments and regulations" (Eph. 2:14). In each case, Christ and his work, as something new, replace the law, making it old.

[251] Note the following: "[T]he New Testament teaches *both* the abrogation of the law of the Old Covenant *and* its abiding moral validity . . ." "Paul views the Old Covenant law as both annulled and binding." Barcellos, *Defense*, 61, 67.

and death of Christ and the inauguration of the New Covenant now condition its application. New Testament scholar Vern Poythress agrees, when he says, "All the commandments of the law are binding on Christians . . . , but the way in which they are binding is determined by the authority of Christ and the fulfillment that takes place in His work."[252]

This quotation would seem to establish beyond doubt the fact that the author holds the more recent understanding. The caterpillar of OT law has been transformed into the butterfly that displays, to use his words, "redemptive-historical maturity" (p. 66). Barcellos is to be commended for leaving behind the older understanding. This very fact, however, leads to two further observations.

First, the redemptive-historical understanding of the change from Old Covenant to New Covenant, as outlined in the extensive quotation above, is a cornerstone of NCT. The reader would hardly realize this from the book. That leads to the following consequence: either there is no real difference between us or one side does not consistently apply the argument as Barcellos has plainly set it forth.

Second, it is clear to me that Barcellos, for whatever reason, draws back from the applications or conclusions that the redemptive-historical understanding demands. I hope to demonstrate this by evidence from the book itself.

How the Author Draws Back from Historical-Redemptive Conclusions

Think again of the parable. In it a caterpillar changes into a beautiful butterfly, representing the change in covenants *and in law* from OT to NT. Steve understood the change, but Ken did

---

[252] Ibid., 64-65. The first ellipsis is my own, but the second was made by Barcellos, quoting Poythress, *The Shadow of Christ in the Law of Moses*, 268.

not. Had Steve been a theologian standing outside the parable, instead of a character within it, he could have adopted Barcellos' explanation above with little or no modification. In these terms, the law, like all else in the transition from OT to NT would undergo transformation.

For Barcellos, however, little or no transformation takes place. What he insists on is this: after the New Covenant has come and after Christ has brought "the whole Old Testament" to redemptive maturity (p. 66), *the Ten Commandments read virtually the same as they did before*. They command the same duties; they forbid the same sins. They still forbid murder, adultery, stealing, and Sabbath-breaking, etc. In other words, nothing has changed, after all. The commandments have retained the same content and even the same form, "Thou shalt not…" What comes after that? You can fill in the words from Exodus 20.

What's wrong with this? In one way nothing, in another everything. There is nothing wrong in saying that believers must not murder, commit adultery and so on through the list. Except for the Sabbath, we all agree on that.[253] What is so wrong about this identification is that a law, largely external and intended for a nation of men, most of whom were unregenerate, is looked upon as the apex of God's moral law even after the

---

[253] If I am asked how I know that Christians must not do these things, I gladly acknowledge that I learn it from Exodus 20. To the objection that if Exodus 20 was only given to Israel then it has nothing to do with me, there is a simple reply. I take nine of those laws to be moral. Whatever is moral binds all men at all times. But knowing what is moral is an extremely complex question, though *in the light of the New Covenant* it is not impossible since we have the embodiment of it in Jesus Christ. To a person under the Old Covenant all the Mosaic laws came with moral force, and they did not need to make this distinction. They simply needed to obey, as we need today to simply obey Christ. See my discussion of *moral law* in chapter 10.

coming of the New Covenant. To put it another way, the caterpillar is still a caterpillar Where is the transformation? Where is "the advanced stage of eschatological realization?" Where is the resplendence promised in the lengthy quotation above? It is apparent for all to see; it is not there.[254] In what is perhaps the most interesting and useful section of Barcellos' book, his exposition of 1 Timothy 1:8-11, he will make it as plain as possible: after all is said and done, the Decalogue, in its ordinary vanilla Exodus 20 form, is the fulfillment of the promise in Jeremiah 31:33.[255] Nowhere in his book does he show us how the promise of Jeremiah 31:33 comes to a transcendently glorious fulfillment. If someone objects that the idea of "transcendently glorious fulfillment" comes as much from my parable as from the paragraph above, I will grant it. But my parable reflects the wonder and grandeur that the OT generally speaks of in describing the last days. In addition, the NT picks up this theme and develops it repeatedly. We must not, then, make Christ look and sound very much like Moses in his approach to moral law.

The answer to this dilemma is twofold: to reflect on the kind of law Christians need, and to look in the NT to see what kind they get from Christ and his writing disciples.

---

[254] "Jesus' concentration on issues of the heart represents a shift of focus in comparison with the law of Moses. *In agreement with the overall external, earthly character of Mosaic worship, the stress of the law is* predominately *on externals.* The Ten Commandments . . . focus in their obvious meaning on the most obvious violations" (Poythress, *The Shadow of Christ in the Law of Moses*, p. 258 [emphasis added]). To make my point another way, the Mosaic Covenant and the Ten Commandments are concerned with crime primarily and sin secondarily, reflecting the concerns of all national societies. Yet this difference must not be over-stressed, since, in a theocracy, every crime is also a sin.

[255] Barcellos' exposition of 1 Timothy 1:8-11 is on pp. 41-57. I treat it on pp. 190-199.

What Kind of Laws Do Christians Need?

This appears to be a speculative question, but a little thought will show that it is not. The NT helps us by describing the kinds of people Christians are. When we know what they are like, we will know what kind of guidance they need.

Christians are those who have been morally and spiritually changed by Jesus Christ.[256] They are controlled by the Spirit (Rom. 8:9), led by the Spirit (Rom. 8:14), indeed, they are God's children (Rom. 8:16), a fact that turns on the truth "like Father, like son." They are men and women chosen to bear fruit that will last (John 15:16), God's workmanship, created in Christ Jesus to do good works which God prepared in advance for them to do (Eph. 2:10). They are new creations (2 Cor. 5:17). Whatever that may mean, it is accompanied by transformation so that Paul can write to the Ephesians and say,

> For of this you can be sure: No immoral, impure or greedy person–such a man is an idolater–has any inheritance in the kingdom of Christ and of God. Let no one deceive you with empty words, for because of such things God's wrath comes on those who are disobedient. Therefore do not be partners with them. For you were once darkness, but now you are light in the Lord. Live as children of light (Eph. 5:5-8).

Three things are clear from this passage. First, no one who is a Christian can be characterized by such things as immorality, impurity or greed. Second, there are deceivers who would seek to tell you that men can practice such things and still be Christians. Third, no Christian is beyond being warned against falling into the vilest sin.

What do we learn from these things? The lesson is clear. A Christian is a godly man, but not perfect. His life is characterized by righteousness. What kind of law does he need?

---

[256] For a book devoted to this subject see Tom Wells, *Christian: Take Heart* (Edinburgh: Banner of Truth, 1987).

The law he needs must be fitted to who he is. It will be characterized by encouragements in heart godliness, but it will include occasional warnings against gross sin.

What Kind of Laws Do Christians Receive from Christ and His Writing Disciples?

The question in the heading is not hard to answer from the NT. Do they need to be told that they must not steal, perjure themselves and commit adultery? Yes. Those are the warnings against gross sin to which I just referred. Their main diet, however, will be something else, encouragement in heart godliness. The Ten Commandments, as they appear in Exodus 20, become a side issue for true believers, not because they are unimportant in themselves, but because when they appear, they appear in company with higher law. This is clear on the face of the NT. No one has to take my word for this. They can read it for themselves all over the NT, but especially in the Epistles. Listen to Paul:

> Therefore, I urge you, brothers, in view of God's mercy, to offer your bodies as living sacrifices, holy and pleasing to God–this is your spiritual act of worship. Do not conform any longer to the world, but be transformed by the renewing of your mind. Then you will be able to test and approve what God's will is . . . .
> For by the grace given me I say to every one of you: Do not think of yourself more highly than you ought, but rather think of yourself with sober judgment . . . . We have different gifts, according to the grace given us. If a man's gift is prophesying, let him use it in proportion to his faith. If it is serving, let him serve; if it is teaching, let him teach; if it is encouraging, let him encourage; if it is contributing to the needs of others, let him give generously; if it is leadership, let him govern diligently; if it is showing mercy, let him do it cheerfully (Rom. 12:1-8) [The passage continues in the same vein through the end of the

chapter. I stop here in the interests of space.]

What kind of advice is this? It is not advice at all. It is the command of God to those whose lives have been changed by Christ. It is the law of Christ. Does it refer to gross sin? Certainly there is an allusion to gross sin in the words, "Do not conform any longer to the pattern of this world" (v.2), but beyond that the tone is different. In fact, that may account for the feeling that this is not law. After all, law is harsh and grates on the nerves. This is gentle and woos the willing heart, but it is law nevertheless.[257]

How Prominent Is the Decalogue in the NT?

Many Christians have only a vague idea of how often the Ten Commandments are referred to in the NT. There are three ways in which we might measure this, with the following results:

1. If we count every explicit mention of them and every clear allusion to them, the total will come to about twenty.[258] This is less than one mention/allusion per NT book.

2. If we count only those places in which the Ten Commandments are explicitly mentioned, the number dwindles to eleven, a little less than one-half mention per book.

---

[257] John Reisinger has a clear and humorous illustration of how law for the Christian becomes undervalued by many in the presence of the *biggies*, the Ten Commandments. Unfortunately it is too long to insert here, but you may read it in John Reisinger, *Christ Lord and Lawgiver Over the Church* (Frederick, MD: New Covenant Media, 1998), 16-17.

[258] My actual count was nineteen, but there is some room for error in this kind of count.

3. If we count only those places where one or more of the laws of the Decalogue is issued as a command, there appear to be only six occasions in the NT. Of these, three of the six occasions transpire while the Lord Jesus and the disciples were still living under the Mosaic Covenant.[259] (Those occurrences appear in the Synoptic Gospels.) That leaves only three places in the last twenty-four books of the NT where the law of the Decalogue is actually quoted in the form of a command. In my judgment one of these is doubtful. However we will assume, for the sake of this discussion, that it is, in fact, a command issued by the Apostle Paul.

The three occasions in the Gospels are as follows. First, there are the words of the Lord Jesus in the Sermon on the Mount in Matthew 5:21ff. As an example, I will take verses 27-28: "'You have heard that it was said, "Do not commit adultery." But I tell you that anyone who looks at a woman lustfully has already committed adultery with her in his heart.'" I include this occasion though it does not meet my own criterion–it is not issued as a command–because I have no doubt that the Lord Jesus could have issued it as a command if he had wanted to.

The second occasion in the Gospels is in Matthew 15:4, where the Lord Jesus rebukes the Pharisees and scribes by reminding them that, "'God said, "Honor your Father and mother".'" (Mark 7:10 is a parallel passage, dealing with the same occasion.)

The third occasion in the Gospels occurs in Jesus' conversation with the rich young ruler, in Matthew 19:17-19. There Jesus said to the man, "'. . . If you want to enter life, obey the commandments.' 'Which ones?' the man inquired. Jesus replied, 'Do not murder, do not commit adultery, do not steal,

---

[259] The survey upon which these figures are based appears as Appendix Five, "A Table for Studying the Decalogue as Commanded by God in the NT," pp. 289-292.

do not give false testimony, honor your father and mother, and love your neighbor as yourself.'" (Mark 10:19 and Luke 18:20 are parallels, dealing with the same occasion.)

What shall we make of these? Though none of them is a command issued to Christians, I have allowed that Jesus *might* have done so on the first occasion. The other two occasions are directed at unconverted men, so there is little material here that would assure us that the Ten Commandments are *the* moral law for Christians.

Are the other three occasions where one or more of the Ten Commandments are issued as commands more promising? Let's see.

The first of these is found in Romans 13:9-10. "The commandments, 'Do not commit adultery,' 'Do not murder,' 'Do not steal,' 'Do not covet,' and whatever commandment there may be, are summed up in this one rule: 'Love your neighbor as yourself.' Love does no harm to its neighbor. Therefore love is the fulfillment of the law." What can we say about this? Once again, I have allowed this as an instance in which several of the Ten Commandments are issued as commands, because I can imagine the Apostle Paul doing so. This is a generous appraisal of this passage, since Paul is discussing these laws much more than he is issuing them as commands. Nevertheless, we will count this as the second occasion on which the Ten Commandments were directed to Christians.

The second of these occasions in the last twenty-four books of the NT (the *third*, overall) is found in Ephesians 6:2-3. (I will add verse 1 for clarity.):

> Children, obey your parents in the Lord, for this is right. "Honor your father and mother"—which is the first commandment with a promise—"that it may go well with you and that you may enjoy long life on the earth."

This instance certainly looks like a command, lifted from the

Decalogue, issued to children at Ephesus. For that reason we will count it as the third instance of a command from the Decalogue being laid on Christians.[260]

That brings us to the final example of the Decalogue being laid on Christians in the NT. Here are the words from James 2:10-11:

> For whoever keeps the whole law and yet stumbles at just one point is guilty of breaking all of it. For he who said, "Do not commit adultery," also said, "Do not murder." If you do not commit adultery but do commit murder, you have become a lawbreaker.

While this is a discussion of the law and not a group of issued commands from the Decalogue, it is fair to count it as another instance, the fourth, in which the writer–in this case, James–could well be imagined to issue such commands if the occasion warranted it. Let's summarize what we have found.

First, we found only four possible instances where a literal command identified as from the Ten Commandments was laid upon Christians. I said at the beginning of this section that I supposed it would surprise most Christians to see how few they are.

Second, in three of the four instances it was clear that they did not, in fact, quite meet the criterion which I established, that is, they were not issued as commands. But I thought it was fair to say that the speaker or writer could well be imagined to issue them.

Third, while that still left us one instance, Ephesians 6:2-3, I have elsewhere argued that the case for it is not at all clear.

---

[260] This is the instance I spoke of as doubtful on page 181. In a forthcoming volume edited by David Hagopian and tentatively titled *Always Reforming: A Dialogue of Differences within the Reformed Tradition* (Phillipsburg, NJ: P&R, forthcoming]), I will argue that in using this passage Paul is applying it typologically and not literally. In that case, of course, it would not qualify for our present list.

Since I have given you no grounds for judging this, however, we will let it stand. Depending, then, on how you look at it, we have found one occasion or four occasions in the NT on which one or more of the Ten Commandments is laid on Christians and identified as from the Decalogue.

What conclusions shall we draw from this? Two things seem clear to me.

First, none of what we have seen disqualifies the Decalogue from being considered moral law.[261] If it is—and that is certainly clear on any current understanding of the phrase *moral law*—there was no reason at all why the writers of the NT could not have applied it as often as they liked. As far as I know, everyone who holds NCT would agree with this.

Second, the very small number of these instances serves to show that the great source of moral and ethical instruction, that is, *law for Christians* as we find it in the NT, is something other than the literal Ten Commandments. Though the speakers in the NT and the writers of its books could legitimately have applied it to Christians hundreds of times without doing anything wrong, in fact they rarely did so. It is even conceivable that they did not do so at all, if you have followed the previous discussion, but it is not at all necessary that you agree to that. What is clear is this: the question at the head of this section, "How prominent is the Decalogue in the NT?" has found an unexpected answer.

Does that mean that the Decalogue is abolished? Not at all. It just means that the fulfillment of Jeremiah 31:33 is a fulfillment that involves a transformation from the Ten Commandments as written in the OT to the teaching of Jesus and his writing disciples. The caterpillar has been transformed. He now looks *very* different. The caterpillar was a promise, the butterfly its fulfillment. How so? He now looks like Jesus. In

---

[261] Since all sides except those who keep a Seventh-Day Sabbath agree that there is some ceremonial element in the Decalogue, this statement can stand as a generalization.

the words of Poythress,

> Doubtless fulfillment may have many ramifications, including Jesus' obedience to the law. But primarily Jesus claims that His own teaching fulfills the *teaching* of the law. . . . All is transformed by the supremacy and weightiness of God Himself [i.e., God the Son] coming to save. The law also undergoes transformation. The final revelation of God is surely in harmony and resonance with the old; indeed, it involves the coming of the old into the destiny to which it pointed. But also this new and climactic revelation bursts the bounds of what anyone could have reckoned from the old.[262]

At times Barcellos seems to recognize this, but when all is said and done, he reverts to the same central thesis: Christ "is not altering the law of Moses in the Sermon on the Mount" (p. 76). The note of transformation and bursting of bounds is gone.

---

[262] Poythress, *The Shadow of Christ in the Law of Moses*, 264.

CHAPTER 12

Critiquing a Friendly Attack (Part Two)

Tom Wells

In the previous chapter I dealt with what I take to be the central challenge of Barcellos' book and its central weakness. The central challenge was to understand the meaning of *my law* in Jeremiah 31:33 as it will apply when we come to the presence of the New Covenant. Though he holds that it is the Decalogue and I expressed doubts about that, I accepted his understanding for the sake of discussion. I tried, after that, to see whether he was prepared to see a transformation of the Decalogue as it passed over into fulfillment. In principle, Barcellos seemed to accept what to me is an obvious fact. I argued, however, that he drew back from that fact in drawing his conclusions, and that is the central weakness in his book. I turn now to the rest of the book.

What Constitutes the Old Covenant?

The second chapter (pp. 25-59) of the book forms a major section of Barcellos' argument. The exegetical work in this section is often quite acceptable and I am glad to give Barcellos credit for that fact. I am genuinely grieved, however, to say that much of his work, as I see it, is based on two misunderstandings.

Barcellos writes on page 25, "According to New Covenant Theology, the Old Covenant is identified as the Ten

Commandments, the Decalogue." Is that true? He certainly had some reason to think so from his sources that he documents in this chapter. Nevertheless, it is not now true and I suspect it never was.

Let me explain.

First, sources for NCT are very limited indeed, if one confines himself, as a critic must, to those who label themselves as its followers. As I tried to show in chapter 1, the basic principle that NCT adopts is, in fact, common to a large segment of biblical conservatives at this time. But most of these men do not adopt the label, perhaps have never heard of it! Barcellos had to work with those who call themselves holders of NCT and have written extensively on the subject. Among them, as he shows, the identification of the Decalogue with the Old Covenant is clearly spelled out in Reisinger's *Tablets of Stone*. He also thinks he finds it in quotations from Fred Zaspel.[263]

The nub of the difficulty is twofold.

To begin with, it is doubtful that this was ever a majority opinion. I have never held it, and I do not know others who have held it, though *Tablets of Stone* has been so influential among us that perhaps a number of others have adopted it.

In addition, I am told that Reisinger no longer holds this position. In light of that fact I am also told that his forthcoming edition of *Tablets of Stone* will contain an appendix disowning his earlier opinion and giving his reasons for doing so. Barcellos has done good work in chapter two of his book (pp. 25-33) in exposing the earlier position's fallacies. It is, however, probably

---

[263] It seems clear that this was not Zaspel's position for two reasons. First, the words that Barcellos quotes on page 25 treat the Decalogue as the "foundational summary statement" of the covenant, showing that they do not exhaust the category of "Old Covenant." Second, a careful reading of the article that Barcellos cites for this quotation makes it clear. In addition, Zaspel has confirmed this to me in telephone conversation.

a thing largely if not entirely of the past.²⁶⁴

Nevertheless, it is useful to mention briefly Barcellos' conclusion to this discussion in the passage of "My law" from the Old to New Covenants, since it illustrates his drawing back from the principle of transformation.

> Reisinger even goes so far as to say, "The Ten Commandments contain much unchanging moral law that is just as binding today as it was on an Israelite." However, due to New Covenant Theology's pre-commitment to the equation that the Old Covenant equals the Ten Commandments, under that view, the Ten Commandments, *as a unit*, can no longer function as covenant law for God's New Covenant people. (p. 34)

I take this to mean that since John Reisinger is not a Sabbatarian, he breaks the unity of the Decalogue and, hence, can only apply part of it to New Covenant believers. But this assumes that the way the Decalogue functions among NCT people is one commandment at a time. In that case, if you drop one out, the unity is broken. In one sense, that is true, but only in one sense, and the least important. For NCT, the Decalogue functions as a unit because it all, every commandment, like all the rest of the Old Covenant and OT is fulfilled in the person, work, teaching and body of Jesus Christ. Only on Barcellos' own assumption that no transformation *of consequence* takes

---

²⁶⁴ Barcellos says, "[O]ne major adherent of New Covenant Theology has recently acknowledged that he will have to modify his understanding of the Old Covenant and revise some of his published works." *Defense*, 7, 8. *If* he is speaking of John Reisinger, and *if* it is on this very point he is now discussing, it would have been a courtesy to both Reisinger and the reader to have made this plain.

place,²⁶⁵ is his criticism is valid. The rest of us feel free to treat part of the Decalogue as moral and part as ceremonial.²⁶⁶ (In the interests of space, this is all I will say about the Decalogue *as a unit*, except in connection with 1 Timothy 1:8-11, which I will take up next.)

For Whom Was the Decalogue Intended?

We come now to the author's exposition of 1 Timothy 1:8-11 (pp. 41-57). There is certainly much to admire in this section, but, as I hope to show, there is another basic misunderstanding that underlies this discussion.

Of this portion of Scripture Barcellos writes, "A final New Testament text that assumes that the Ten Commandments function outside the Old Covenant *as a unit* [italics added] is First Timothy 1:8-11" (p. 41). In saying this, he shows what his primary interest in this section is. Since I have just discussed the question of the Decalogue *as a unit* and what that ought to mean in the light of redemptive history, I might excuse myself from treating this further. But I want to do so because Barcellos uses this section to prove that the Ten Commandments apply

---

²⁶⁵ Barcellos would perhaps cry "Foul!" here since he makes a great deal of the transition from law being written in stone to law being written on hearts. That *is* important. But in his view it is no transformation of the content of the Decalogue, as he shows throughout his discussion.

²⁶⁶ This should *not* give rise to the observation, "So do Barcellos and those who think like him!" While that is literally true, we remove an entire commandment from what they deem to be moral law, while they simply remove one part of one by championing a change of day. This is an important difference, even though we do not think a partial removal makes sense in the light of redemptive history. For us, it destroys the typological relation between the whole Decalogue and the teaching of Christ.

Critique: Part Two

directly to Christians. He makes that point repeatedly and once again it destroys the typological relationship between the whole Decalogue and the teaching of Christ. It is as if someone said, "Christ is a prophet; he issues the same prophecies as the OT prophets. Christ is a priest; he offers the same sacrifices as the OT priests. Christ is a king; he gives the same orders as the OT kings."

Barcellos continues on page 41:

> In considering this passage, four questions will be asked to frame the outline for its exposition. 1) Why does Paul bring up the issue of the law? 2) What is said about the law? 3) To whom is Paul referring when he says "the law is not made for a righteous person"? 4) What law is Paul referring to in verses 8 through 10?

The author is to be commended for framing his outline in advance. That is helpful. More than that, it would seem to be easy to do a good job of expounding the passage under these headings. Several of the headings would serve to answer the question, "For whom was the law intended?" since Paul spells out the answer in detail when he writes, "the law is not made for a righteous man." But Barcellos gives very little time to this issue, though you have to read him carefully to see that.

We take no exception to his answer to the first question he poses. His second question, "What is said about the law?" offers an opportunity which he passes up. The third question, however, seems to demand a discussion of to whom the law is given. So let's see how he handles the question. If it is not for the righteous, for whom is it?

The first thing to see is that the author spends much of his space defining who a *righteous person* is. Is that wrong? No, but it puts the emphasis where Paul does *not* put it. That is why, earlier, I said that this section also turns on a misunderstanding. Paul is concerned to tell us for whom the law is intended, and the phrase "not for a righteous person" is the foil against which he works. Since the author, however, wants to use the passage to show that the law is intended for Christians as well as non-Christians, establishing who a *righteous person* is becomes very important.

I have no fault to find with his definition of a righteous person as "anyone in *external* conformity to the law whether Christian or non-Christian" (p. 43), though I think that requires some proof. I also agree that the law may be "given to deal with people who are specifically violating its sanctions and to warn them against their specific sins (as the list in vv. 9b-10 goes on to do)" (p. 43).[267] But nothing in either of these concessions, whether they are true or false, demands the broad conclusion that Barcellos draws from it. Before I defend what I have said in detail, in fairness to the author let us look at his conclusion in context:

> In the sense that the law defines proper behavior and rebukes those not in conformity to it, it is not for "a righteous person" for such a person is already conforming to it. However, what about the person who is not conforming to the standards of the law? He is obviously not "a righteous person" in the sense intended by Paul. It is this person or persons that this use of the law is for.

Having laid this groundwork, he draws the conclusion, "This understanding of the passage makes conformity to the law the responsibility of believers and unbelievers alike" (p. 44). Since I grant that moral law applies to everyone, I could grant this *in theory*. But it does not and cannot apply to the present passage. Several observations will bear this out. First, Paul does not give us a list of vices to answer the question, for whom is the law intended? He gives us a list of *unrighteous persons*. Immediately this ought to alert us that what we primarily need to know is not who a righteous person is, but who an unrighteous person is.

Second, the persons in the list have a specific character, and

---

[267] Knight, *The Pastoral Epistles*, 83.

in no case is it the character of a Christian. This is evident in several ways. When Paul chooses "lawbreakers" to start his list, he is signaling this fact. The Greek word translated *lawbreakers* (ἄνομος) appears ten times in the NT. In 1 Corinthians, Paul uses it four times in one verse (9:21) with no negative connotation.[268] That is obviously not the use here. In every other instance (Mark 15:28; Luke 22:37; Acts 2:23; 2 Thess. 2:8; 1 Tim. 1:10; 2 Pet. 2:8) not only is the connotation negative, but it applies to lost people, unless this verse in Timothy is the exception. In 2 Thessalonians 2:8 Paul uses it as the title of the one "whom the Lord Jesus will overthrow with the breath of his mouth and destroy by the splendor of his coming."

Not only that, but Paul's other lists of sinful persons bear this out. In Romans 1:18-32, Paul lists sinners against whom "[t]he wrath of God is being revealed from heaven" (v.18). That wrath is revealed in God's giving "them over" to all kinds of wickedness (vv.24, 26, 28). Clearly this list of persons is not intended to include believers in Christ. The list in 1 Corinthians 5:9-13 at first looks ambiguous, since Paul speaks of men in the church who call themselves brothers. But Paul evidently means to treat these men as unbelievers. After saying "God will judge those outside," he commands that they be put outside. "Expel the wicked man from among you," he writes, adopting a repeated sentence from Deuteronomy that leaves little doubt of how Paul views their character. A glance at a few of the Deuteronomy passages will make this clear. (In each case Paul's vocabulary is the same as the words I will italicize. Only a verb form differs.)

> The hands of the witnesses must be the first to put him to death, and then the hands of all the people. *You must purge the evil from among you.* (17:7)
> If a malicious witness takes the stand to accuse a man of a crime,

---

[268] In this verse it means "those without [the Mosaic] law."

> ... [t]he judges must make a thorough investigation, and if the witness proves to be a liar ... then do to him as he intended to do to his brother. *You must purge the evil from among you.* ... Show no pity: life for life, eye for eye, tooth for tooth, hand for hand, foot for foot. (19:16-21)
> If a man has a stubborn and rebellious son .... [His parents] shall say to the elders, "This son of ours is stubborn and rebellious. He will not obey us. He is a profligate and a drunkard." Then all the men of his town shall stone him to death. *You must purge the evil from among you.* All Israel will hear and be afraid. (21:18-21)

There are three other examples of this same language in Deuteronomy, all involving the death sentence (22:21, 24; 24:7). In the Corinthian list, then, Paul is telling the church to treat anyone who professes faith as an outsider, if these things characterize him.

Paul has still another list of ungodly persons in 1 Corinthians 6:9-11. Using the same kind of language he uses in 1 Timothy 1:8-11, he makes their fate clear.

> Do you not know [he writes] that the wicked will not inherit the kingdom of God? Do not be deceived: Neither the sexually immoral nor idolaters nor adulterers nor male prostitutes nor homosexual offenders nor thieves nor the greedy nor drunkards nor slanderers nor swindlers will inherit the kingdom of God.

Here Paul not only gives us a list of persons, but he makes sure that we understand this is in no sense a list of Christians. Such people "will not inherit the kingdom of God." Someone might reasonably ask, "Don't you know, Paul, that Christians can commit some of these sins?" But Paul would reply, "I am not giving you a list of sins. I'm giving you a list of people. They are lost because these things characterize them."

One more example will make plain what Paul is doing, this time from 2 Timothy 3:1-5:

> But mark this: There will be terrible times in the last days. People will be lovers of themselves, lovers of money, boastful, proud, abusive, disobedient to their parents, ungrateful, unholy, without love, unforgiving, slanderous, without self-control, brutal, not lovers of the good, treacherous, rash, conceited, lovers of pleasure rather than lovers of God—having a form of godliness but denying its power. Have nothing to do with them. [Verses 6-9 continue in the same vein, characterizing people who do not have power for godliness.]

It is time to draw our conclusion. It is important to differentiate Paul's "vice lists" from his "lists of ungodly persons." It is common for commentators to discuss these two things as if they were one, but they need to be distinguished. In the former, he recognizes that Christians may commit the sins he lists. In the latter, however, he excludes Christians and characterizes the ungodly. The passage under discussion, 1 Timothy 1:8-11, falls into this group. It characterizes unbelieving godless men. In words quoted by Barcellos himself, Alfred Plummer makes this point: "[T]he first five commandments of the Second Table are taken one by one, *flagrant violators being specified in each case*" [italics added] (p. 50).[269] This answers the question, "For whom was the Decalogue intended?" *In the intention of Paul, the passage has nothing to do with Christians.* Barcellos has done good work in further identifying the references to the Decalogue that Knight expounded (pp. 46-57), but that is another subject.

---

[269] Alfred Plummer, *The Pastoral Epistles* (NYC: Hodder & Stoughton, n.d.), 45.

One or two other things in this section of his book call for comment. In a footnote to page 52, the author writes as follows:

> Isaiah's prophecy [of the Sabbath] poses an insurmountable problem for New Covenant Theology's view of the Sabbath. New Covenant theologians identify the Sabbath, the fourth commandment of the Decalogue as *the* sign of the Old Covenant and therefore as abrogated, in total, with the Old Covenant. This view seems to preclude any future, eschatological Sabbath, i.e., the Sabbath of Old Testament prophecy (Is. 56; 58; and Ezek. 44) without the reinstitution of the Old Covenant. Either the Old Covenant will be reinstituted (impossible according to New Covenant Theology), or the New Covenant has a Sabbath (also impossible according to New Covenant Theology)[270]. Since New Covenant Theology denies the former, then New Covenant Theology must affirm the latter, but cannot, due to identifying the Sabbath as the sign of the Old Covenant. If New Covenant theologians affirm that the New Covenant has a Sabbath, then non-premillennial New Covenant theologians must affirm a present (i.e., interadvental) Sabbath and premillennial New Covenant theologians must affirm a future millennial Sabbath in fulfillment of Old Testament prophecy. If the Sabbath is *the* sign of the Old Covenant, exclusively, what is it doing in a *New Covenant* prophecy?

What shall we say about this? Two things: first, this is another case of misunderstanding NCT. In our view, everything without exception in OT redemptive history points to Christ. Why not, then, the Sabbath? Second, presumably the author believes that circumcision was the sign of the Abrahamic Covenant. In that case we might ask him, what is it doing in Colossians 2:9-12? The answer would be the same in both

---

[270] In my judgement there is no Sabbath day for Christians. Nevertheless, NCT only demands that Jesus Christ be given logical priority on this question as on all others. It is conceivable, then, that someone holding NCT could also be a Sabbatarian.

Critique: Part Two

cases. The OT and the NT stand in typological relation to one another. Everything in redemptive history in the OT points to Christ. In some cases, but only in some, we are able to specify how these things *individually* are fulfilled in him.

Finally in this section, I need to examine successive arguments from page 53. They are built on Barcellos' observations on how the Decalogue is the foundation of 1 Timothy 1:8ff. for which I have already expressed appreciation.

> [1 Timothy 1:9] comes in a context applicable to both believers and unbelievers.
>
> This answers the objection often brought against the perpetuity of the fourth commandment, which says that since it is not repeated, it is not binding, and the objection which says it was unique to Israel as God's Old Covenant nation. If the understanding of this text offered above is correct, then the fourth commandment is both *repeated* in the New Testament and *binding* on all men.

Let me make several observations on this. First, while I have been glad to agree with Barcellos that the Decalogue underlies this passage, it must be clear that the relation between the passage and the Decalogue is a *formal* relation. That is, Paul used the Decalogue as a pattern for what he had to write, but his content was his own.

Why do I say this "must be clear?" Because no one, I think, in applying what Paul says would limit the sins suggested by Paul's list of persons to the ones specified in the Ten Commandments.

Suppose for a moment, as Barcellos does, that "the ungodly and sinful, the unholy and irreligious" all allude to individual commandments among the Ten. That still leaves the question, did Paul mean to specify only violators of those particular commands in using this language?

Granting that the author is right in finding an allusion to the Sabbath in the word "profane" ("irreligious" NIV),[271] does Paul mean to exclude all the other kinds of profane or irreligious actions that those words might cover? Is it even clear that he means to include Sabbath-breakers at all? Adopting Moses' forms and adopting Moses' content are clearly two different things.[272]

The second observation follows from the first. If my understanding is correct, the conclusions he draws in the quotation above are unwarranted. That is, nothing here demands the "perpetuity of the fourth commandment" in the sense he uses the phrase; nothing here repeats it in the sense of laying it upon anyone under the New Covenant, and nothing here makes it "binding on all men."

---

[271] Note how cautious Knight is on this point (as quoted on pages 52-53): "Since the keynote of the sabbath is to keep it holy (... Ex. 20:8 ...) and since Paul's list is in negative terms, the single term, . . . [profane], might well characterize those who profane that day, putting the command negatively in terms of its violation. . . ." Barcellos follows this immediately with a categoric statement: "This sin is a violation of the fourth commandment of the Decalogue."

[272] To illustrate this point we may take the conjecture that the framework of "the elementary teachings about Christ" in Hebrews 6:1-2 is a Jewish catechetical form. F.F. Bruce (*NIC: The Epistle to the Hebrews*, [Eerdmans, Grand Rapids, 1964], 112) writes, "When we consider the 'rudiments' one by one, it is remarkable how little in the list is distinctive of Christianity, for practically every item could have its place in a fairly orthodox Jewish community. Each of them, indeed, acquires a new significance in a Christian context; but the impression we get is that existing Jewish beliefs and practices were used as a foundation on which to build Christian truth." He continues the discussion on the following page. (It goes without saying, of course, that Bruce's analysis need not be correct for it to illustrate my point.)

The other issues that Barcellos touches on in this section are discussed in my chapter on moral law.[273]

The Meaning of Matthew 5:17-20.[274]

Richard Barcellos understands that the exegesis of Matthew 5:17-20 is critical both to his own case and to the NCT position. In an effort to distance himself from a wrong view of these verses, he writes as follows:

> A common understanding of this text goes like this: Jesus is saying that He will make the law null and void for His people and is declaring that they will have nothing to do with the Old Testament Law of God because He will fulfill or complete it for them. This understanding often pits law and grace against each other, as if law keeping, or works, saved Old Testament saints; and faith, or grace, saves New Testament saints. (p. 62)

Let me make some comments on what he writes. First, I have already shown that making negative remarks about the law is done by all sides (including Barcellos) in the interests of taking the general standpoint of Jesus or Paul in a given context.[275] We can illustrate this from page 61. The author writes, "[T]he New Testament teaches *both* the abrogation of the law of the Old Covenant *and* its abiding moral validity under the New Covenant." It would seem that there is not much to choose between saying the law is abrogated and saying what amounts to the same thing, the law is made "null and void."

---

[273] See chapter 10.

[274] Since Fred Zaspel has supplied a thorough exegetical study of Matthew 5:17ff. as chapters 5-8 of this book, I will confine myself to critiquing Barcellos' view.

[275] See my remarks on p. 174.

Second, though someone somewhere may have innocently spoken of the law made "null and void" in the sense I have just cited, it is hard to imagine who among Christians could be characterized as saying that Christians "will have nothing to do with the Old Testament Law of God because He will fulfill or complete it for them." It would be truer to say that the Christian will carry out the law of God as it comes to him through Christ. It may indeed be the OT Law, but it will be the OT law after it has passed through the hands of the Lord Jesus in its transformed fashion.

Third, I need to say something about pitting "law and grace against each other, as if law keeping, or works, saved Old Testament saints; and faith, or grace, saves New Testament saints." I suspect our author shows here that he has confused the NCT position with some views of classical dispensationalism. Their theologians sometimes made statements of this kind.[276] Barcellos, however, must not attribute these things to NCT as he seems to do by repeating the words "this view" throughout pages 62-63.

Fourth, alluding again to "this view" he writes,

[T]his view cannot adequately explain 2 Timothy 3:16. In 2 Timothy 3:16-17, we read: "All Scripture is given by inspiration

---

[276] It is only fair to add that among scholars of dispensationalism, both within and outside the movement, it is now generally conceded that such unguarded statements did not, in fact, represent the real position of most of these men. Like the rest of us, they sometimes were inconsistent in what they said. An egregious example is the Old Scofield note on Matthew 6:14: "This is legal ground. . . . Under law forgiveness is conditioned upon a like spirit in us; under grace we are forgiven for Christ's sake . . . ." Contrast that with the note at Romans 4:2 where Scofield says of Abraham's justification, "Paul speaks of that which justifies man *before God*, viz: faith alone, wholly apart from works; . . ." He seems to make this a generalization which applied to all redeemed men of all ages.

> of God, and is profitable for doctrine, for reproof, for correction, for instruction in righteousness, that the man of God may be complete, thoroughly equipped for every good work." . . . The Holy Scriptures are said to be both "able to make you wise unto salvation through faith which is in Christ Jesus" and "profitable for . . . instruction in righteousness" (verse 17). It is the whole of Holy Scripture[277] that Paul is referring to, not merely selected parts which are repeated in the New Testament by Christ and His apostles. This passage teaches us that the whole Old Testament is inspired of God and still profitable for men in Christian ministry under the New Covenant. (pp. 63-64)

Though I have excused NCT of holding what the author calls "this view," this passage presents an opportunity to clear up confusion that often accompanies the quotation of 2 Timothy 3:16-17. Let me repeat it with a portion of its context:

> [F]rom infancy you have known the holy Scriptures, which are able to make you wise for salvation through faith in Christ Jesus. All Scripture is God-breathed and is useful for teaching, rebuking, correcting and training in righteousness, so that the man of God may be thoroughly equipped for every good work.

This passage is often quoted as if it could be taken literally without any important qualification. No one believes that, of course, as I will show in a moment, but that is the way it is often inadvertently used. If that were the case, however, it would amount to this: "The OT is all we need; we don't need the NT at all. The OT can make a person 'wise for salvation,' so we don't need the NT for that. The OT can make the minister 'thoroughly equipped for every good work,' so we don't need the NT for that either." Let me repeat: *no Christian believes this*, but the passage is often quoted as if this were its point. (I must

---

[277] In Barcellos' context, "the whole of Holy Scripture" must mean the whole OT, as reference to parts of it being repeated in the NT shows.

emphasize this distinction because I want to make it clear that neither Pastor Barcellos nor any who share his views take this position.)

Paul's point in 2 Timothy 3 is simply this: the OT is useful both for pointing men to Christ and for equipping gospel ministers *when it is read in the full light of Christ's coming*. In other words, we may make extensive use of the OT provided we are aware of the transformation it has undergone with the coming of our Savior. The point is well illustrated in the story of the Ethiopian eunuch in Acts 8 who was reading Isaiah 53. When Philip asked him whether he understood what he was reading, he replied, "How can I, unless someone explains it to me?" (8:31). He needed the light of the coming of Christ–the very thing now contained in the NT–to grasp its meaning. No Christian, I think, would disagree with this, but it is easy to forget in the heat of theological controversy. Let's see how this applies to the paragraph I have quoted from Barcellos above.

The author rightly says that the OT is "profitable for . . . instruction in righteousness." But what does that mean? It must mean that the OT is profitable for instruction in righteousness when read in the full light of the coming of Jesus Christ. That fact explains why applicability becomes so important. If, after the coming of the Lord Jesus, we apply OT law just as the OT prophets applied it, we have failed in our understanding. That, it seems to me, is what our author wants to do. He tells us that "Christ came to bring the Old Testament to an advanced stage of eschatological realization and application" (p. 65). But when he presses the application of the Decalogue on us, he does it in the most literal terms as it appears in Exodus 20. There seems to be no advance at all. What we need, and what in my judgment Barcellos does not supply, is a clear explanation of the change that he describes as "eschatological realization and application." Otherwise readers are bound to conclude that those words, correct in themselves, have no clearly defined meaning in the mind of the author. This problem continues on the following pages. Again on page 65 he writes the following excellent statements, "What Jesus is saying [in Matthew 5:17] is that the Old Testament is still binding upon His people, *but not in the same way it used to be. The Old Testament is still authoritative as far as our sanctification goes, but the coming and death of Christ and the inauguration of the New Covenant now condition its application.*" We applaud these statements and others like them in the context, but when we ask how that changes the application of the Decalogue, with one exception we seem to be met with silence. The one explanation that Barcellos gives follows:

> It is very clear from this passage [Eph. 2:14-16] and other explicit statements of the New Testament that the Old Covenant and its law, *as Old Covenant law*, has been annulled by Christ's death. Though the law of the Old Covenant still exists and is *called* law, it no longer *functions* as the law of the Old Covenant, because the Old Covenant has been replaced by the New Covenant. (p. 67)

What can we say to this? It looks very much like a truism meaning "since the Old Covenant has passed away and no one is now under it, Old Covenant law no longer applies to men under the Old Covenant." This implies that it is now given to different people, New Covenant believers, *and it is applied exactly as it always was, in the literal words of Exodus 20*.

This seems to be the import of the following quotation from Barcellos:

> Ephesians 2:14-16, and other New Testament texts, speak of the abrogation of the Old Covenant as a covenant with ancient Israel, but in no way makes the law of the Old Covenant as New Covenant law obsolete. The law of the Old Covenant is simply assumed into New Covenant law and applied as such by the New Testament. (p. 69)

Once again this is followed by language about "redemptive-historical change" and a change of application, but we are given no new light on what that means. If, in fact, the "law of the Old

Covenant now functions as part of New Covenant law" (p.69), how has that part changed or been modified?[278] To discuss the answer of Barcellos to that question we will turn now to the Sermon on the Mount.[279]

Has NCT Mistaken the Import of the Sermon on the Mount?

An important part of Barcellos' critique of NCT has to do with the words "But I say to you," as they are expounded, rightly in my judgment, by John Reisinger. He summarizes the problem he sees by writing,

> According to New Covenant Theology, the "But I say to you" statements of the Sermon on the Mount indicate to us that Christ is about to reveal new and higher truth, which contrasts [with] the law of Moses. But to "contrast" different things means "[t]o set in opposition in order to show or emphasize differences."[280] Is Christ setting His new laws in opposition to the Law of Moses in order to show and emphasize differences between them? If so, then we would expect Christ's laws to be found in the Sermon on the Mount and the epistles, but *not* in the Law of Moses or the rest of the Old Testament. (p. 73)
>
> The question the author raises is an important one: if Christ is transforming OT law at the turn of the ages, how is it that we

---

[278] One obvious answer, the Sabbath day has been changed to Sunday, is right as far as it goes on Barcellos' presuppositions. But such a small change can hardly be all that sweeping language about "redemptive-historical change" can refer to.

[279] Since Fred Zaspel discusses the Sermon on the Mount in chapters 5-8, I will again confine myself to a critique of Barcellos' understanding rather than making extensive positive statements about the Sermon itself.

[280] The definition comes from William Morris, editor, The American Heritage Dictionary of the *English Language*, s.v. "contrast."

find some of the same teaching in the OT? To illustrate the difficulty he cites Matthew 5:27-28, "'You have heard that it was said, "You shall not commit adultery." But I say to you that whoever looks at a woman to lust for her has already committed adultery with her in his heart.'" What can NCT say, if words very much like these *in content* are found in Moses or elsewhere in the OT? Specifically, will Reisinger still be able to maintain that this commandment "has a higher and deeper meaning when applied by Christ under the New Covenant than it could have ever had when merely written on stone" (p. 73)?[281]

A number of factors enter into any answer to this question. First, Barcellos provides one answer to this question by his next quotation from Reisinger: "The correct way to approach Mt. 5:27 is *just let it mean exactly what it says*. Let it really contrast the difference between rule under covenant law and rule under grace . . ." (pp. 73-74).[282] As I have contended elsewhere, at its most basic level the Old Covenant law was national law for a national society. As "covenant law," then, it demanded that men be *righteous* in the sense spelled out by Barcellos on page 43: "The 'righteous person' is anyone in *external* conformity to the law . . ." For the most part the "covenant law" has this kind of national reference. One evidence of that fact is the addition of the tenth commandment against coveting. It would not have been necessary if the commandments against stealing and adultery were thought to include desire. This will also help us see the answer to the author's further question, "Did an Old Covenant man honor God by committing lust, the type of heart adultery forbidden in Matthew 5:28?" (p. 74). The answer is "No, of course not." But he could meet the demands of the national covenant and remain an unpunished member of society. For more than that he needed the work of the Holy

---

[281] John Reisinger, *But I Say Unto You* (Southbridge, MA: Crown Publications, Inc., 1989), 21-22.

[282] Ibid., 22.

Spirit, a subject too broad to look into in detail here.[283]

Second, even though the Ten Commandments contain a command against coveting, it is not at all certain that the command intends to say what Jesus said, "whoever looks at a woman to lust for her has already committed adultery with her in his heart." Again, national interests may be in view along the lines of the English proverb, "the wish is the father to the deed." The Israelite could know that he was not to covet from the command, but could he know (and was the law intended to tell him?) that his coveting was adultery? This is not an idle question since the penalty for adultery under the Mosaic law was death.

Third, it is doubtful that such proverbs as Proverbs 7:25 forbid "heart adultery." In keeping with the practical nature of the book, the "simple youth" (7:7) was being warned about the danger to himself in letting his "heart turn to her [the adulteress'] ways or stray into her paths." Why? Because "[m]any are the victims she has brought down; her slain are a mighty throng. Her house is a highway to the grave, leading down to the chambers of death" (7:26-27). One may call this a warning against "heart adultery," but its point is to warn against the *eventual* sin of adultery and its disastrous consequences, as the following verses show. There is no suggestion here that the simple youth has already committed adultery in verse 25. The most we could do here would be to argue that in ignoring the command in verse 25 he would in fact sin against God by despising his counsel.

Fourth, the last point brings us to the question of the presuppositions we bring to a text. Assuming that Solomon is the author of Proverbs 7, can we imagine that the things not mentioned there, love for the husband, for example, compassion

---

[283] The question of regeneration in the OT is difficult. My assumption is that there has never been anyone brought to God in any age that did not come by the new birth, including heart transformation.

for the straying wife and the dread of sinning against God in sexual matters *for God's own sake* are presupposed? We have no reason to think so. But all of these matters would have been part of the moral matrix from which Jesus spoke. No, he did not mention them here, but we know he held them. So his observation on "heart adultery," when looked at in light of his fuller revelation of God's character, has "good things" for us that cannot be reduced to prior revelation.

Finally, there is another answer to this entire question, which I suggested earlier. It is the whole revelation of OT redemptive history that is transcended in Jesus Christ. It is of great interest to us to see how a certain promise, threat or law is transcended, though that is often beyond us. It is the OT *as a unit*—the Law and the Prophets (Matt. 5:17)—that is fulfilled in Christ. The point to remember is this: there is no reason to make the Decalogue an exception.

Is There a Rule of Thumb for Knowing Which Laws Bind the Christian?[284]

Richard Barcellos has written the following:

> A sixth area of challenge for New Covenant theologians concerns hermeneutical presuppositions. New Covenant theology seems to hold to the maxim: Not repeated, not binding. Let me illustrate. New Covenant theologians say, "Since all of the Ten Commandments are not repeated in the New Testament, and only those repeated are still binding, therefore, not all ten are still binding." For instance, John Reisinger says, "Nine out of the ten are repeated in the New Testament Scriptures and are *therefore* [emphasis added] just as binding on a Christian as they were on an Israelite." This position is very common. Whatever is repeated in the New is for the Christian; whatever is not is fulfilled in

---

[284] I am skipping over Barcellos' discussion on NCT and the Moral Law since I have devoted chapter 10 to this question.

Christ and not for the Christian. (p. 85)

Let me make two observations.[285]

First, Barcellos was in a position to know that "not repeated, not binding" is not the doctrine of some who hold NCT, since he used the *Reformation & Revival* issue on the New Covenant as one of his sources.[286] In it I make plain that my position is more elastic than that.[287] John Armstrong, however, is clearer yet. After writing, "The sober and wise warning of one commentator needs to be heard by all advocates of new covenant thinking . . ." he quotes Craig Blomberg:

> It is inadequate to say either that none of the Old Testament applies unless it is explicitly reaffirmed in the New or that all of the Old Testament applies, unless it is specifically revoked in the New. Rather, all of the Old Testament remains normative and relevant for Jesus' followers (2 Tim. 3:16), but none of it can be rightly interpreted until one understands how it has been fulfilled in Christ.[288]

I am sure that Blomberg's statement represents the thinking

---

[285] I'll discuss the substance of the quotation in the main part of the text, but here I want to point out some formal problems. First, the author gives no source for his first lengthy quotation concerning what "New Covenant theologians say." Second, John Reisinger asserts which OT commandments are certainly binding. He says nothing about the rest. The position that is characterized as "very common," then, may or may not be. I suspect it fits the older dispensationalism, however, better than it fits NCT.

[286] John H. Armstrong, ed., *Reformation & Revival* 6, no. 3 (summer 1997).

[287] Ibid., 47-48. Cf my chapter 10 in this volume.

[288] Ibid., 16-17. The quotation is from Craig Blomberg, *Matthew, The New American Commentary* (Nashville: Broadman & Holman, 1992), 103-104.

of NCT as well.

A Few Final Matters.

Barcellos closes his examination of NCT with two final challenges to NCT. They are titled, "New Covenant Theology and Canonics" and "New Covenant Theology and Historical Theology."

Under the first heading there is little new with which to grapple, but perhaps this is the heart of it:

> The New Covenant theology position, practically speaking, reduces the canon for ethics to the New Testament alone. As Zaspel says, "We would rather expect that for new covenant believers divine law would be codified in the new covenant."[289] Put another way, the New Covenant theology position appears to leave us with a revelational canon—the Old and New Testaments—and an ethical canon—the New Testament. The canon of Scripture is *functionally* reduced in this approach.(p.88)

Since I have handled this in great detail already, let me give just two hints here. First, with respect to the quotation from Fred Zaspel, it would be well for all of us to remind ourselves again, that old/new language is used by all sides, and rightly so, because it reflects the variety of the NT itself. Second, that the OT is indeed an ethical canon along with the New, but only when the full light of Christ's fulfillment is shed on it. Third, see Zaspel's own treatment of this in chapter 9, particularly his remarks about a whole-Bible hermeneutic.

What shall we say about NCT and historical theology? For the most part I would like to let Richard Barcellos rest on this matter. In this final section of his book he has done some good work in this area. My own opinion of "strict subscription" to

---

[289] Zaspel, "Divine Law: A New Covenant Perspective," *Reformation and Review* 6:3 (summer 1997): 155.

creeds will be apparent in chapter 15 of this book. As for the views of John Calvin and John Bunyan, they lie outside the parameters set for a student of the Scripture. It may well be that Barcellos has done his homework on both Calvin and Bunyan. I will commend him for that and leave things there.

Summing Up.

Richard Barcellos set a demanding task for himself in trying to survey and critique NCT. He recognized the difficulties at the outset. NCT, he wrote, "is not a monolithic movement. New Covenant theologians differ on some of the nuances involved with defining New Covenant Theology"(p.7). He was right about that! He also recognized that there has been no definitive work written on NCT. Again he was right! Finally, he noticed that at least "one major adherent" of NCT has recently changed his views, and that would cause some difficulty for him. Once again he hit the bull's-eye, and I have discussed one important change.

It is unfortunate that the process of critique is so obviously confrontational or "contrastive," but it cannot be helped. Nevertheless, Barcellos has rendered good service to the Christian community by holding NCT's feet to the fire. We obviously do not agree with all his views, but reading his book has sharpened our wits. We commend the spirit in which he has tried to write, and we hope that we have shown an equally good spirit in our answer. May the Lord bless all who try, even feebly, to question and answer the wisdom of men! And may that blessing be subjection to the word of God.

CHAPTER 13

The Sabbath: A Test Case

Fred G. Zaspel

It may be an oversimplification to say that disagreements regarding the subject of divine law are all settled on the question of the Sabbath. Then again, perhaps in some sense this is no oversimplification at all. It is common knowledge that disputes concerning the subject of divine law eventually and almost inevitably make their way to this subject and often with considerable energy. Moreover, much of what has been discussed in this book regarding the anticipatory function of the law of Moses would—at least could—find wide acceptance on all sides of today's theological fences. Even with this much agreement, the question of the Sabbath remains. Did the Sabbath have a similar forward look? If not, why not? If so, does it also retain its former shape and significance? What transformation, if any, has the Sabbath undergone with the coming of Christ? And what warranted such changes?

The Sabbath question is admittedly complex and problematic, and it would be rash to claim to have settled the matter for all concerned. This chapter will offer an attempt to demonstrate that the Sabbath need be treated no differently and with no different hermeneutic than the one expounded throughout this book and which is commonly employed in the NT treatment of all other aspects of OT law. It can serve as an illustration and a test case for the thesis presented thus far. Answer cannot be given to every opposing opinion at each step of this discussion, but some of the leading alternatives will be considered along the way.

Old Testament

Genesis 2

Sabbath discussion usually begins in Genesis, chapter 2. Although the word "Sabbath" does not appear at this climax of the creation narrative, there is enough relevant material here for all sides to recognize at least a small and suggestive beginning to a larger discussion.

> Thus the heavens and the earth, and all the host of them, were finished. And on the seventh day God ended His work which He had done, and He rested on the seventh day from all His work which He had done. Then God blessed the seventh day and sanctified it, because in it He rested from all His work which God had created and made. (Gen. 2:1-3)

This passage is significant as the capstone of the creation narrative (Gen. 1:1-2:3). God has spoken the whole world into being and has clothed it with beauty and grandeur and has given it inhabitants. Now he has "finished" (*kālāh/sunteleō*) his work, and in his own estimation it is all "very good" as it stands in its completeness and perfection (1:31-2:1). His handiwork—"all the host" of it—displays his glory, and God "rested" (*šābat/katapauō*) and was "refreshed" (Exod. 31:17) from his labors. To be sure, God has never tired or needed rest or refreshment. This is the rest of accomplishment, the rest of satisfaction. On the seventh day, God sat back, as it were, and took pleasure in what he had done. Twice it is stated "God rested." This is in every sense *God's* rest (Ps. 95:11), *his* delighted rest in his finished work. The creation narrative climaxes in God's contentment.

This was *God's* rest. But was this a delight to be enjoyed by himself alone? Why does the week end in the Creator's rest? In what way is this significant? Notice that the closing formula "the evening and the morning" is absent—the day remains open. Also, in Genesis 2:2-3a "the seventh day" is mentioned three times, each in a sentence composed of seven words (Hebrew text). Moses has carefully and creatively built a sense of anticipation into the narrative and even the sentence structure itself. Further, God "blessed" the seventh day and "sanctified" it. For whom was it thus made sacred? There seems to be both an outward and a forward look. Indeed, we have it on Jesus' own authority—"The Sabbath was made for man" (Mark 2:27). Clearly, Moses has structured this passage (Gen. 1:1-2:3) in such a way that it reaches its high point, not in the creation of man (day six), but in divine, contented rest (day seven). This, God's rest, is the point to which the passage drives. Put another way, Moses is portraying the fact that creation—human history—finds its goal in God's rest. God's rest is a rest in which creation itself is to enjoy and have a share. "The declaration mounts, as it were, to the place of God himself and testifies that with the living God there is rest. . . . The way is being prepared, therefore, for . . . the final, saving good."[290] Little more information is given here, but the note of anticipation is sounded already, an anticipation of universal rest. Will newly-created man enjoy this rest also?

In the next chapter (Gen. 3), Moses records for us how the enjoyment of God's rest was forfeited. As a result of his rebellion, mankind has fallen under a curse, a curse which involves labor, toil, sweat, pain, and death. The state of sin and death now dominates, and rest is but a hope. Life now is one of toil and labor and sin and death. Indeed, Moses has told us that God's work ($'\bar{a}\acute{s}ah$ and $b\bar{a}r\bar{a}'$) was "finished . . . ended . . . done" (2:1-2). Now, after man's sin, God begins to work again; he "made ($'\bar{a}\acute{s}ah$) garments of skin for Adam and his wife and

---

[290] G. von Rad, *Genesis*, 60. Cited in Derek Kidner, *Genesis* (reprint, Downers Grove, IL: InterVarsity Press, 1979), 53. This of course is the interpretation given by the author of Hebrews (3:7-4:13).

clothed them" (3:21). On the seventh day God rested. "But not for long. As soon as man sinned God went to work again."[291] God has again taken up the work of preparing rest, even for his fallen creatures. This is evidently Jesus' point of reference in John 5:17 (in context)—"My Father has been working until now, and I have been working."

That the initial seventh day had this sense of anticipation built into it is precisely the affirmation of Hebrews 4:4, which will be surveyed later. There are other later Biblical passages that seem to view Genesis 2:1-3 similarly, and they will be noted in due course. But it should be recognized at the outset that this passage (Gen. 2:1-3) is *intended* to be understood as a small beginning of a much larger theme which later biblical writers will progressively unfold. It is a theme that is pregnant with hope and anticipation.[292] Creation has as its goal the divine rest.

---

[291] Donald Grey Barnhouse, *Genesis* (Grand Rapids: Zondervan Publishing Co., 1976), 14. See also James M. Boice, *Genesis*, vol. 1 (Grand Rapids: Baker Book House, 1982), 104.

[292] In light of this, the view that Genesis 2:1-3 establishes and enjoins Sabbath observance as a creation ordinance, whether right or wrong in itself, seems to miss the main point. Von Rad spoke more strongly: it "would be a complete misapprehension of the passage" (*Old Testament Theology*, vol. 1; cited by Ralph Smith, *Old Testament Theology* [Nashville: Broadman & Holman Publishers, 1993], 185). No command regarding Sabbath day observance can be found here. Nor is there any religious significance attached to the day, so far as man's obligations or behavior are concerned. No mention at all is made as to what bearing this day has on man, if any. See James M. Boice, *The Gospel of John*, vol. 2 (Grand Rapids: Baker Book House, 1985), 368. The passage reveals that God rested on the seventh day and that he gave it a special, sacred significance. With this is an intimation of God's purpose to open this rest beyond himself. There is a note of expectation. But beyond this the text does not go. Exegetical ground for the Sabbath as a "creation ordinance" must be found elsewhere. Notice John Bunyan's more thorough response to

As Oehler noted,

> That the whole course of human history is not to run on in dreary endlessness; that its events are to have a positive termination; are to find a completion in an harmonious and God-given order, — is already guaranteed by the Sabbath of creation. . . . The Divine rest of the seventh day of creation, which has no evening, hovers over the world's progress, that it may at last absorb it into itself.[293]

Keil and Delitsch remarked similarly: The original seventh day—

> "was the beginning and type of the rest to which the creation, after it had fallen from fellowship with God through the sin of man, received a promise that it should once more be restored through redemption, at its final consummation."[294]

So Genesis 2:1-3 sounds the first note of eschatology in Scripture, and this anticipatory function of the seventh day of creation week, in turn, provides the interpretive clue to understanding this rest/Sabbath motif as it is revealed throughout the history of divine revelation.

---

this issue in Appendix 6, pp. 293-294.

[293] Gustav Friedrich Oehler, *Theology of the Old Testament*, trans. George E. Day (1873; reprint, Minneapolis: Klock & Klock Christian Publishers, 1978), 332.

[294] Keil and Delitsch, *Commentary on the Old Testament*, vol. 1 (reprint, Grand Rapids: Wm. B. Eerdmans Publishing Co., 1986), 70.

The Pentateuch

As the narrative of human history unfolds, there are subtle reminders along the way of mankind's want for rest (e.g., Gen. 2:15; 3:16-17; 5:29, etc.). The reality of toilsome restlessness is never absent and is brought to the fore again in the opening chapters of Exodus, with the people of Israel in bondage, and at this point the "rest" theme moves a large step forward.

The first record of seventh day/Sabbath observance by men appears in connection with the Exodus, just prior to Sinai (Exod. 16).[295] Murmuring because of hunger, Israel is given "manna" (literally, "what is it")—to eat and be filled. Each day, God graciously provided plenty for each person, but it must not be hoarded. Each day will see new provision. Israel must learn to trust God. On the sixth day the Lord provided double, and each was to take two days' supply. No manna would be harvested on the seventh day, for on the seventh day "the Lord has given you the Sabbath" (šāḇāṯ/sabbaton, v. 29). "So the people rested (šābbaṯ/sabbatizō) the seventh day" (v. 30). Rest is provided, and God's people were reminded weekly of God's grace. This is not yet the Jewish Sabbath as such; it is much less restrictive than the Sabbath soon to be given at Sinai. The only restriction here concerns the manna specifically. There is no prohibition from work of any other kind. But this does prepare Israel for what is to come shortly, and it is itself a regular and vivid reminder that rest can come only by God's provision.

It was at Sinai that God "made known His holy Sabbath" to Israel (Neh. 9:14). In Exodus 19-20, God constituted Israel as a nation and gave them his law, a law summarized in the Ten

---

[295] Attempts to find a reference to Sabbath observance in the expression "in the end of days" (miqēṣ yāmim/met' hēmeras, Gen. 4:3) are merely speculative. See 1 Kings 17:7 where the identical expression occurs and connotes, simply, "in the course of time," "many days later," or the like. Cf. Jeremiah 13:6.

The Sabbath: A Test Case

Commandments (Exod. 20:2-17).[296] The fourth command assigns to Israel strict and regular Sabbath day observance.

> Remember[297] the Sabbath day, to keep it holy. Six days you shall labor and do all your work, but the seventh day is the Sabbath of the LORD your God. In it you shall do no work: you, nor your son, nor your daughter, nor your male servant, nor your female servant, nor your cattle, nor your stranger who is within your gates. For in six days the LORD made the heavens and the earth, the sea, and all that is in them, and rested the seventh day. Therefore the LORD blessed the Sabbath day and hallowed it. (Ex. 20:8-11)

---

[296] Cf. Warfield, "The Sabbath in the Word of God," 311.

[297] Some argue that "remember" (Exod. 20:8) indicates that the day was observed before this command was given, perhaps as far back as creation week. But this places more weight on "remember" than the word need sustain, particularly given that there is no evidence in Genesis 2 that such a command was then given. "Remember!" is a common way of phrasing commands, one which every parent will recognize immediately. So also in Scripture it may simply connote, "keep" or "observe" or "obey" or "act in accordance with" (Lev. 26:42, 45; Judg. 8:34; Eccles. 12:1, 6 [cf. vv. 13-14]; Jer. 14:21; Amos 1:9; Mal. 4:4; Luke 1:72; Heb. 13:7). In fact, when Moses repeats the Sabbath command in Deuteronomy 5:12, he simply uses the word "observe" (šāmăr). Frequently in the Bible, "remember" is followed up immediately with the appositional phrase "to keep" or "to do" which serves to define it (Num. 15:39-40; Ps. 103:18; 1 Cor. 11:2). It is not necessary to read any more than this into the command (Exod. 20:8). The word by itself does not require any prior observance. Perhaps the "remember" of Exodus 20 refers to the Sabbath first given in Exodus 16. But we should note that here (Exod. 20) Moses gave instruction as to *how* the Sabbath was to be remembered; God forbad *all* labor. This appears to be new legislation. Finally, Nehemiah 9:14 specifically states that the Sabbath was "made known" to Israel at Sinai. When all this is considered, the command to "remember" the Sabbath day does not seem to reflect a prior observance of the day as a creation ordinance.

The first four and the last six commands of the Decalogue are today commonly referred to as "the first table" and "second table" of the law, respectively. Kline has shown by a comparison with suzerainty treaties of this time period that such covenant documents are written out in their entirety on *both* tables.[298] It seems that our terminology needs revision, then, for both "tables" of the law would have contained the entire Decalogue. Further, Kline shows that in the center of the document appears the suzerain's dynastic seal. Of course, God has no such "image" with which to seal the document; instead, it is the Sabbath law that is central to the document and which stands as the "sign" or "seal" of God's covenant with Israel. This is the repeated affirmation of Exodus 31:12-18—"You must observe my Sabbaths. This will be a sign (*'ôṯ*) between me and you for the generations to come" (Exod. 31:13; cf. Ezek. 20:12, 20). As the rainbow stood as the sign of the Noahic covenant (Gen. 9:12, 13, 17), and as circumcision stood as the sign of the Abrahamic covenant (Gen. 17:11), so also the Sabbath stood as the sign of God's covenant with Israel. This explains the expression in Isaiah 56:4-6, "hold fast My covenant." This also explains the command's frequent repetition in the Torah (e.g., Exod. 23:12; 34:21; 35:2-3, etc.). This also explains why Israel's neighboring nations, though condemned for many sins, were never criticized for a failure to observe the Sabbath day—it was the sign of God's covenant with Israel.[299]

That the Sabbath stood as the sign or seal of God's covenant with Israel further explains the careful strictness and importance

---

[298] Meredith Kline, *The Structure of Biblical Authority* (1989; reprint, Eugene, OR: Wipf & Stock, 1997), 120.

[299] Boice is more direct: "It is difficult to see how anything other than prejudice could apply these words to any nation other than Israel or miss the fact that the sabbath was a part of the law and as such was intended to distinguish the nation of Israel from others." Boice, *The Gospel of John,* vol. 2, 369.

attached to its observance. Violation of Sabbath in any way resulted in death (Exod. 31:14). No work was to be done (Exod. 20:10; 31:14-15). Singular importance was associated with Sabbath observance, for to violate it was to violate the very covenant sign. For example, as wrong as it would be for an angry husband to throw a chair or a lamp across the room, it would be viewed with much more concern if it were his wedding ring being thrown; to throw away the ring would carry more symbolic, and thus more solemn, connotations. The wedding ring is the solemn sign of the marriage covenant, and to treat it lightly or with contempt would be a very serious matter. So also, it was a matter of utmost concern to God for Israel to give the Sabbath due respect, and to violate it was an act worthy of death. Plowing and harvesting (Exod. 34:21), bearing burdens (Jer. 17:21), merely gathering sticks (Num. 15:32-36), or even lighting a fire (Exod. 35:3) were all to be carefully avoided. Israel's violation of God's Sabbath was the reason assigned to her destruction and captivity (Ezek. 20:10-26; 22:8, 26, 31).[300] God had given Israel "rest," and this rest, the very token of the covenant, was to be duly honored and observed. God's rest must not be profaned (*ḥālal*) by man's work (Ezek. 22:26).

But the seventh-day/Sabbath day is more than a weekly reminder. Grounded as it was, not in God's nature, but in his work, it had a ritual/ceremonial character. In the Mosaic economy, it served "as the foundation for all Israelite festivals."[301] In Exodus 23:12 and Leviticus 23:1-3, the Sabbath command begins the transition to the commands regarding

---

[300] Israel's continued violation of the Sabbath year for a period of approximately five centuries meant that the people owed seventy years to the Lord, and they were made to pay this back in Babylon (2 Chron. 36:21; Jer. 25:11; cf. Ezek. 20:10-26).

[301] Paul R. House, *Old Testament Theology* (Downers Grove, IL: InterVarsity Press, 1998), 146.

Israel's annual festivals to the Lord (Exod. 23:14ff; Lev. 23:4ff). In Exodus 35:2-3, Leviticus 19:30, and 26:2, the Sabbath command appears in association with matters concerning the tabernacle. The Sabbath day forms the rationale for the Sabbatical year and the year of Jubilee (Lev. 25:1ff). These, and the feast of trumpets (23:24-25), the day of atonement (16:29, 30), and the feast of tabernacles (23:34)are all Sabbath-rests to the Lord.[302] Perhaps most compelling of these for our purposes are the Sabbatical year and the year of Jubilee, both of which shout of rest, freedom, and restoration (Lev. 25). The theme born at the climax of creation week continues to grow as God multiplies these reminders of his rest.

The Sabbath had a still more significant feature. It was both commemorative and prospective. The Mosaic command reaches back to find its significance in God's creation rest—"For in six days the LORD made the heavens and the earth, the sea, and all that is in them, and rested the seventh day" (Exod. 20:8-11). This Sabbath observance was reminiscent of God's rest, which itself is prospective of a rest to come—the toil and labor imposed on man by sin and a curse is to end in final rest, and of this rest there is a weekly reminder.

This connection explains why the Sabbath command in Deuteronomy 5:12-15, unlike the command in Exodus 20:8-11, was grounded not in God's creation rest, specifically, but in God's deliverance of Israel from slavery.

> "And remember that you were a slave in the land of Egypt, and the LORD your God brought you out from there by a mighty hand and by an outstretched arm; therefore the LORD your God commanded you to keep the Sabbath day." (Deut. 5:15)

This note of labor giving way to rest, and rest as a gift from God, links this to the "rest" theme introduced in Genesis 2.

---

[302] Hence, the plural, "Sabbaths" (Lev. 19:3, 30).

The Sabbath: A Test Case

Since earliest times, man's toil was reminiscent of the curse (Gen. 3:17-19) and prospective of divine rest (Gen. 5:29[303]), and here the theme is highlighted again. The idea of divine redemption is not foreign to that of divine rest but of a piece with it. Indeed, for fallen man, rest *is* redemption.

The Old Testament as a Whole

In this regard it should be noted that Israel's "rest" was realized not in the seventh day only, but in Israel's land itself (e.g., Exod. 33:14; Deut. 3:20; 12:9-10; 25:19; Josh. 1:13; 21:44; Ps. 95:11, etc.; cf. Lev. 25:2).[304] Similarly, in Babylon, Israel "found no rest" (Lam. 1:3; cf. 5:5). The OT emphasizes that this "rest" or "resting place" is God's own provision for his people, and in this connection Israel is described as an heir of a divine inheritance (e.g., Exod. 15:17; Deut. 4:20). So the promised land also is taken up into this theme of divine rest; it too is both a token of God's gracious provision and prospective of a fulness of rest still to come.

Similarly, when Israel enjoyed deliverance from her enemies, the resulting peace is described as a time of "rest" (Josh. 11:23; 14:15; 21:44; Judg. 3:11, 30). David was a "man of war" (1 Sam. 17:33; 2 Sam. 17:8), so named for his successful defeat of all Israel's enemies. But by his labors he brought Israel into rest (2 Sam. 7:1, 11). Thus his son Solomon was "a man of rest" (1 Chron. 22:9; cf. 1 Kings 8:56). Here also, as Solomon's name

---

[303] "Noah" means "rest." "Comfort" translates *nûaḥ* /*dianapauō*. Cf. the *nûaḥ* group of words below. Note also the echo of Genesis 3:15ff.

[304] The primary terms used for "rest" are *nûaḥ/m^{e}nûḥāh*, and then *šāqaṭ* which the Septuagint translate with *katapauō* and sometimes *kopazō* or *hēsuchazō*. See Walter C. Kaiser, Jr., "The Promise Theme and the Theology of Rest," *BibSac* (April 1973), 4-51.

implies, the language of "peace" is brought into the theme of rest—"Behold, a son shall be born to you, who shall be a man of rest; and I will give him rest from all his enemies all around. His name shall be Solomon ($š^e lōmōh$), for I will give peace ($šālôm$) and quietness ($šěqěṭ$) to Israel in his days." This link appears to provide warrant to include in this "rest" theme the various prophetic announcements of the coming age when peace will prevail in the rule of God's Servant and as a result of God's intervention in human history (Isa. 11, 65, etc.).

Further, there is a frequent association of rest with the presence of God/dwelling place of the ark in Zion (Ps. 132:8, 14; Isa. 66:1; etc.).[305] This is reminiscent of God's promise to Moses—"My presence will go with you, and I will give you rest" (Exod. 33:14). This highlights again the ideas of rest as found in God and rest as God's gracious provision.[306]

The Psalms offer only a few, but highly suggestive, references to this theme of rest. In Psalm 116:7, the psalmist expects to return to God's rest in his resurrection.[307] And in Psalm 94:13 ($šěqěṭ$) and 95:11 ($m^e nûḥah$), two enthronement psalms heavily loaded with an eschatological outlook, rest "from days of adversity" and rest in the promised land are made the object of happy expectation. These contributions to the theme are suggestive in that they associate the fulness of rest with the eschaton.[308] Psalm 95 adds to this an invitation to this divine rest and warns, by the example of the wilderness generation, of missing this rest by rebellion and unbelief. Rest here takes a decidedly soteriological as well as eschatological connotation.

---

[305] Cf. Kaiser, "Promise Theme," 140.

[306] A. T. Lincoln, "Sabbath, Rest, and Eschatology in the New Testament" in Carson, *From Sabbath to Lord's Day*, 208.

[307] Cf. Kaiser, "Promise Theme," 140, 148-149.

[308] Kaiser, "Promise Theme," 142-3.

The Sabbath: A Test Case

This eschatological fulness of rest is an often-repeated hope resounding in the prophets also, particularly Isaiah. Over and again God's "salvation" is promised with great excitement, and the related terms "rest" and "peace" and "safety" often highlight the announcement (Isa. 52:7; 55:12; 57:2; Jer. 30:10; Ezek. 34:25; 37:26). The close association of this rest with Jehovah's Servant (Isa. 52:7; cf. 9:6-7) points again to the idea of redemption.

The Sabbath, then, as the word itself indicates, speaks of rest. It is not a human rest only but a divine rest in which man may one day share. The Sabbath speaks of grace, of divine provision, and of redemption. It is not surprising, then, that the worship of the Israelite religion was elevated on the Sabbath. The Sabbath offered time and reason for praise in the house of the Lord, as Psalm 92, "A Psalm for the Sabbath Day" and a psalm of deliverance and provision, illustrates. It was a day of special sacrifice and offering (Num. 28:9-10; cf. Ezek. 46:1-3). There is no indication that the observance of the Sabbath by the Israelite people at large was to be marked by any special religious functions other than the fact that true observance of the day involved a "delighting in the Lord." Proper observance of the Sabbath focused on a cessation from work. Since this rest pointed to divine provision, the note of worship is not far behind, at least insofar as the day's redemptive-historical purpose is concerned. The Sabbath speaks of more than cessation of human activity. It is more than a sign by which God's covenant people are identified. It is a ceremony which points beyond itself. It looks ahead to a fulness of rest which in God's grace and time will be given to his people. It remains for the NT to reveal how this rest will come to fruition, but the expectation of it is a matter of constant and repeated reminder throughout the OT.

New Testament

As with all Biblical themes, it is in the NT that this Sabbath-rest motif is given clearest and final definition. As noted above, the OT associated the promised rest with the Servant of Jehovah and with the ideas of redemption and eschatology. Although the OT did not give great detail to the discussion, it did give enough information that the fulfillment realized in the Lord Jesus Christ should not strike us as surprising. He is, after all, the Servant-Redeemer, and he is the Eschatos (*eschatos*, Rev. 22:13). "All the promises of God in Him are Yes, and in Him Amen" (2 Cor. 1:20). In the NT, the revelation of Jesus Christ, we expect to see the theme made clear and brought to full realization.

With the note of redemption and peace brought by the Lord's Servant already sounded in connection with the rest motif in the OT, as we turn to the NT, we are tempted to include in our tracing out of this theme all the passages which treat of Christ and his work in any way. This would be entirely legitimate, as passages like Hebrews 4 will make clear. For our purposes here, we must be more restrictive, though it sometimes is difficult to know precisely what constraints to observe. Simeon's words in the temple could surely be taken into account—"Lord, now You are letting Your servant depart in peace, according to Your word; For my eyes have seen Your salvation" (Luke 2:29-30). A still closer link may be found in Matthew 1:21 where "Jesus" is the name given to the Savior who is born. "Jesus," of course, translates into the Greek from the Hebrew "Joshua"—in the same way that "Caesar" translates to "Czar" in Russian and "Kaiser" in German, or as the Greek *kuriakon* ("belonging to the Lord") becomes "church" and "Kirche" in English and German respectively. This identification of Jesus with Joshua immediately points to him as the one who, like the earlier Joshua, will lead God's people into rest. There are other passages, such as Luke 4:16ff, where Jesus announces himself to be the Servant of the Lord who has come to proclaim the Sabbatical year of release (Jubilee), and Matthew 11:28ff, where Jesus offers his "rest" to the weary who come to him for it. So also Romans 8:18-24, with echoes of Genesis 2-3, notes with the prophets that not mankind alone, but all of creation awaits a coming rest. Just as the narrative of Genesis 1-2 culminates in God's rest, so also shall history itself (cf. Eph. 1:10). These kinds of notes along the way illuminate the study considerably and confirm that the OT Sabbath looked forward to the reality to be enjoyed in Christ. It was the "shadow" of which Christ is the "substance" (Col. 2:16-17). But lest this chapter rival the size of the book, we will restrict our remarks here primarily to those passages in which the "Sabbath" theme is treated explicitly.

The Gospels – Jesus and the Sabbath

Jesus' most memorable teaching about the Sabbath came in the context of controversy. Sampey remarked,

> "It is worthy of note that, while Jesus pushed the moral precepts of the Decalogue into the inner realm of thought and desire, thus making the requirement more difficult and the law more exacting, He fought for a more liberal and lenient interpretation of the law of the Sabbath. Rigorous sabbatarians must look elsewhere for a champion of their views."[309]

This may be so, particularly in reference to the many regulations which had been added to the Sabbath law in the various rabbinic traditions. And "while none of [Jesus'] actions clearly infringes the written law, the non-emergency healings of Jesus

---

[309] *The International Standard Bible Encyclopedia*, s.v. "sabbath."

certainly 'stretch' it."³¹⁰ But Jesus' comparative "leniency" with regard to the Sabbath must be understood within its proper framework.

In Matthew 12:1-8 (cf. Mark 2:23-28; and Luke 6:1-5), Jesus comes under attack for his disciples' actions. On a Sabbath day, while walking along the edge of a grainfield, the disciples plucked some of the heads of grain to eat. Luke adds the detail that the disciples were rubbing the grain in their hands (6:1), doubtless to winnow away the chaff. The Pharisees were aghast, and since it was Jesus' disciples who had done this, the Pharisees rightly assumed that it was with Jesus' approval; implicitly, they accused Jesus of contravening the Mosaic law. Moses specifically allowed one to take of his neighbor's grain by hand (Deut. 23:25), but harvesting on the Sabbath was specifically forbidden (Exod. 34:21). Further, the Pharisees may well have perceived the disciples' "rubbing out of the grain as threshing and their blowing away of the chaff as winnowing."³¹¹ It is significant also that the charge was never brought against Jesus or his disciples formally; it evidently would not have stood even in their own religious court.³¹² The disciples' actions were hardly what was in view in the Mosaic prohibition.

What first strikes us about Jesus' response is that he does not answer on these grounds. He does not argue that they have over-extended Moses, however accurate such an argument would have been. Instead, he argues from 1 Samuel 21:1-6 that

---

³¹⁰ Moo, "The Law of Christ as the Fulfillment of the Law of Moses," 354.

³¹¹ D. Edmond Hiebert, *Mark: A Portrait of the Servant* (Chicago: Moody Press, 1974), 77. For a list of thirty-nine classes of prohibited work extrapolated from the prohibition of Exodus 34:21, see Mishna Shabbath 7.

³¹² For that matter, not even at Jesus' trial was the accusation of Sabbath violation brought against him. He lived "under the law" successfully (Gal. 4:4).

The Sabbath: A Test Case

he constitutes an exceptional case.[313] David and his soldiers, during their flight from King Saul, took and ate the showbread in the house of God. This action constituted a violation of the law; the consecrated bread was to be eaten by the priests only (Lev. 24:5-9). Yet David, when hungry and in need, allowed—demanded—this exception from the priest, and that on the Sabbath day.[314] So Jesus' opponents are faced with a dilemma: they must choose between their traditions and interpretations of the law on the one hand, and David their great and revered king on the other. In opting for David, they would thereby both exonerate the activities of Jesus' disciples, whom they have already pronounced guilty, and implicitly acknowledge the narrowness of their own teachers. The conclusion was an obvious one, however difficult it would have been for them to admit it.

The justification for the actions of David and his men, and by extension, the actions of Jesus' disciples, is still unexplained. Jesus makes mention of David's hunger, thus demonstrating a parallel situation. David "needed" (*chreian eschen*) to eat, and so now do Jesus' disciples. But this is not the point at issue, really, for unlike David's men, the disciples of Jesus were not hungry to the point of exhaustion. David's was an extreme case; not so for the disciples of Jesus. By implication Jesus lends some insight into the nature of the Sabbath law itself. If the Sabbath were, as is often assumed, a part of God's "unchangeable moral law," it would be very difficult indeed to admit such an exception as this, especially given that this is an exception

---

[313] This reference to David's "unlawful" activity seems to allow, at least for the moment, the validity of the charge. Wilson, *Luke and the Law*, 33.

[314] So says rabbinic tradition; see B. Men. 95b.

grounded in human concerns.[315] Jesus does not classify the Sabbath as unchanging moral law, and this brought him into conflict with the Pharisees. The Sabbath was not an end in itself, an absolute that admitted no exceptions. "The Sabbath was made for man, and not man for the Sabbath" (Mark 2:27). It was intended for man's benefit, his well-being. To elevate it to a place of tyranny over man is to make more of it than was intended; indeed, it would overthrow it altogether.[316]

More to the point, it is *Jesus* who possesses the authority to decide these things—he is "Lord, even [ascensive *kai*] of the Sabbath" (Matt. 12:8). "As lord of the sabbath he stands above the law and implicitly claims the right to define it. . . . It is the Son of Man who decides what is and what is not acceptable behavior on the sabbath."[317] That is, the question is not so much Jesus' relation to the Sabbath but its relation to him. As B. B. Warfield stated, "It [the Sabbath] belongs to him. He is the Lord of it; master of it — for that is what 'Lord' means. He may do with it what he will: abolish it if he chooses."[318] Jesus

---

[315] Cf. Ezra P. Gould, *A Critical and Exegetical Commentary on the Gospel According to Mark*, ICC (NY: Charles Scribner's Sons, 1913), 50. Nor does this statement lend weight to the idea that the Sabbath was a creation ordinance, and to press *egeneto* so would be unwarranted. See M. Max B. Turner, "The Sabbath, Sunday, and the Law in Luke/Acts," in Carson, *From Sabbath to Lord's Day*, 103.

[316] See *Dictionary of Jesus and the Gospels*, ed. Joel B. Green and Scot McKnight, s.v. "sabbath."

[317] Wilson, *Luke and the Law*, 33. Wilson later continues in this vein: "The general drift, however, seems clear. The disciples disobey the sabbath law and Jesus defines their action by allusion to the OT and, above all, by a claim to personal authority which implicitly gives him the right to make or break sabbath commands" (p. 35).

[318] Warfield, "The Sabbath in the Word of God," 310.

The Sabbath: A Test Case

"continually subordinates the Sabbath to the demands of His own mission."[319] It is not so much a question of the extent of Sabbath regulations but of Jesus' lordship. In the words of Plummer, "The Son of man controls the sabbath, not is controlled by it."[320] This is the point at issue, and this is the high point of Jesus' defense (*hōste*, Mark 2:28[321]). If David had the right to make an exception to Israel's ceremonial laws, Jesus has more. Jesus' defense claims the highest possible ground: he has an authority that surpasses even the Sabbath itself. His greatness gives certain rights to his disciples: they may pluck this grain and eat, even on this day of rest.

As a second illustration of his point, Jesus continues, "'Or have you not read in the law that on the Sabbath the priests in the temple profane the Sabbath, and are blameless?'" (Matt. 12:5). The priests continue their work on the Sabbath; indeed, on the Sabbath they are busier than on any other day! But this does not "profane" the Sabbath, for (it is implied) the temple takes precedence over the Sabbath. Again, Jesus claims higher ground—"'in this place there is One greater than the temple'" (v.6). Jesus' rights surpass not only those of the priests but even the temple itself. He is greater. He is greater than David, greater than Jonah (v. 41), greater than Solomon (v. 42), greater than the temple (v. 6), and greater even than the Sabbath (v. 8). Jesus justifies his disciples' actions on the ground of his

---

[319] Turner, "Sunday, the Sabbath, and the Law in Luke/Acts," 113.

[320] Cited in Carson, *From Sabbath to Lord's Day*, 65.

[321] "Therefore" (*hōste*) identifies the statement of v.28 as a conclusion that has been reached by what has preceded. Mark explicitly affirms that the passage is intended to show the authority of Christ. See also Boice, *The Gospel of John*, vol. 2, 364-5.

unsurpassed lordship.³²² "This does not mean that Jesus here actually breaks the Sabbath or overrides it, at least as far as Torah is concerned, but it does mean He claims authority to do so, and in a sense questions the Pharisees' right to question Him."³²³

Jesus only hints here that the Sabbath is being transformed. Some significant change is taking place. He does not specify exactly what that change is, but it is impossible to think that his lordship over the Sabbath will not be exercised in some way. A claim to authority over the Sabbath demands definition. Accordingly, there are some contextual clues as to what changes the Sabbath would undergo. In the preceding paragraph, Jesus offers "rest" to those who are weary (Matt. 11:28), and it is in connection with this ("at that time," 12:1) that Jesus asserts his lordship over the Sabbath. Matthew seems to imply that the "rest" which Jesus offers is that to which the Sabbath pointed. Here, *in Jesus*, the Sabbath finds its true meaning. Mark casts this incident more explicitly in redemptive-historical terms. The question of fasting was used to show something of the epochal significance of Jesus' person and presence on earth and the newness of this Messianic age (2:18-22—the question of fasting, the new cloth, the new wineskin). The epochal shift marked by the coming of Jesus Christ had ramifications even in regard to the Sabbath day and how it is to be observed in this age. The Lord Jesus has ushered in an age in which God's promised rest is realized. The fuller details of this await the apostolic writings (see below), but our Lord himself here lays the groundwork for that teaching. The statement, as it is, neither confirms nor disallows the continuation of Sabbath observance, in explicit terms. But it emphatically affirms Jesus'

---

³²² Note the explanatory conjunction "for/because" (*gar*), Matthew 12:8.

³²³ Carson, "Jesus and the Sabbath in the Four Gospels" in *From Sabbath to Lord's Day*, 67.

The Sabbath: A Test Case

inherent right to do with the law as he pleases, and so the foundation for an epochal change is clearly implied. The arrival of God the Son has forever changed the whole significance of the Sabbath day. He has brought about that which it only anticipated.

It was most often Jesus' works of healing on the Sabbath that gave rise to controversy (e.g., Matt. 12:8-14/Mark 3:1-6/Luke 6:6-11; 13:10; 14:1-6; John 9:1-41). Brown asserts that Jesus *"went out of his way* to heal on the Sabbath," but he offers no explicit support.[324] He does note later that Jesus intends by his Sabbath healings to demonstrate his lordship over the day, and this may lend some weight to the point. Jesus remarked that it was "necessary" (*dei*) for the woman with the spirit of infirmity to be healed on the Sabbath, and Moo concludes from this that "Jesus regarded the day as a particularly appropriate time for his ministry of healing."[325] It would seem then, that Jesus' Sabbath healings are designed to illustrate the rest and release from Satanic "bondage" (Luke 13:16) that Jesus brought and which is typified in the Sabbath. Jesus' emphasis in these passages, however, generally falls on the harshness of the rabbinic Sabbath regulations and the appropriateness of doing good on *any* day of the week, Sabbath included.

In John 5:1-18, however, there is a further twist. Jesus' emphasis here is similar to that of Matthew 12:1-8 (and parallels)—it is his inherent right to determine what is good on the Sabbath. "'My Father has been working until now, and I have been working'" (John 5:17). Moreover, his superior authority affects not only his own behavior on the Sabbath, but also that of others (namely, the man whom Jesus commanded to rise and carry his pallet). Beyond that, the illustrative

---

[324] Michael L. Brown, *Israel's Divine Healer* (Grand Rapids: Zondervan Publishing House, 1995), 221.

[325] Douglas Moo, "Jesus and the Authority of the Mosaic Law," *JSNT* 20 (1984), 17.

function of his healings is something Jesus himself notes. This particular sickness was evidently due to sin (v. 14), and thus "this Sabbath cure is more directly related to the soteriological work for which the Lamb of God came into the world (1:29)."[326] This is both Jesus' and his Father's "work"—a work which they had been at for some time. Presumably, this statement—"'My Father has been working until now, and I have been working'" (John 5:17)—points back to mankind's fall into sin and Genesis 3:15 and the work of redemption/rest which God then took up. It also presupposes a soteriological/eschatological view of Genesis 2:2-3.[327] This is the Father's work which Jesus has come to do (John 4:34; 9:4), and it is a work of redemption (John 6:37-40). "Until now" seems to imply that the work is soon coming to completion; this Jesus affirms later—the work will be "finished" when he dies on the cross (John 19:30; cf. 17:4). With these connections in place we have clearer indication of the meaning of the Sabbath—it pointed to a finished work of God in providing redemptive rest for his people through the death of his Son.

Hebrews — Entering into Rest

Hebrews 3:7–4:13 confirms that our tracking of this theme has been on the right lines. First, the inspired writer explicitly connects the rest which we enjoy by faith in Christ (4:2, 6), with God's creation rest (vv. 3-4), with the rest of the land under Joshua (v. 5), and with the rest of the Sabbath (*sabbatismos*, v. 9). For the writer to the Hebrews, this observation arises from a simple chronological reading of the Bible. He notes that in Psalm 95:7b-11, the psalmist invites the people of his day to partake of that rest which that first

---

[326] Carson, " Jesus and the Sabbath in the Four Gospels," 81.

[327] Lincoln, "Sabbath, Rest, and Eschatology," 204.

wilderness generation forfeited because of rebellion and unbelief. He further notes that the psalmist inserts the word "today." From this, he reasons that since in the day of the psalmist (tenth century B.C.) God's "rest" was still available, then clearly Joshua's rest, although of a piece with it, did not exhaust it (v. 6). He further concludes that this offer of Sabbath-rest (*sabbatismos*, v. 9) "remains" for us "today." In calling the creation rest a "Sabbath-rest" (v. 9) he links together the ideas of creation rest, the Sabbath day, the rest of Canaan, and the soteric rest that is yet available.

There are indicators that this rest involves still more, a future blessing of which all these have been but a preview.[328] This rest "remains" for the people of God (v. 9). This rest is that of Genesis 2:3 (v. 9); that is, it is the final goal for which history was created. Verse 11 also hints of the believer's prospect of rest – "Let us therefore be diligent to enter that rest, lest anyone fall according to the same example of disobedience." The concept is an eschatological one, and all these previous "rests" are but pointers and samples of it.[329] The point is that this rest is available "today," for those who believe (v. 2) and "cease from their works" (v. 10). So the writer to the Hebrews, like the psalmist, extends the same invitation along with the same warning – "The gospel is preached to you, and this rest is available; be careful that you do not miss it by unbelief as they did." All this is to say that the creation Sabbath portrays a rest which God intended to share with redeemed mankind; all Sabbaths and "rests" since have been in view of this. "Today" the rest of salvation—yes, the rest of the eschaton—is available to those who cease from works and believe.

---

[328] The eschatological outlook of Psalm 95 was noted above. For details, see Kaiser, "Promise Theme," 142-3. Also Thomas Kem Oberholtzer, "The Kingdom Rest in Hebrews 3:1-4:13" in *BibSac* 145, no. 578 (April 1988), 187-8.

[329] Note also Rev. 14:13 (*anapauō*).

Conclusion

Several ideas have now converged. Finished work, rest, Sabbath, peace, Christ, redemption, cessation of works, faith – these all are taken up into the concept of rest which was first announced at the end of creation week. It is difficult not to notice further connections, such as the "new creation" passages of the Epistles (2 Cor. 5:17; Eph. 2:10). Likewise, it is doubtlessly beyond coincidence that it was on the sixth day of the week that Jesus finished God's work of redemption (Mark 15:42). Further, unlike the Mosaic priests who must "stand ministering daily and offering the same sacrifices which can never take away sins" (Heb. 10:11), Jesus "sat down," having accomplished the work of redemption "once for all" (Heb. 9:12; 10:12; cf. 1:2). Redemption is done, and rest may now be enjoyed. "No work allowed," is the watchword of this new creation. "Do not even pick up that stick!" "No gathering of manna today! God has provided plenty—just trust him." "No sowing or harvesting this year—God has given enough—believe it!" "This is the year of Jubilee, the year of release – by the work of his Son, God has declared all debts canceled for all who believe!" "Behold, now is the accepted time; behold, now is the day of salvation" (2 Cor. 6:2). "Do not work," God says, "just trust me." Only that person who "does not work but believes on Him who justifies the ungodly" (Rom. 4:5) enters this rest. This rest is a celebration of *God's* work, a work taken up long ago and now accomplished in the Lord Jesus Christ. The invitation is to faith in the Lord Jesus Christ and *his* work that saves. To enter this rest we must come, saying (to borrow the words of Isaac Watts),

> *No more, my God, I boast no more*
> *Of all the duties I have done.*
> *I quit the hopes I held before*
> *To trust the merits of Thy Son.*
>
> *The best obedience of my hands*

> *Dares not appear before Thy throne;*
> *But faith can answer Thy demands*
> *By pleading what the Lord has done!*

Observing the Sabbath Today

This is the meaning that is given to the Sabbath since it has reached its fulfillment in the Lord Jesus. Robert Garner, the seventeenth century English Particular Baptist, wrote,

> Therefore by Sabbath here, we are to understand the Lord Jesus only, Who Alone is the Sabbath or Rest of Believers under the Gospel. And to keep this Sabbath from polluting it, is to believe in Him only unto righteousness. For to do any work, I mean to seek righteousness, or peace, or reconciliation with God by any work, is to pollute this Sabbath or this Rest; by Whom Alone, such as believe in Him, do and shall enjoy a glorious, an everlasting rest.[330]

It is here the Sabbath finds its true significance, and only by resting in faith in him do we truly observe what the day symbolized. Like circumcision (Col. 2:11), the feast of tabernacles (John 7:37), the Jubilee Sabbath (Luke 4:16-21), the cities of refuge (Heb. 6:18), the Passover (1 Cor. 5:7), the day of atonement (Heb. 10:1-14), and all the ancient Mosaic institutions, the Sabbath has reached its fulfillment in Christ (Col. 2:17; Heb. 4), and it is by trusting in him that we preserve its significance today. Justin Martyr hints of this interpretation in his criticism of Trypho the Jew:

> You have now need of a second circumcision, though you glory greatly in the flesh. The new law requires you to keep perpetual sabbath, and you, because you are idle for one day, suppose you

---

[330] Robert Garner, *A Treatise on Baptism* (1645; reprint, Paris, AR: The Old Faith Baptist Church, n.d.), 30.

are pious, not discerning why this has been commanded you.[331]

Just as the temple with all its rituals and sacrificial system gives way to Christ, the reality to which it pointed, so also the Sabbath. These Mosaic institutions are not thereby nullified; they are fulfilled. Moreover, it is our Lord himself who led in this direction—"he redirects attention from the law to himself, the Lord of the Sabbath, and thereby sets in place the principle on which the later church would justify its departure from Sabbath observance."[332]

Only this can account for the reckless way in which the apostles write of the Sabbath's abrogation. The stronger brother does not observe any day as holier than another (Rom. 14:1-6), and no one must be judged in such terms (Col. 2:16). The shadow has given way to the substance (Col. 2:17), and we dare not look back to the "weak and beggarly elements" (Gal. 4:9-11) of the Old Covenant. The sign and seal of the Old Covenant has given way to the reality of Christ in the New Covenant (Matt. 26:28). The Sabbath no longer has significance *as a day*; its significance is in that to which it pointed—in him who gives rest (Matt. 11:28) and in whom we have ceased from our works (Heb. 4:10). For those who rest in Christ, every day is a Sabbath (cf. Rom. 14:5).

Observing the Sabbath Forever

Unlike the wicked who have followed the beast, who in the end will have "no rest day or night forever" (Rev. 14:11), we

---

[331] Justin Martyr *Dialogue with Trypho*, chap. 12. The chapter is entitled, "The Jews Violate the Eternal Law, and Interpret Ill that of Moses."

[332] Moo, "The Law of Christ as the Fulfillment of the Law of Moses," 356.

who have followed the Lamb will one day find "rest from our labors" (Rev. 14:13) in the very presence of God (Rev. 21:3). All the painful toils of this life will be "no more" (Rev. 21:4; 22:3, 5). John's "back to Eden" allusions at the end of the book of Revelation (e.g., the bride, the tree, the river) hint further of the fulness of rest that awaits the return of the one who gives rest. History will reach its goal, and in that day fulness of rest will be realized in his "glorious resting place" (Isa. 11:9-11).

CHAPTER 14

The Sabbath: Some Critical Texts in Paul

Tom Wells

Earlier I have written that the correct way to treat the Bible is to give logical priority to the NT.[333] Why is that so? Because revelation is progressive and we have come to its high point in this age and in the NT. To ignore this is to invite misunderstanding. We are standing at the pinnacle of redemptive history, and are wise to use that vantage point to survey it all.

You can feel the weight of this by imagining a man without Bible knowledge seeking to find out how to be right with God. To which part of Scripture would you direct him? Wouldn't it be to the NT? That seems clear. Suppose a third party wanted to argue over this. He might say that the OT is also filled with Christ, what then? If you were wise you would not deny that. Not at all! But you would know instinctively that the best way to help someone to the truths of salvation would be to set before them the apex of revelation first.

I may illustrate this fact by the advantages one finds in reading the latest critical commentaries.[334] Successive

---

[333] See pp. 7-14.

[334] By "critical commentaries" I mean, of course, not those that criticize the Bible, but those that give the reasons for the positions they take and the names and arguments of those who oppose their positions. A *critical* commentary is different from a *devotional*

commentators stand on the shoulders of those who go before them. Each gets the advantage of surveying his predecessors' work, and we who read receive the benefit from the process.

This approach applies to the subject of the Sabbath as well. What does the NT say on this important subject? Both Fred Zaspel and I have already made extensive comments on this subject, but in this chapter I want to examine two critical texts on the subject.

Galatians 4:8-11

In Galatians, Paul is dealing with a problem that threatened the very existence of the Galatian church, defection from the gospel as Paul had preached it (1:6-9).[335] For Paul, the Lord Jesus was a sufficient Savior who did not need to be augmented by other things. In Paul's view, no one needed more than knowledge of the Lord Jesus to be saved, and no one needed more than the Lord Jesus to arrive at maturity in the Christian life.

When the Galatians were evangelized they understood this, at least in a rudimentary way. But now they were in doubt. Other preachers had come from elsewhere, probably ultimately from Jerusalem, and had cast doubt on the full sufficiency of Christ. The Galatians listened to them and began to wonder if they needed to add the Mosaic law, or some portion of it, to the work and teaching of Christ, so that they might ultimately be saved.

---

commentary, in that the latter often takes one position on a given text and expounds it without defending it.

[335] For the purposes of this study it is not important whether Paul is dealing primarily with legalism as most commentators have historically held, or whether he is dealing with the desire of some to make Gentile converts conform to Judaism for other reasons.

The Sabbath: Some Critical Texts in Paul

And they had done more than wonder! Evidently they had not yet accepted circumcision (5:2), but had adopted the keeping of days as necessary to the Christian life (4:10). (We get the sense of present practice and the sense of necessity from the verb as Paul uses it.[336]) Paul was genuinely *afraid* of where this would lead them. "I fear for you," he wrote, "that somehow I have wasted my efforts on you" (4:11). There was not much that could plant fear in Paul, but the Galatians had managed to do it.

The evidence Paul cites here is, "You are observing special days and months and seasons and years!" (v.10).

Paul's evidence invites a number of observations.

First, the group of words Paul uses that describe time ("days," "months," "seasons and years") include the kinds of calendrical celebrations in use among the Jews.

Second, if Paul puts any special emphasis on any part of this, it will be on "days."[337] A prominent mention of days, with Judaism as its background, could hardly exclude the weekly Sabbaths.

Third, in spite of my first point above, the list lacks the specificity of Colossians 2:16, where the relation to Judaism is spelled out in no uncertain terms. This allows Paul to make a statement that addresses any and every kind of calendrical celebration, and leaves us with the sense that whatever it is about such celebrations that he opposes he will oppose across the board, whether of Jewish origin or not. (The focus of his opposition will become clearer when we examine Romans 14:1-

---

[336] Note the present tense of the verb translated "observing." In all its uses in the NT it also implies extreme or scrupulous care. Besides Galatians 4:10 it appears in Mark 3:2; Luke 6:7, 14:1, 20:20 and Acts 9:24. Cf. also the present tense verb, "turning back," in v.9.

[337] The list may be a convenient summary without focusing on any one part, but the word translated "days" stands emphatically at the beginning of the sentence in Greek.

6).

Beyond these three things, his state of mind, described as "fear" in v.11, shows that Paul senses a matter of (eternal) life and death here. By insisting on something more than the ministry of the Lord Jesus on earth and, through his apostles, from heaven, the opponents of Paul are threatening the eternal destiny of the Galatian believers. This explains the intensity of his earlier condemnatory words:

> But even if we or an angel from heaven should preach a gospel other than the one we preached to you, let him be eternally condemned! As we have already said, so now I say again: If anybody is preaching to you a gospel other than what you accepted, let him be eternally condemned! (1:8-9)[338]

It seems fair to conclude, then, that Paul is prepared to find fault, in some respect, with practices that arise from the laws concerning time. The general way he speaks of calendrical practices shows that the principle he adopts extends, however, to the observance of all such time-bound programs. It may also be that Paul especially emphasizes the dangers in keeping days.

Romans 14:1-6

In this passage, Paul is dealing with matters that cause disputes among Christians. He cites two such matters that probably were

---

[338] Some commentators take both Paul's list in verse 10 and his "fear" in verse 11 as ironic. For this view we may mention his apparent assurance of the reality of the Galatians' Christian experience (3:3; 5:1). But the harshness and extremity of Paul's assigning the interlopers to hell shows beyond doubt, or so it seems to me, that Paul took the danger as so real that unfeigned fear was the appropriate response.

The Sabbath: Some Critical Texts in Paul

debated in Rome, the question of what foods are proper for consumption and the question of whether Christians are to celebrate special days. Then he makes the following applications:

> One man considers one day more sacred than another; another man considers every day alike. Each one should be fully convinced in his own mind. He who regards one day as special, does so to the Lord. He who eats meat, eats to the Lord, for he gives thanks to God; and he who abstains, does so to the Lord and gives thanks to God. (14:5-6)

Several details call for comment.

First, Paul treats one's attitude toward "days" as a special concern. Questions of Christian liberty can take many forms, but Paul again makes "days" a main focus.

Second, it is clear that his concern is not to settle an argument between keepers of days and non-keepers, but to inspire mutual respect among the two parties.

Third, this shows us that so far as Paul is concerned, the question is largely a matter of indifference. There is no sin necessarily involved in either practice. I say *"largely* a matter of indifference" because by calling one group "weak" and the other "strong," he implies that there is a better understanding among the strong, since it is the strong who feel liberty in such matters. No one, of course, must feel bound to do everything he is at liberty to do, but the strong position is clearly the one Paul identifies with.

Fourth, since the two views represent two levels of progress in understanding, it is clear that the strong are the more mature in this matter.

Fifth, Paul again, as in Galatians, uses language broader than the designation of a specific day or days. The *prima facie* impression left with the reader is that Paul has laid down a comprehensive rule for approaching the whole question of keeping or not keeping specific days. Such a general rule would take in both the OT Sabbath and any day or days that Christians keep as sacred.

Preliminary Synthesis of These Two Passages

At first glance, a comparison of Galatians and Romans on the subject of keeping days suggests that Paul is inconsistent with himself. The very thing, keeping of days, that called forth his anathema in Galatians, appears to meet with his qualified approval in Romans. How can we reconcile these two attitudes? Several possibilities suggest themselves:

1. In light of the longstanding practice of keeping a Sabbath day, Paul simply excludes the Sabbath from his thinking in both passages. Hence, a Sabbath still binds all men.

2. Though Paul includes the Jewish Sabbath in his exposition of keeping of days, he does not include the Lord's Day. Hence, the Lord's Day binds all men.

3. Since Paul speaks comprehensively about days in these passages, we must look for the cause of his frustration with the Galatian interlopers in something other than the keeping of days.

The first solution ignores the fact that a passage parallel to both of these, Colossians 2:16-17, explicitly includes the Sabbath in a larger framework of language that summarizes the holy days and seasons of the OT.

> Therefore do not let anyone judge you by what you eat or drink, or with regard to a religious festival, a New Moon celebration or a Sabbath day. These are a shadow of the things to come; the reality, however, is found in Christ.

The second solution above also seems extremely unlikely since it demands a restriction on the comprehensive language of

The Sabbath: Some Critical Texts in Paul

Paul in both Galatians and Romans. In Galatians, he certainly uses comprehensive language: "You are observing special days. . . . I fear for you, that somehow I have wasted my efforts on you" (4:10-11). To the Romans, he speaks of "one day more sacred than another" and "every day alike. Each one should be fully convinced in his own mind" (14:5). In neither case does he suggest that the keeping of another day or days would change his basic position. There is no reason to exclude any day from this statement.

The second solution also fails for other reasons. For example, can we really believe that in a society with a majority slave population, as Roman society was, that many would have the leisure to devote an entire day to the worship of the Lord Jesus?[339] Again, it seems clear that some early converts to Christianity retained an attachment to the synagogue which entailed Sabbath attendance. At Ephesus, Paul taught in the synagogue and received an invitation to remain. Instead, leaving Aquila and Priscilla behind, he promised a return visit (Acts 18:19-21). Sometime later Priscilla and Aquila are still there when Apollos arrives as a man who had been instructed in the way of the Lord.

> [H]e spoke with great fervor and taught about Jesus accurately, though he knew only the baptism of John. He began to speak boldly in the synagogue. When Priscilla and Aquila heard him, they invited him to their home and

---

[339] Since "works of necessity" are generally recognized as legitimate by Sabbath-keepers, one might argue that the labor of slaves and the very poor would fall into this category, though it must be admitted that the category was probably not first described with this in mind. Even if we make this allowance we are left with the uncomfortable fact that from the outset of the Christian era, a sizeable minority (majority?) of Christians would have had no ability to carry out the Christian Sabbath or Lord's Day as it is recommended to us by its proponents.

explained to him the way of God more adequately. (18:25-26)

How long this was after Paul left we do not know. Luke places it after the arrival of Paul in Antioch of Syria (18:22-23), whether for convenience in not breaking Paul's story into too many parts, or simply because it did happen some little time later. Whatever the time lapse, Priscilla and Aquila are apparently still part of the synagogue while Paul makes a circuit of more than eight-hundred miles that takes in Jerusalem.

Eventually Paul returns to the same synagogue where the previous invitation still stands, and he preaches there for three months (19:8). This raises the important question: is it conceivable that Priscilla and Aquila or other Christians had caused a division in the synagogue during the year or so that Paul was away? If they did not, what became of the Lord's Day in this period? If they did not make such a breach with the synagogue and they also met on the Lord's day, the difficulties for slaves and no doubt many others would have become insuperable. On the other hand, if they had made such a breach, can we imagine that the same synagogue would have allowed Paul to proselytize in it for three months?

Questions like these have led many scholars to conclude, in the words of M. M. B. Turner,

> The earliest Jewish Christians, almost without exception, kept the *whole* law and were theologically committed to it. There is no indication of their sensing the inner freedom that would be required to allow for so fundamental a manipulation. On the contrary, the period witnesses to a retreat from Jesus' stance with respect to the law.[340]

That might well have been the end of the story if it had

---

[340] Turner, "The Sabbath, Sunday, and the Law in Luke/Acts," 134.

not been for the conversion of Gentiles. We have already seen how other parts of the Mosaic law, such as the cleanness or uncleanness of foods, remained unchanged in the minds of Jewish Christians.

> The needed inner freedom came when the entry of the Gentiles brought the claims of Christ into sharp conflict with those of the law and led to a new realization of the total subordination of the whole law to Christ and to His teaching. It is during this period that the understanding of Jesus' relationship to the law . . . may well have become widespread; the law was binding on Christians only in so far as it was taken up in Jesus' teaching.[341]

The sum of this is: the law among the early Jewish Christians overshadowed the liberty that we have in Christ. Since, however, the church lived with this, it is clear that they were not aware of any rule laid down by the Lord Jesus that instituted the Lord's Day as a replacement for the Jewish Sabbath. If there was such a rule, and they later discovered it, we have no record of it. If the apostles or a council made such a rule, the Bible is silent on it. What is more striking yet, in either case we have no record of the inevitable discussion and turmoil such a change would have brought about.[342] If we add to these facts the detail that the Lord's Day is thought by many to be a universally binding moral law, we may close this section by pointing out that it was beyond the ability of the early church to have made this known to all but the tiniest fraction of mankind.[343]

---

[341] Ibid.

[342] The discussion in Romans 14 would not qualify. If it included the Lord's Day, it would rule it out as binding.

[343] If those who hold that the Sabbath was a "creation ordinance" are correct, the various races of mankind have only

That brings us to the other alternative stated above: since Paul speaks comprehensively about days in the passages we have examined, we must look for the cause of his frustration with the Galatian interlopers in something other than the keeping of days, which he pronounces innocent in itself.

What can that be? It seems clear that Paul's vigorous opposition is to the *imposition of days*.

Paul has nothing against the keeping of certain days as either convenient or cultural. He makes that clear in Romans.

What is equally clear, however, is the fact that all sides in this issue must receive one another as equals so that a category of second-class Christians (or worse!) is not tolerated. This is much the same issue he defended against Peter in Galatians, where table fellowship was about to make the Gentiles into second-class believers (2:11-21).

The sum of Paul's understanding is this: every Christian is free to keep whatever days he cares to keep as long as he does not impose them on others, though Paul himself feels it shows a certain lack of Christian maturity to impose such laws *as a religious obligation* on one's self. For Paul, to acquiesce in days of obligation was a species of slavery (Gal. 4:8-11). The intruders in Galatia were singularly vulnerable to Paul's rebuke because they wanted to impose much more than special days on the Galatians. The extent of their insistence on Moses led to Paul's withering condemnation. In light of this, we must all ask ourselves whether we impose upon the consciences of men and women without authorization from the Lord Jesus, and we must correct our practice accordingly.

When certain days are represented as holy in themselves, when one day is distinguished from another on

---

themselves to blame for the loss of the knowledge of the seventh-day Sabbath. But if the first day of the week began to bind men in the first century, the Lord apparently had made no provision for most of those in the world to learn this fact.

religious grounds, when holy days are reckoned a part of divine worship, then days are improperly observed. . . . When we, in the present age, make a distinction of days, we do not represent them as necessary, and thus lay a snare for the conscience; we do not reckon one day to be more holy than another; we do not make days to be the same thing with religion and the worship of God; but merely attend to the preservation of order and harmony. The observance of days among us is a free service, and void of all superstition.[344]

Paul and the Remainder of the New Testament

In the eyes of some, the conclusions I have drawn about Paul are thought to be contradicted by other statements in the NT. Major books have been written on this subject, so I can do no more than suggest the answer to these challenges.

One passage often cited is Mark 2:27-28. The words were spoken to the Pharisees after they accused the Lord's disciples of profaning the Sabbath by working on it. The Lord came to the defense of his disciples with these words: : "'The Sabbath was made for man, not man for the Sabbath. So the Son of Man is Lord even of the Sabbath.'"

Two arguments for Sabbath keeping have been found in this passage, one from each sentence. The first goes something like this: since God made the Sabbath for mankind at creation, the assumption is that such a good provision of God will continue throughout redemptive history. In response we need to say that all that God created was made for man. Unfallen man both supervised and enjoyed all of creation, and that is redeemed man's future destiny as well. But it does not

---

[344] John Calvin, *Commentaries on the Epistles of Paul to the Galatians and Ephesians* (Grand Rapids: Eerdmans, 1948), 124. This passage captures the truth although it seems to many that Calvin is not always consistent with this position.

follow from this truth that all of God's good gifts were intended to last throughout history. Some of the animals are now extinct. The tree of life, in its literal form, has passed away. The entire Mosaic system eventually benefitted all mankind in its instruction and its providing the circumstances that produced the Messiah and the rest of the word of God. It could be said in the most literal sense, "It was made for man, and it passed away."

The second argument for Sabbath keeping here is found in the statement, "So the Son of Man is Lord even of the Sabbath" (2:28). The argument is a simple one: would the Lord Jesus assert his authority over the Sabbath only to abolish it? The question is a fair one and we must answer it.

Two things must be kept in mind in answering this question. First, the mere fact that Jesus claims lordship over the Sabbath means that he has the option to abolish it if he so chooses. The idea of lordship would be largely emptied of meaning if that were not the case. No argument, then, for the permanence of the Sabbath can be sustained simply from Christ's declaration of lordship over it.

Second, and equally important, we have to ask what abolishing the Sabbath might mean. And here we come to the recurring problem that we may call "the tension reflected in old/new language." If we ask the question, "Does the Sabbath still exist or has it been abolished?" we are driven to an ambiguous answer as we are with so much in the Mosaic system. We are contending that the Sabbath finds its fulfillment in Christ, specifically in the rest he promises in Matthew 11:28-30. Is it then abolished in every sense? Certainly not! While many may disagree with our contention that the rest in Christ fulfills the Sabbath, all must see that if we are right, in a very important sense indeed, the Sabbath goes on and is not abolished at all. That remains true even if a great part of that "rest" awaits eternity. It is one thing, then, to say we are wrong; it is quite another to say we have abolished the Sabbath. Lordship over the Sabbath means that the Lord Jesus can do

The Sabbath: Some Critical Texts in Paul

with it as he pleases.

Another passage that is often referred to as teaching a NT Sabbath or sacred day is in 1 Corinthians:

> Now about the collection for God's people: Do what I told the Galatian churches to do. On the first day of every week, each one of you should set aside a sum of money in keeping with his income, saving it up, so that when I come no collections will have to be made. (16:1-2)

A glance at this passage shows that it refers to the first day of the week and a collection or collections. Because these two things are joined together here many Christians have concluded that this is a clear reference to a weekly meeting of the church at Corinth. There are some important difficulties with this view as one can see by consulting the standard commentators. Nevertheless, I will not spend my time on these since I too think that the church met on the first day of the week, so I will simply concede that point for the sake of the discussion.

What I must insist on, however, is this: *if this passage teaches that the church met on the first day of the week, that is all it teaches that is relevant to our subject.* It does not tell us whether they met at that time as a matter of convenience or as a sacred obligation laid upon them by the Lord himself. The passage is simply silent on that matter. Because of this, the passage leaves us exactly where it found us, trying to take seriously the alarm that Paul feels about the keeping of days when he writes to the Galatians and balancing that against his relative indifference in Romans 14.

Did the Corinthians know that Christ rose on the first day of the week? Of course they did. Would that strike them as a reason to meet on that day? It is perfectly possible. Did they think of it as a sacred day, that is, a day that bound their consciences beyond its convenience? We have no reason at all to think so.

The same thing is true with the two final verses I wish to discuss, Acts 20:7 and Revelation 1:10. Let's look at them together.

> On the first day of the week we came together to break bread. Paul spoke to the people and, because he intended to leave the next day, kept on talking until midnight (Acts 20:7) On the Lord's Day I [John] was in the Spirit, and I heard behind me a loud voice like a trumpet . . . .(Rev. 1:10).

Along with 1 Corinthians 16:1-2, these are the NT verses that are thought to show that the early Christians kept a Sabbath on the first day of the week. Several things are clear in looking at them.

First, again along with 1 Corinthians 16:1-2, these verses say nothing about a Sabbath and nothing about one day being more sacred than another. Second, so far as Bible evidence is concerned, we have no way of knowing whether they both refer to the same day, because the Bible does not tell on what day of the week the "Lord's Day" fell.[345] Third, we know that if the church is to meet it must settle on a day. Any day, then, in the absence of a command from the Lord or his agents, may have been specified for convenience and for no other reason.

Many Christians, however, have not been content to leave the matter there. They have argued that the very name, *the Lord's Day*, shows that we are dealing with a sacred day of obligation. I want to try to hear them fairly, without allowing the reader to forget the absence of any command to this effect

---

[345] It is clear from later church history that already in the second century, if not before, the phrase "the Lord's Day" was another designation for the first day of the week. See Richard J. Bauckham, "The Lord's Day" in Carson, *From Sabbath to Lord's Day*., especially 227ff.

The Sabbath: Some Critical Texts in Paul

in the NT. There is a certain field for speculation here due to the fact that the Lord's Day is mentioned by that name just once in the NT Scriptures. Hence, all of us must be careful not to allow our desires in this matter to run away with our reason.

The phrase, *the Lord's Day*, is a striking phrase. In itself it would be an appropriate name for a sacred day of obligation if there were one designated by Christ for his people to keep. It would be hard to imagine a better phrase. We have reviewed how Christ claimed to be Lord of the Sabbath, so there would be nothing intrinsically wrong in his laying this day upon his people to be kept in any and every way he might deem correct. More than that, he entered upon his own universal Lordship as God's prime minister on this very day, when he was raised from the dead.[346]

Nevertheless, we must remember that the NT is silent on this. (The situation, in fact, is much like the NT's silence on infant baptism, a doctrine often wrongly argued from the OT almost entirely.)

Some scholars, however, have noted that the Greek word for "Lord's" appears only one other place in the NT and that its appearance there is sufficient to show what it means here. That place is 1 Corinthians 11:20 where Paul is rebuking an apparent chronic disorder in the Corinthian church. In context, we read:

> In the following directives I have no praise for you, for your meetings do more harm than good.... When you come together, it is not *the Lord's Supper* that you eat, for as you eat, each of you goes ahead without waiting for anybody else. One remains hungry, another gets drunk. Don't you have homes to eat and drink in? Or do you despise the church of God and humiliate those who have nothing? What shall I say to you? Shall I praise

---

[346] I assume here that Jesus' statement about universal Lordship in John 17:2 is proleptic, anticipating his resurrection from the dead and the Father's bestowal of "all authority" (Matt. 28:18) on him. Cf. Philippians 2:9-11.

you for this? Certainly not!

For I received from the Lord what I also passed on to you: The Lord Jesus, on the night he was betrayed, took bread, and when he had given thanks, he broke it and said, "This is my body, which is for you; do this in remembrance of me." In the same way, after supper he took the cup, saying, "This cup is the new covenant in my blood; do this, whenever you drink it, in remembrance of me." For whenever you eat this bread and drink this cup, you proclaim the Lord's death until he comes. (11:17-26)

The arguments go something like this.

First, in the phrase, *the Lord's Supper*, Jesus declares his Lordship over the meal that the disciples are to engage in. Second, in instituting it, he exercises his Lordship over this meal by making it a sacred obligation for his people and regulating how it is practiced. Third, it follows, then, that when John in Revelation speaks of *the Lord's Day*, he means for us to understand that Christ has made this day a sacred obligation for his people and reserves the right to regulate it as he pleases, not as we might please.

How shall we respond to this?

First, we must note that what we know about the Lord's Supper we know from the direct command of the Lord Jesus himself. That is very important. We have no record of any such institution or explanation of the Lord's Day from the lips of the Lord Jesus or from any of his apostles or agents.

Second, the fact that the same adjective, "the Lord's," is used in both cases can tell us nothing by itself beyond the fact that in some way or other the day is related to the Lord Jesus. All of us who believe it refers to the first day of the week grant this. The question is, "What is that relationship?" Even if "Lordship" is the point of the word in 1 Corinthians 11:20, that does not prove that John means to emphasize the same point in Revelation 1:10. That question must be investigated on its own merits.

Third, it is very doubtful that the point in calling the meal

The Sabbath: Some Critical Texts in Paul

"the Lord's Supper" is to emphasize the Lordship or ownership of the Lord Jesus over the "supper."[347] That seems clear from the context. Remember, unless the context informs us, we cannot know why Paul used this phrase since he does not tell us. Is the context any help, then? It has seemed clear to the church in all ages that the point of the passage is to say that it commemorates the Lord in his death. It is the Lord's supper because in partaking of it we are remembering the Lord, not in his sovereign power, but in his weakness and humiliation (cf vv. 23-26). If we then turn to Revelation 1:10 to discuss the parallel phrase, "the Lord's Day," we see immediately that a commemorative understanding would be fitting as well. That is, it is called the Lord's Day to remember something else that Jesus did, his resurrection. We need no further explanation than that. Is this conclusive? No, but it does two things. Number one: it shows that there is no compelling reason to take it any other way. If there is one alternative, there might be many others. Number two: it makes a case for a different parallel understanding that is contextually arrived at, whether right or wrong.

It is true that the Lord's Supper is a special Christian religious observance that was instituted by Christ and regulated by him. But the conclusion that these are the points of comparison with the phrase, "the Lord's Day," may or may not be true. I have given another understanding that is contextually derived from 1 Corinthians 11. That would seem to be the better way, but in either case we are left where we were before. Revelation 1:10 does not tell us why the word "Lord's" is used in the phrase "the Lord's Day." We simply must leave the matter there and do as Paul commanded us in Romans 14:5,6:

---

[347] Note carefully how I have phrased this. No Christian doubts that the Lord Jesus "owns" or is Lord over the supper as he is Lord over everything, including every day of the week. But the question is, is that the reason why it is called the Lord's Supper in 1 Corinthians 11:20?

"One man considers one day more sacred than another; another man considers every day alike. Each one should be fully convinced in his own mind."

In the light of these truths, we may add again that since the Lord Jesus rose on the first day of the week, there is an appropriateness to meeting on that day. If this has occurred to us, we may be sure that it occurred to the early church.

Summing Up

Early on we contended that the only way to survey the meaning of redemptive history is to stand at the apex of revelation, the NT, and look back.

Taking this stance I have allowed the apostle Paul to speak his mind on the subject of special days. Here is what we have found as we listened to him and compared his utterances in Galatians and Romans to a number of other verses in the NT.

First, Paul can treat those who keep days very tenderly or very roughly.

Second, the determining factor in his treatment is whether or not *days are imposed*. If one professed believer imposes days on another as part of a larger (Mosaic) system, Paul is prepared to consign the one who commits the imposition to hell (Gal. 1:8-9). We do not know what eternal assignment he would give those of us who are less systematic and consistent in our demands on others, but the clear message is to avoid anything like this sin. He is much more lenient, however, on those who impose sacred days on their own consciences.

Third, we have seen that the other verses that are sometimes thought to teach a Sabbath or religiously binding Lord's Day are inconclusive at best so that they in no way modify Paul's clear directions in Galatians and Romans.

Fourth, without *imposition* of days, Paul himself can make a great deal of them when it suits his purposes, including a day to meet. And if you asked him for a suggestion, I have no doubt he would have chosen the first day of the week.

Paul's contribution to our quest, then, is limited but of significance. While he forbids us from stating that Christians may *not* observe Sunday as the Christian day *par excellence*, he also forbids us from imposing such observance as a duty upon our fellow believers. Since, at least in much of the world, Sunday is allowed to the majority of us as a day of rest and a day suitable for worship, we may surely gratefully receive it as such; but our study of Paul forbids us from erecting any theological edifice upon this convenient, but fortuitous fact.[348]

Except for changing "fortuitous," into "providential," I will let de Lacey have the last word.

---

[348] D. R. de Lacey, "The Sabbath/Sunday Question and the Law in the Pauline Corpus" in Carson, *From Sabbath to Lord's Day*, 185-186.

CHAPTER 15

Our Creeds and How They Affect Our Understanding

Tom Wells

The barriers to unity among Christians are formidable and no one must imagine that solutions that arise from unaided human intellect will overcome them. The problems are spiritual. We are divided because of our sinfulness, and our divisions are one aspect of the loss of objectivity within a fallen race. Yet objectivity eludes us. I have it, of course; who could doubt it! But your inability to see beyond your hastily conceived, narrow convictions guarantees that our minds will never meet. We are doomed to division until a brighter day dawns forever. Why can't you see things my way? Who shall deliver us from this body of conceptual death?

As with other spiritual problems, however, the Scriptures demand our efforts. The fact that a problem arises from sinfulness is a call to attack it with fervor. Individually we must repent of our arrogance in not listening with sympathy to our brothers and sisters in Christ. But corporately—what can we do corporately? In this chapter I would like to discuss a single barrier to unity. What I want to say may be summarized in two short sentences:

1. *Our creeds and confessions are one immense barrier to unity.*
2. *There is no easy or obvious way to cross this divide.*

If my first sentence sounds to you like an indictment against treasured historical and doctrinal landmarks, I would simply remind you that one function of creeds is to exclude; no one should be surprised at this. If the second seems pessimistic, keep in mind that there can be no solution without a frank recognition of the problem created by the documents for which some among us are prepared to die.

Creedal unity has a long and honorable history. Beyond gathering for minor events such as ice cream socials and softball tournaments, whatever the church of Jesus Christ does is done on a doctrinal foundation. The absence of a written creed is no real exception. United effort means the presence of common convictions wherever men and women enter intelligently into labor for the Lord. This is nicely and authoritatively illustrated in the earliest church as seen in the book of Acts. We need not confine their "one mind" (Acts 2:46) to doctrine, to the exclusion of all else, to see that if they did not share the Apostles' doctrinal teaching they could not have joined as heartily in the fellowship, breaking of bread and prayer (2:42).

Nor is that all. Paul insists on doctrinal unity in reminding the Ephesians,

> There is one body and one Spirit, just as also you were called in one hope of your calling: one Lord, one faith, one baptism, one God and Father of all who is over all and through all and in all.. (4:4-6)

Such teaching makes it impossible to think that any and every opinion may be called *Christian* and used as a basis for united effort.

It is sometimes thought that the Bible itself is a sufficient basis for unity. After all, any doctrine that can be called *Christian* must finally be traced to the written word of God. Why not, then, simply rest upon the Scriptures? In recent years we have heard men and women respond to traditional categories like *Calvinist* and *Arminian* with the assertion that they are *Biblicists*. What is wrong with that?

There is nothing wrong with the word *Biblicist* itself. But what does it mean? If it is the simple assertion, "I believe the Bible!" we may approve of it, even applaud it, but we cannot

How Our Creeds Affect Our Understanding

help remembering the large number of cultists who say the same thing with the same eager enthusiasm. If it means more than "I believe the Bible!" then those who unite on it have some common understanding about what the Bible teaches. There is no middle ground here. A creedal basis of some greater or lesser degree of precision, written or understood, undergirds all common activity among Christians. A creed asserts, in the words of a booklet issued by the Free Reformed Churches of North America, that

> We are united, not merely by a vague respect for Scripture, but by a deep-rooted commitment to a common understanding of its message. Our creeds are a declaration of the doctrines which we hold in common.[349]

Groups that have opposed writing down their common convictions have had them nevertheless. And they have held them tenaciously!—witness the groups that are called the *Plymouth Brethren* and the *Churches of Christ*.

In writing this book we have been very conscious of this fact. We have been pleading with you to address Scripture directly. Most Christians, of course, agree that we must all do this. Perhaps, however, we have commitments to creeds and confessions that deflect to some degree the thrust of Scripture. We do not want that to be true, but we must reckon with the possibility.

While the points I have made above are widely accepted, it seems to me that most Christian groups have not given sufficient thought to the magnitude of the difficulties created by our creeds and confessions.

There are, to be sure, exceptions to this judgment. At the departure of our Pilgrim forefathers for the new world, their

---

[349] *Introducing the Free Reformed Churches of North America* (St. Thomas, Ontario: Free Reformed Publications, 1996), 15.

pastor, John Robinson, made a speech described for us by Edward Winslow:

> We were now ere long to part asunder; and the Lord knoweth whether ever he [Robinson] should live to see our faces again. But whether the Lord had appointed it or not; he charged us, before God and his blessed angels, to follow him no further than he followed Christ: and if God should reveal anything to us by any other instrument of his, to be as ready to receive it, as ever we were to receive any truth by his Ministry. For he was very confident the Lord had more truth and light yet to break forth out of his holy Word.
>
> He took occasion also miserably to bewail the state and condition of the Reformed [i.e., Protestant] Churches, who were come to a period in religion; and would go no further than the Instruments of their Reformation. As, for example, the Lutherans: they could not be drawn to go beyond what Luther saw, for whatever part of God's will He had further imparted and revealed to Calvin, they will rather die than embrace it. And so also, saith he, you see the Calvinists. They stick where he left them, a misery much to be lamented.[350]

While we recognize that Robinson was speaking of groups of Christians rather than written creeds per se, several things call for comment. First, Robinson himself, though an independent, was no doubt a Calvinist so that this is not a criticism from wholly outside the circle of those he seeks to correct. Second, he believes that there is yet more truth for Christians to discover in God's word. Unless he thought this further truth would not contradict any tenet already held by Lutherans and Calvinists, a thing very unlikely in itself, he is implicitly calling for creedal

---

[350] The quotation comes from Edward Winslow, *Hypocrisie Vnmasked*, London, 1646. It is found in Walter H. Burgess, *John Robinson: Pastor of the Pilgrim Fathers, A Study of His Life and Times* (London: Williams and Norgate, 1920), 239-240. (This reference was kindly provided to me by Michael Haykin.)

corrections and additions. Third, he thinks he detects an unwillingness among his fellow Protestants to do such correcting and addition. Sadly, history bears out this judgment. Only the slightest changes have been made in most of the creedal forms that arose as a result of the Reformation.

Let me illustrate the difficulty with the words of Matthaeus Flacius, a 16th-century Lutheran:

> Every understanding and exposition of Scripture is to be in agreement with the faith. Such [agreement] is, so to speak, the norm or limit of a sound faith, that we may not be thrust over the fence into the abyss by anything, either by a storm from without or by an attack from within (Rom. 12:6). For everything that is said concerning Scripture, or on the basis of Scripture, must be in agreement with all that the catechism declares or that is taught by the articles of faith.

Several proposals call for comment here. First is the demand for all interpretation of Scripture to agree either with the Lutheran catechism or with "the articles of faith." i.e., presumably, the Augsburg Confession.[351] For someone standing outside the Lutheran tradition this seems to be a demand to give up *sola scriptura*. We need not deny the importance of Martin Luther and Philip Melanchthon in the providential

---

[351] *The Book of Concord*, 1580, contains a number of documents going back to the Apostles' Creed that might be described as "articles of faith" by Lutherans, but Flacius wrote this in 1567. He may have intended much more than the Augsburg Confession, however. In addition to a number of creeds from the early church, other candidates for articles of faith would include the "Apology of the Augsburg Confession" (1531), the "Smalcald Articles" (1537) and the "Treatise on the Power and Primacy of the Pope" (1537), all of which appear in the later *Book of Concord*. It is plain to see that if any of these were also in Flacius' mind, it complicates the problem immensely, especially in the view of someone outside the Lutheran tradition.

arrangements of God to see that they have no right to stand between us and God's revelation in his Word.

What most of us must see, however, is that this situation is just as egregious if our tradition looks to John Calvin or John Wesley or to the authors of the Thirty-Nine Articles or the Westminster Confession. In each case we must allow Scripture to speak for itself. As Daniel Fuller has written in commenting on Flacius' statement above,

> This statement of Flacius shows how Luther's use of the analogy-of-faith principle had made church tradition, fixed in creeds and catechisms, the key for the interpretation of scripture. Even though this tradition was now of a Protestant rather than of a Roman Catholic variety, yet the barrier which it erected against letting biblical exegesis improve or correct that tradition was exceedingly hard to surmount.[352]

Christians of all persuasions must seek to take this seriously. What has developed in church history is the claim that Scripture alone is our standard, joined to the quiet and often unrecognized co-principle that our confessions are the traditions by which we must read God's word.

We must also examine Flacius' reference to Romans 12:6. There Paul has written, "And since we have gifts that differ according to the grace given to us, *let each exercise them accordingly:* if prophecy, according to the proportion (*analogian*) of faith." Commentators are divided on the understanding of "the proportion [or analogy] of faith," but even if we take it as a standard to which all exegesis must conform, it is clear that it must be a standard that existed prior to Paul's writing of Romans. That does not mean that there

---

[352] Both the quotation from Flacius and Fuller's comment are taken from Daniel P. Fuller, "Biblical Theology and the Analogy of Faith" in *Unity and Diversity in New Testament Theology*, ed. Robert A. Guelich (Grand Rapids: Eerdmans, 1978), 198.

could be no growth in it as more of the NT was written, but to suppose that it conforms exactly to one of the post-Reformation confessions strains credulity beyond reasonable limits. Again, on the assumption that a standard is in view, the most it may demand of us is to understand more obscure Scripture in the light of what is clearer and simpler. (This is, in fact, the way the phrase "the analogy of faith" has often been used in church history.)

While the confessions have tended to control our understanding of Scripture, something even less frequently recognized has added to our difficulty. At least until the present century, our conservative systematic theologies have tended to be expositions of the confessions even when that was not immediately apparent. The reason for this is not far to seek: the systematic theologian doing the writing was usually already bound to a confession by being a member or theologian of a confessional church. He could keep neither his credentials as a minister nor his post as a theological professor if he varied appreciably from the confession of his church.

This does not mean—and I do not want to be understood as saying—that such men compromised their convictions for the sake of their positions. I have no way of knowing their motives and, more than that, I am an admirer of the men in my theological tradition. It does mean, however, that they were producing theological works that did very little to question confessional stances, however pure their motives may have been.

Now you will see immediately how all of this bears on unity among believers. Surely we must unite on truth, but as I wrote earlier, the confessions and creeds are a barrier between us. This is what we might have expected, but that is not all. The little impact that Lutherans have had on Calvinists, and vice versa, bears witness that some constraint has kept them from freely and openly working to eliminate their differences in the last three-hundred years. Creedal statements were intended to unite, but also to exclude, and they have succeeded on both fronts. Is there a single substantive area in which Lutherans have convinced their Calvinistic brothers? Has any change been made in the Lutheran confessions of the last three-hundred years that demonstrates the cordial embrace of any Calvinistic idea? Is it any consolation for those who long for unity among believers in Christ, that each side can say, "But we are right!"? Each side—and every other side that may reasonably be called *Christian*—has had the responsibility before God to strive for unity in a Scriptural way. Can anyone doubt that the large measure of failure can be traced, humanly speaking, to strict subscription to creeds? On the other hand, it is with heavy heart that I admit that finding a solution to this problem is more difficult than simply describing it. I have shown earlier that the abandonment of creedal statements cannot be the cure-all. Too much is at stake.

What can we do? The central matter is that those who study the Scriptures must have liberty to follow them wherever they may lead. How can we obtain such liberty in a creedal world?

The possibilities, it seems to me, must lie somewhere along the following lines. None of these solutions will commend itself to everyone, but we need to consider them.

1. A major simplification of our creeds. I have already alluded to the large number of confessions upheld by Lutherans. They are by no means exceptional. A number of Calvinistic denominations subscribe to the Apostles' Creed, the Nicene Creed, the Athanasian Creed, the Belgic Confession, the Heidelberg Catechism and the Canons of Dort. Other groups subscribe to fewer creeds, but their confessions of faith are lengthy and detailed. Each group must seriously ask itself if all this detail is necessary.

2. A looser subscription to creedal statements. Would anyone today defend the following subscription terms that the French churches adopted in 1620?

> I N[ame]. N[ame]. do Swear and Protest before God, and this Holy Assembly that I do receive, approve and imbrace [sic] all the Doctrines taught and decided by the Synod of *Dort*, as

perfectly agreeing with the Word of God, and the Confession of our Churches. I Swear and Promise to persevere in the Profession of this Doctrine during my whole life, and to defend it with the utmost of my power, and that I will never, neither by Preaching nor Teaching in the Schools, nor by Writing depart from it.[353]

Certainly "loose" subscription is preferable to swearing never to change one's mind in one's "whole life!"

The problem here, of course, is "How loose is loose?" If this looseness is defined in detail, the result is likely to be a slightly smaller confession to which all must strictly subscribe! Yet in the past, some groups have apparently found a way to do this. Let me cite one illustration, the Baptists of the Philadelphia Association, who subscribed to the Philadelphia Confession (a slight variant of the *1689* or *Second London Confession*). Each year this association issued a circular letter to all the churches. The following is taken from the letter of 1798, entitled *Religious Worship and the Sabbath Day*.

[I]t is to be wished that all Christians were unanimous on this subject; but there is little hope of this being the case, till we drop all traditions and traditional modes of speech; for these things will cause many mistakes.

The compilers of our confession of faith were desirous to use the same language with other Christians, as far as was thought consistent with a good conscience; and it may be, on this subject, they conformed more than can be supported by the Holy Scriptures, or any arguments justly drawn from them. . . . [W]e proceed to show that the fourth command was not moral, notwithstanding it is sometimes placed with moral commands . . .[354]

---

[353] Quoted in Brian G. Armstrong, *Calvin and the Amyraut Heresy* (Madison: Univ. of Wisconsin, 1969), 134.

[354] David Jones in *Beloved Brethren: Circular Letters of the Philadelphia Baptist Association from 1774 to 1807*, ed. Norbert Ward

As suggested by his own words, the writer, David Jones, goes on to argue against the language of his confession, showing that in at least one important respect he was a loose subscriptionist.

3. Encouragement for change within the confessions themselves. Perhaps our confessions of faith must include more than a general statement that all writings of uninspired men are bound to err. Perhaps in addition they need a statement to the effect that *this confession itself* falls under this general condemnation. And perhaps they must last of all include a statement of willingness and expectancy to be reproved from Scripture. When the confessions of men genuinely challenge others to question them without fear of consequences, then we will have arrived at confessions that demand our respect in a new way. At least one solid gain would come from such an approach. Questions about the truth or falsity of statements in the confessions would now come from within the groups of adherents. Of those men who think they find a flaw in their confessions, who is better to raise questions, the man whose integrity now forces him to abandon them when he agrees with most of what is written, or the man who stays within the group of adherents and keeps his reservations to himself? Can there be any doubt as to the answer to this question?

4. To be creative let's invent something on the spur of the moment. It may be that a denomination, an association or even a local church could rate deviations from its standards as to the degree of departure it will tolerate. In this scenario

---

(Nashville: Baptist Reformation Review, n.d [ca 1970's]). Though Ward was editor, the chapter from which the quotation was taken apparently has no editorial work within, since it seems plainly to be photocopied from a 19th-century page.

each item in the confession would be awarded a score. A few basic matters would be awarded an "N" for non-negotiable. The rest would be rated from one to ten, ten representing the most important matters. If a member or deacon or elder compiled a score of, say, more than fifty, he would be excluded, unless he could persuade the others of the rightness of at least part of his cause, enough to get him down below fifty again! Ridiculous? Maybe, but this problem must find a solution!

5. Some combination of the above.

It may be that none of these solutions commends itself to you. That is all right, if you will expend your time and effort to address the problem.

Is there any hope that a solution to this problem will be found? We are not the first generation to recognize the difficulty. In 1787, J.P. Gabler attacked dogmatic (systematic) theology with being far removed from Scripture. He proposed that going back to studying the text of Scripture was the way ahead. Systematics must rest on Biblical texts.

> The first part of Gabler's proposal, the rupturing of the link between biblical study and confessional application, was soon widely adopted, but the second part, that the results of such biblical theology should then be deployed in the construction of dogmatics, was largely ignored. . . . [As a result] the drift of biblical theology was toward the increasingly atomistic, cut off from any obligation to traditional dogmatics.[355]

Once again we are seeing a revival of biblical or exegetical theology, a searching for the meaning of texts and books and testaments prior to, or more accurately, accompanying systematization. This time many conservatives and evangelicals

---

[355] *Dictionary of the Later New Testament and Its Developments*, ed. Ralph P. Martin and Peter H. Davids, s.v. "New Testament theology."

are at the forefront of the effort. We must not let this opportunity be lost. The presence of strict subscription to creeds fosters fear — fear of being ostracized — in men who might otherwise tackle this problem.

At first, questioning a creedal statement will require godly courage in such groups, but when done intelligently and prayerfully it will be worth the cost. The fearful trend in our day is to follow the battle cry: "Love Unites, but Doctrine Divides!" Certainly we must emphasize love . . . and unashamedly! I would like to think that this chapter itself is such a plea. But if this one-sided slogan were to prevail, it would mean the abandonment of truth in the church of Jesus Christ. Yet experience suggests that, humanly speaking, the fear inspired by our creedal stances keeps us from pursuing unity both in love and in truth.

As I began this chapter I set before you the facts we must wrestle with:

1. *Our creeds and confessions are one immense barrier to unity.*
2. *There is no easy or obvious way to cross this divide.*

Neither of these two things has changed in the time it took you to read this. Perhaps, then, you will want to join me in this brief prayer: Lord, grant us a marriage between exegesis and systematic theology resulting in greater unity in understanding your word.

Is this too much to hope for? Not at all, given the nature of our God who holds men and opinions in his mighty hands. The truth is certain to prevail, but it will not do so automatically, without God-inspired effort. He will use sinful humans, opposing their own sinful subjectivity, to do his work.

APPENDIX 1

The Relation of Law to the Work of Evangelism

Tom Wells

The way Luther and others of the Reformers married law and gospel together has proven fruitful in evangelism. The idea that men must see their need for salvation before they seek it seems fairly obvious, and this idea was exploited by the Puritans and others to bring men to Christ. While the idea itself is only partially true, it is in fact the route that many take in coming to Christ. More than that, it proves a fruitful starting point in making conversation or bringing messages addressed directly to the unsaved. Speaking of, and preaching, moral law under the blessing of the Spirit of God often turns men from their preoccupation with "felt needs" to their real need, salvation from the sin that cripples their lives here and will eventually send them into eternal hell.

The following observations, however, will help us to better understand the relations between evangelism and moral law. First, there is no reason to limit moral law to the Decalogue as has often been done in Reformed evangelism. There *is* an obvious sense in which all law is demand, though that is not what the NT generally means when it speaks of law. The command to repent of sin is law. Such a demand does not necessarily need any other command to make it effective, given the relics of moral law in the conscience of some individuals. (I say "some" because Paul contemplates the possibility of a conscience past feeling in 1 Timothy 4:2.)

Second, the attractiveness of Christ must not be discounted as a motive for seeking him. A sense of the majesty of his person, words, and work of dying for poor sinners is no doubt enhanced by understanding his death in detail, including its bearing on sin, but it may not be necessary to regeneration and conversion. Not all men and women are motivated by the same appeals.

Finally, we need to remember that the way to eternal life was left relatively obscure, even in Israel, for many centuries. Does that mean that there were no men and women of faith during that time? Not at all! But if the Pharisees and Sadducees could argue over whether there was any reference whatsoever to immortality in the Pentateuch, it seems unlikely that such men and women came to faith by contemplating salvation in the eternal sense.

How, then, could they have come to faith? The answer must lie in the attractiveness of the character of Yahweh that led them to trust him and his promises. I am not suggesting that men and women are saved on that basis today, apart from knowledge of Christ, because faith in Yahweh must have always been dependent on the available level of revelation concerning God. Today God is revealed in Christ. We see God in him and we come to faith in God by contemplating him. That does not mean, however, that we can specify in detail what it is about him that men and women must believe. J. Gresham Machen wrote years ago:

> At this point, a question may be asked. We have said that saving faith is acceptance of Christ, not merely in general, but as He is offered to us in the gospel. How much, then, of the gospel, it may be asked, does a man need to accept in order to be saved; what, to put it baldly, are the minimum doctrinal requirements in order that a man may be a Christian? That is a question which, in one form or another, I am often asked; but it is also a question which I have never answered, and which I have not the slightest intention of answering now. Indeed it is a question which I think no human being can answer. Who can presume to say whether the other man's attitude toward Christ, which he can express but badly in words, is an attitude of saving faith or not? This is one of

Appendix One: Law and Evangelism

the things which must be surely left to God.[356]

The safest path for us to take in evangelism is to tell men and women as much truth about God, Christ, and their souls as we have opportunity to give them. God honors his word, sometimes in relatively small amounts.

Should we use moral law in telling men of Christ? By all means! But not because the word of God is bound without it. Those who made law and gospel two parallel tracks through all of history on which the engine of salvation had to run were mistaken. That is simply not the way the Bible presents those two things.

That, however, does not prove that moral law has no place in preaching the gospel. Gospel and moral law are not opposing categories. The gospel is the good news that God's king and agent has come to reign. What would we think of such a king without his own laws? But when we ask what those laws are, they turn out to include whatever can be called moral law plus all else that Christ commands, including repentance and faith.

The law of Christ is not opposed to the gospel. It is part and parcel with it. "Believe on the Lord Jesus Christ and you will be saved" is both gospel and law. Christ has a law that is also gospel. As the Servant of Yahweh he has his own torah (law) that brings confidence. "In his law the islands will put their hope" (Isa. 42:4).

In the words of John Calvin on Ezekiel 18:23,

> How, then, does God wish all men to be saved? By the Spirit's condemning the world of sin, of righteousness, and of judgment, at this day, *by the Gospel*, as he did formerly by the law and the

---

[356] J. Gresham Machen, *What Is Faith?* (Grand Rapids: Eerdmans, repr. 1974), 154-155.

prophets (John xvi. 8.).[357]

---

[357] John Calvin, *Commentaries on the First Twenty Chapters of the Book of the Prophet Ezekiel* (Grand Rapids: Baker, repr. 1984), 247 (italics added).

APPENDIX 2

The Relations Between the Biblical Covenants

Tom Wells

The heavy emphasis on the Old and New Covenants in the historical section of chapter one raises important questions. What of the other covenants? Are they important? Are they relevant to the history of redemption? And are they relevant to our lives? The answer to each of these last three questions is yes, of course. Any comprehensive treatment of this subject would show their importance and relevance in some detail, but here I will simply outline what I perceive to be the kind of relationship that exists between them.

1. The Relationship between the Covenants is a Teleological Relationship.

In Ernest Kevan's book, *The Grace of Law*, he makes very few criticisms of the Puritans. Kevan did an excellent job in surveying the Puritan uses of the law. His own convictions were very much those of the men he wrote about, but in one important point he faulted them.

> It is true, as many have pointed out, that some of their detailed expositions suffered from a defect in historical perspective and were based upon a kind of mathematical unity rather than a teleological one. It is also true that proof-texts were frequently cited by them as if every verse of Scripture were of universal

validity irrespective of considerations of time and place.[358]

The two points made here are both important and related. A *mathematical unity* suggests that each of the covenants functions in the same way, much as links in a chain do. This conviction would, of course, have been accompanied with the idea of progress from covenant to covenant. Keeping to my figure, then, each link would have been larger than the previous one. For example, when we pass from the Old Covenant to the New Covenant we see great progress in that relatively few were saved under the regimen of the Mosaic Law while many more came to Christ under the New Covenant. Each link was different in size, but each carried out the same program. Each sought to bring men of their generations to God. This idea of the unity of Scripture would invite 'proof-texting' because there would be little difference in the contents of the covenants as we pass from one to another.

A *teleological unity*, however, would work in a different way. It would be a unity in which each covenant contributed something to the fulfillment of redemptive history, but what each contributed could be quite different from the contributions of the other covenants. For example, the Noachic Covenant (Gen. 9:8-17) provided a continuing earthly scene on which redemption could take place. The Abrahamic Covenant with its promises outlined the course of redemptive history, while setting forth two kinds of redemption and two peoples to experience them. Then the Mosaic Covenant regulated the course of redemptive history by producing the people who would write the Scriptures and bring forth the Messiah. Each of these covenants, if they did no more than I have suggested here, would serve the same ultimate purpose, to bring glory to God in the salvation of a people that no man can number.

---

[358] Kevan, *Grace*, 255.

2. The Abrahamic Covenant Offers the Framework for Understanding All the Following Redemptive History.

We have already noticed that working out the distinctions between the Old and New Covenants has been the focus of covenantal investigation in most of church history. Further than that, I have suggested that such a focus was correct. That seems to imply that the Abrahamic Covenant is of secondary importance. I would like to correct that impression now.

One reason that working out the distinctions between the two later covenants is so important is this: it enables us to see the full import of the Abrahamic Covenant. Here again, looking back from the high point of revelation clarifies something that otherwise would have remained cloudy. From the NT we can see that the Abrahamic Covenant spoke of two distinct peoples, Israel and the church, that would experience two kinds of redemptive histories with two covenants to guide them. They stand in *typological* relation to one another. One would experience a physical and national redemption, starting with deliverance from Egypt and guided by the Old or Mosaic Covenant. The other would experience a spiritual, transnational redemption, starting with deliverance from sin and guided by the New Covenant.[359] In retrospect this is easy to see in some detail; in prospect we could not grasp it in any comprehensive way.

---

[359] For the possibility that this does not preclude some future importance for Israel see Fred Zaspel, *Jews, Gentiles & the Goal of Redemptive History* (Hatfield, PA: Interdisciplinary Biblical Research Institute, 1995).

3. The Mosaic Covenant Illustrates This Difference in Many Ways.

The Mosaic Covenant was given in celebration of the most remarkable physical deliverance in history, the Exodus of the people of Israel from Egypt (Exod. 19:3-6; 20:1-2). It was clearly given to guide the nation throughout its history as a physical and national entity. The terms of the covenant, to the extent that it was a national constitution,[360] could have been kept by Israel and she would have prospered in her land and fulfilled her national destiny. By the prospects of national life set forth in the Mosaic Covenant Israel pictured the church and its spiritual prosperity under the New Covenant. In neither case could this prosperity exist without warfare. So the physical wars that God commanded Israel to engage in, on the way to prosperity, prefigured the battles that the church engages in on its way to perfection.

More than anything else, however, Israel under the Mosaic Covenant illustrates the fact that the salvation of individual Israelites was not its *immediate* goal. As part of redemptive history this covenant contributed its part to the ultimate salvation of God's regenerated people, but as an immediate goal *the covenant is virtually silent on this subject*! This is true of the whole Mosaic legislation in its historical context. There is not a word directly about eternal life anywhere in the legal code. In part, that may be why the Lord Jesus received congratulations from the scribes in Luke 20:39. They were normally his enemies, but they no doubt were hard pressed to answer the Sadducees who did not believe in eternal life, and Jesus gave

---

[360] If and when it was turned into a means of spiritual justification before God, it became a demand for moral perfection and no one could keep it for a moment. But as a national constitution it assumed that no one under it was perfect and it made provision for many failures by its ceremonies.

them a sound argument for it from the Pentateuch (Exod. 3:6), the only part of the OT that the Sadducees accepted as authoritative.

The point is this: if the Mosaic legislation was explicitly aimed at teaching men about eternal life, how could there ever have been a shortage of arguments to prove its existence? Could anyone read the NT for more than a few pages without realizing that Christ came to save men eternally? The emphasis of the Mosaic Covenant, however, lies in another direction. As far as individual salvation is concerned, it can show man his sin, but it nowhere explicitly calls him to seek an eternal remedy. That was not its main purpose. It was not just another link in a monotonous chain of such links. It had its own justifications that served the final purposes of God. The unity of the covenants was teleological.

4. The New Covenant Brings God's Purpose of Redemption to Its Conclusion.

The goal of God's redemptive activity is the New Covenant. Each preceding covenant had its part to play in redemption's story. Building on a stable earth provided by the Lord in the covenant with Noah, God announced to Abraham worldwide blessing for those to whom he would be a father. At first this blessing was seen in the establishment of the nation of Israel, a nation that typified the coming church and provided a remnant of godly men and women who perpetuated the hope of the Lord's coming salvation. Along the way this people produced both the OT scriptures and the family of David to bring God's blessing to its apex.

Finally, "in the fulness of time," God sent forth his Messiah, the agent of his eternal salvation toward which all of history tended. *Already* this Messiah, the Lord Jesus, is creating a new nation to inhabit a new heavens and a new earth. The citizens of that nation are the members of God's universal church, now united to the Lord Jesus in the body of Christ. Beyond this lies glory. It is not yet clear to us what all that will mean. "But we know that when he appears, we shall be like him, for we shall see him as he is" (1 John 3:2).

In glory we will enjoy the manifest presence of God forever.

APPENDIX 3

"Covenant" and its Cognates in the New Testament

Tom Wells

Although three Greek words are translated by cognates of our English word *covenant* in the English NT, only one is used theologically of God's redemptive work. There appear to be thirty-three occurrences of this word for *covenant* in the NT. They may be divided as follows:

1. Three references to purely human covenants: Galatians 3:15; Hebrews 9:16, 17.
2. Two references as part of a title: Hebrews 9:4; Revelation 11:19.
3. Twenty-eight references to covenants within redemptive history or to eternal covenants.

We may further divide the last category of covenants into those that plainly imply a plurality of covenants and those that do not.

References that Plainly Imply a Plurality of Covenants

1. There are sixteen references that imply a plurality of covenants by using the plural or by introducing comparative modifiers such as *first, new,* etc.: Luke 22:20; Romans 9:4; 1 Corinthians 11:25; 2 Corinthians 3:6, 14; Galatians 4:24; Ephesians 2:12; Hebrews 7:22; 8:6, 8, 9(twice), 10; 9:15(twice); 12:24.
2. There are nine references that imply a plurality of

covenants in some other way:
> (1) Two references are parallel to other verses that speak of the New Covenant: Matthew 26:28 and Mark 14:24 are parallel to Luke 22:20 and 1 Corinthians 11:25 They too, then refer to the New Covenant.
> (2) Four references refer to the Abrahamic Covenant as shown by their contexts: Luke 1:72; Acts 3:25; 7:8; Galatians 3:17.
> (3) Hebrews 9:4 refers to "the tables of the covenant," clearly a reference to the Mosaic Covenant.
> (4) Hebrews 9:20 shows by its context (vv.18ff.) that it refers to the Old or Mosaic Covenant.
> (5) Hebrews 10:16 is clearly a reference to the New Covenant (cf. 8:7-12).

The Remaining References Using the Word *Covenant*.

There are now just three references left that might conceivably be used as "covenant-of-grace" language is used by theologians:
> 1. Romans 11:27, whether it alludes to Isaiah 27:9; 59:20-21 or Jeremiah 31:33-34, is a reference to a *future* covenant. That must, then, be the New Covenant.
> 2. Hebrews 10:29 "alludes to Exodus 24:8, quoted in Hebrews 9:20 (cf. v. 18), and reapplies it by implication to the covenant established by the sacrifice of Christ (cf. 13:20)."[361]

---

[361] Paul Ellingworth, *NIGTC: The Epistle to the Hebrews* (Grand Rapids: Eerdmans, 1993), 540. I have quoted Ellingworth rather than making my own statement since earlier on the same page he says of this verse, "The author's present concern . . . is with the *continuity of God's covenant* (→ 7:22)" [italics added]. Even though he makes this *theological* judgment about the continuity of "God's covenant," he sees clearly that the New Covenant is in view after all.

3. Hebrews 13:20, with its reference to an "eternal covenant" is left as the only instance of a possible usage for a panhistorical covenant. For a discussion of this verse see the reference in chap. 3, p. 45, footnote 53, with its reference to further literature.

The conclusion seems clear: when NT writers use the word *covenant*, they normally want to assert *dis*continuity.

APPENDIX 4

The Promises of the Abrahamic Covenant

Tom Wells

Promises of the Abrahamic Covenant may be read in two ways, depending on the sense of the word *seed* one uses.

Though the word *covenant* is first applied to the Abrahamic Covenant in Genesis 15, I have included the promises that start in Genesis 12. (The reason for this is contained in footnote 68, p. 60 .)

		Fulfilled:	
Ref.	Promise	by Israel	by the Church
12:2	God would make Abraham a great nation.	Deut. 26:5	Rev. 5:9
12:2	God would make Abraham's name great	Obviously true throughout Bible history in both groups.	
12:3	God would bless those who blessed Abraham.	Gen. 39:5	Matt. 10:42

Ref.	Promise	Fulfilled: by Israel	by the Church
12:3	God would curse those who cursed Abraham.	Ps. 149	Rev. 6:9-11
12:3	God would bless all men through Abraham.	The giving of Scripture and Christ fulfills this in both groups	
12:7	God would give the land to Abraham	Josh 21:43	Rev. 21:1-8
13:15	[Reproduces the promise of 12:7.]		
13:16	God would make Abraham's seed innumerable.	1 Kings 3:8	Rev. 7:9
15:5	[Reproduces the promise of 13:16.]		
15:7	[Reproduces the promise of 12:7.]		
17:6	God would cause Abraham to father kings.	2 Sam. 12:24	Rev. 3:21
17:8	God would be God to Abraham and his seed.	Ps. 77:13-15	Rev. 21:3
17:19	God would make the promises come through Isaac.	Josh. 24:3-4	Lk. 3:21-38

Note: I have selected only one reference per promise from each category, but you can easily find more for most of the promises.

APPENDIX 5

A Table for Studying the Decalogue as Commanded by God in the NT
(See p. 60)

Tom Wells

BOOK	REF:	ALLUSIONS	PARALLELS	COMMANDMENTS	SPOKEN TO	OCCASION
Matt.	15:21ff.	None		Several (Seventh quoted)	Disciples	Number 1
	15:4		Mk 7:10	Fifth	Scribes & Pharisees	Number 2
	19:18-19		Mk 10:19; Lk 18:20	Fifth to Ninth	Rich young ruler	Number 3
Mark	Parallel only	2:27-28				
Luke	Parallel only	23:56				
John	None	8:11				
Acts	None	20:33				
Rom.	7:7			Tenth	Paul when unconverted	
	13:9			Sixth, Eighth, Tenth	Romans	Number 4
1 Cor.	None	6:9-10				

Appendix Five: Studying the Decalogue in the NT 291

BOOK	REF:	ALLUSIONS	PARALLELS	COMMANDMENTS	SPOKEN TO	OCCASION
2 Cor.	None					
Gal.	None					
Eph.	6:2-3	4:28, 5:5		Fifth	Children	Number 5
Phil.	None					
Col.	None	3:5, 20				
1 Thess.	None					
2 Thess.	None					
1 Tim.	None	1:9-10				
2 Tim.	None					
Titus	None					
Phm.	None					
Heb.	None	13:4				

BOOK	REF:	ALLUSIONS	PARALLELS	COMMANDMENTS	SPOKEN TO	OCCASION
James	2:11-12			Sixth, Seventh	"Twelve Tribes"	Number 6
1 Pet.	None					
2 Pet.	None					
1 John	None	3:12-15				
2 John	None					
3 John	None					
Jude	None					
Rev.	None	21:8				

The reference to *Occasion* is intended to enumerate the times I think or allow that one or more of the Ten Commandments is actually applied to someone as a law in such a way that the Ten Commandments are clearly the source. There is a certain subjectivity involved in a table like this with reference to allusions, but I hope it will commend itself to fair-minded readers.

APPENDIX 6

John Bunyan on the Creation Sabbath

Fred Zaspel

Bunyan responded more thoroughly: "But I answer, as I hinted before, that God did sanctify it to his own rest. 'The Lord also hath set apart him that is godly for himself.' But again, it is one thing for God to sanctify this or that thing to an use, and another thing to command that that thing be forthwith in being to us. As for instance, the land of Canaan was set apart many years for the children of Israel before they possessed that land. Christ Jesus was long sanctified— that is, set apart to be our Redeemer—before God sent him into the world. (Deut. xxxii. John x. 36.)

"If, then, by God's sanctifying of the seventh day for a sabbath you understand it for a sabbath for man, (but the text saith not so,) yet, it might be so set apart for man long before it should be, as such, made known unto him. And that the seventh-day sabbath was not as yet made known to men, consider—

Secondly. Moses himself seems to have the knowledge of it at first, not by tradition, but by revelation; as it is Exodus xvi. 23: 'This is that (saith he) that the Lord hath said,' (namely, to me, for we read not, as yet, that he said it to anybody else,) '*To-morrow is the sabbath of the holy rest unto the Lord.*'

"Also holy Nehemiah suggesteth this when he saith of Israel to God, 'Thou madest known to them thy holy sabbath.' (Neh. ix. 14.) The first of these texts shows us that tidings of a seventh-day sabbath for men came *first* to Moses from heaven; and the second, that it was to Israel before unknown."[363]

---

[363] *The Complete Works of John Bunyan*, vol. 3 [4], 197-8.

A
Bibliography of Quoted Sources

BOOKS

A

Armstrong, Brian G. *Calvin and the Amyraut Heresy*. Madison: Univ. of Wisconsin, 1969.

Armstrong, John H. ed. *Reformation & Revival* 6, no.2 (summer 1997).

Aquinas, Thomas. *Summa Theologica* in *Basic Writings of Saint Thomas Aquinas*. Vol. 2. Edited by Anton C. Pegi. NYC: Random House, 1945.

Augustine, Aurelius *City of God*.

------. *Reply to Faustus the Manichaean*.

------. *Two Letters against Pelagius*.

B

Bahnsen, Greg L. *Theonomy in Christian Ethics*. Nutley, NJ: The Craig Press, 1979.

Banks, Robert. *Jesus and the Law in Synoptic Tradition*. Cambridge: Cambridge University Press, 1975.

Barbieri, Louis A. *Matthew* in *The Life of Christ Commentary*, edited by John F. Walvoord and Roy B. Zuck. Wheaton, IL: Victor Books, 1989.

Barcellos, Richard. *In Defense of the Decalogue: A Critique of New Covenant Theology*. Enumclaw, WA: Wine Press, 2001.

Barnhouse, Donald Grey. *Genesis*. Grand Rapids: Zondervan Publishing Co., 1976.

Barrett, C. K. *The First Epistle to the Corinthians*. New York: Harper and Row, 1968.

Bauer, Walter, William F. Arndt, F. Wilbur Gingrich, and W. Danker. *A Greek-English Lexicon of the New Testament and Other Early Christian Literature*. 2nd ed. Chicago: The University of Chicago Press, 1979.

Beasley-Murray, George R. *Gospel of Life: The Theology of the Fourth Gospel*. Peabody, MA: Hendrickson Publishers, Inc., 1991.

Blomberg, Craig. *Matthew, The New American Commentary*. Nashville: Broadman & Holman, 1992.

Boice, James Montgomery. *The Gospel of John*. Grand Rapids: Baker Book House, 1985.
Bolton, Samuel. *The True Bounds of Christian Freedom*. 1645. Reprint, Carlisle, PA: Banner of Truth, 1964.
Brown, Michael L. *Israel's Divine Healer*. Grand Rapids: Zondervan, 1995.
Brown, John. *Discourses and Sayings of our Lord Jesus Christ*. Reprint, London: Banner of Truth, 1967.
------. *An Exposition of the Epistle to the Galatians*. Reprint, Marshallton, DE: Sovereign Grace Publishers, 1970.
Bruce, F.F. *NIC: The Epistle to the Hebrews*. Grand Rapids: Eerdmans, 1964.
------. *Paul: Apostle of the Heart Set Free*. Grand Rapids: Eerdmans, 1977.
Bunyan, John. *Complete Works of John Bunyan*. Marshallton, DE: The National Foundation for Christian Education, 1968.
Burgess, Walter H. *John Robinson: Pastor of the Pilgrim Fathers, A Study of His Life and Times*. London: Williams and Norgate, 1920.

C

Calvin, John. *Commentaries on the First Twenty Chapters of the Book of the Prophet Ezekiel*. Reprint, Grand Rapids: Baker, 1984.
------. *A Harmony of the Gospels: Matthew, Mark and Luke*. Vol.1 of *Calvin's Commentaries*. Translated by A. W. Morrison. 1555. Reprint, Grand Rapids: Wm. B. Eerdmans Publishing Co., 1972.
------. *Institutes of the Christian Religion*. Vol. 1. 1559. Reprint, Grand Rapids: Wm. B. Eerdmans Publishing Co., 1979.
Carson, D. A. *Matthew*. Vol. 8 of *The Expositor's Bible Commentary*, edited by Frank E. Gaebelein. Grand Rapids: Zondervan Publishing House, 1984.
------, ed. *From Sabbath to Lord's Day*. Grand Rapids: Zondervan, 1982.
Chafer, L. S. *Grace: The Glorious Theme*. 1922. Reprint, Grand Rapids: Zondervan, 1978.
------. *Systematic Theology*. 1948. Reprint, Dallas, TX: Dallas Seminary Press, 1978.
Chantry, Walter J. *God's Righteous Kingdom*. Carlisle, PA: Banner of Truth Trust, 1980.
Childs, Brevard S. *The New Testament as Canon: An Introduction*.

Philadelphia: Fortress Press, 1985.
Coxe, A. Cleveland, ed. *The Ante-Nicene Fathers*. Vol. 9. 1887. Reprint, Grand Rapids: Eerdmans, 1990.
Cranfield, C.E.B. *ICC: The Epistle to the Romans*. Reprint, Edinburgh: T. & T. Clark, 1981.

D

Dabney, R. L. *Lectures in Systematic Theology*. 1927. Reprint, Grand Rapids: Baker Book House, 1985.
Davids, Peter. *NIGTC: Commentary on James*. Grand Rapids: Wm. B. Eerdmans Publishing Co., 1982.
Davies, W. D., and Dale C. Allison. *A Critical and Exegetical Commentary on the Gospel According to Saint Matthew*. Edinburgh: T. & T. Clark, 1988.
DeHaan, M. R. *Law or Grace?* Grand Rapids, Zondervan, 1965.
Dunn, James D. G. *Jesus, Paul, and the Law*. Louisville: Westminster/John Knox Press, 1990.

E

Ebeling, Gerhard. *Word and Faith*. Philadelphia: Fortress, 1963.
Ellingworth, Paul. *NIGTC: The Epistle to the Hebrews*. Grand Rapids: Eerdmans, 1993.
Elwell, Walter A. ed. *Evangelical Dictionary of Biblical Theology*. Grand Rapids: Baker, 1996.
------, ed. *Evangelical Dictionary of Theology*. Grand Rapids: Baker, 1984.
Estep, William R. *The Anabaptist Story*. Rev. ed. Grand Rapids: Eerdmans, 1975.

F

Fairbairn, Patrick. *The Revelation of Law in Scripture*. 1869. Reprint, Winona Lake, IN: Alpha Publications, 1979.
Fee, Gordon D. *The First Epistle to the Corinthians*. Grand Rapids: Eerdmans, 1987.
------, and Douglas Stuart. *How to Read the Bible for All It's Worth*. Grand Rapids: Zondervan, 1982.
France, R. T. *TNTC: The Gospel According to Matthew*. 1985. Reprint, Grand Rapids: Eerdmans, 1990.
------. *Matthew: Evangelist and Teacher*. Grand Rapids: Zondervan Publishing House, 1989.

Friedlander, Gerald. *Jewish Sources of the Sermon on the Mount.* New York: KTAV, 1969.

G

Garner, Robert. *A Treatise on Baptism.* 1645. Reprint, Paris, AR: The Old Faith Baptist Church, n.d.

Gaebelein, Arno C. *The Gospel of Matthew.* Neptune, NJ: Loizeaux Brothers, 1961.

Gould, Ezra P. *A Critical and Exegetical Commentary on the Gospel According to Mark,* ICC. NY: Scribner's Sons, 1913.

Green, James Benjamin. *A Harmony of the Westminster Presbyterian Standards.* n.d. Reprint, Collins/World, 1976.

Green, Michael. *Matthew for Today.* Dallas, TX: Word, 1988.

Guelich, Robert A. *The Sermon on the Mount: A Foundation for Understanding.* Waco, TX: Word, 1983.

H

Hiebert, D. Edmond. *Mark: A Portrait of the Servant.* Chicago: Moody Press, 1974.

Hendriksen, William. *New Testament Commentary: Ephesians.* Grand Rapids: Baker, 1967.

------. *Exposition of the Gospel According to Matthew*, New Testament Commentary Series. Grand Rapids: Baker, 1979.

Henry, Carl F. H. *Christian Personal Ethics.* Grand Rapids: Wm. B. Eerdmans Publishing Co., 1957.

Hoch, Jr., Carl B. *All Things New.* Grand Rapids: Baker, 1995.

Hodge, Charles. *Commentary on the Epistle to the Romans.* Grand Rapids: Eerdmans, 1965.

House, Paul R. *Old Testament Theology.* Downers Grove, IL: Intervarsity Press, 1998.

I

Introducing the Free Reformed Churches of North America. St. Thomas, Ontario; Free Reformed Publications, 1996.

Irenaeus. *Against Heresies.*

------. *Fragments from the Lost Writings.*

J

Jeremias, Joachim. *The Sermon on the Mount.* Translated by Norman Perrin. Edited by John Reumann. Facet Books: Biblical Series,

No. 2. Philadelphia: Fortress, 1963.
------. *New Testament Theology. Part One: The Proclamation of Jesus.* New York: Scribner's, 1971.
Johnson, Sherman E. *Matthew* in *The Interpreters Bible.* Vol. 7. New York: Abingdon, 1951.

K

Kaye, Bruce, and Gordon Wenham, eds. *Law, Morality and the Bible.* Downers Grove, IL: InterVarsity Press, 1978.
Keil, C. F., and F. Delitsch. *Commentary on the Old Testament.* Reprint, Grand Rapids: Wm. B. Eerdmans Publishing Co., 1986.
Kaiser, Walter. *Toward An Old Testament Theology.* Grand Rapids: Zondervan, 1978.
Kevan, Ernest F. *The Grace of Law.* Grand Rapids: Baker, 1976.
------. *The Moral Law.* Jenkintown, PA: Sovereign Grace Publishers, 1963.
Kidner, Derek. *Genesis.* Reprint, Downers Grove, IL: InterVarsity Press, 1979.
Kissinger, Warren S. *The Sermon on the Mount: A History of Interpretation and Bibliography.* Metuchen, NJ: The Scarecrow Press, Inc., 1975.
Kline, Meredith. *The Structure of Biblical Authority.* Eugene OR: Wipf & Stock, 1997.
Knight III, George W. *The Pastoral Epistles: A Commentary on the Greek Text.* 1992. Reprint, Grand Rapids: Eerdmans, 1996.

L

Lange, John Peter. *Commentary on the Holy Scriptures: The Gospel according to Matthew.* Reprint, Grand Rapids: Zondervan, 1960.
Larkin, Clarence. *Rightly Dividing the Word.* Phila.: Rev. Clarence Larkin Est, n.d.
Lenski, R. C. H. *The Interpretation of St. Matthew's Gospel.* Columbus, OH: The Wartburg Press, 1943.
Lightfoot, J. B. *The Epistle of St. Paul to the Galatians.* Reprint, Grand Rapids: Zondervan, 1966.
Longenecker, Richard N. *Paul, Apostle of Liberty.* 1964. Reprint, Grand Rapids: Baker Book House, 1980.
Louw, Johannes P., and Eugene A. Nida. *Greek-English Lexicon of the*

New Testament Based on Semantic Domains. 2nd ed. New York: United Bible Societies, 1989.

Luther, Martin. *The Works of Martin Luther*.

M

McArthur, Harvey K. *Understanding the Sermon on the Mount*. 1960. Reprint, Westport, CT: Greenwood Press, 1978.

Machen, J. Gresham. *What Is Faith?* Reprint, Grand Rapids: Eerdmans, 1974.

Martin, Ralph P., and Peter H. Davids, eds. *Dictionary of the Later New Testament and Its Developments*. Downers Grove, IL: IVP, 1997.

Martyr, Justin. *Dialogue with Trypho*.

Meier, John P. *The Vision of Matthew*. NY: Paulist Press, 1978.

Minear, Paul S. *Images of the Church*. Phila.: Westminster, 1960.

Moo, Douglas. *NIC: The Epistle to the Romans*. Grand Rapids: Eerdmans, 1996.

------. *The Letter of James*. Grand Rapids: Wm. B. Eerdmans Publishing Co., 2000.

Morris, Leon. *The Apostolic Preaching of the Cross*. Grand Rapids: Eerdmans, 1955.

Morris, William, ed. *The American Heritage Dictionary of the English Language*. NYC: American Heritage, 1969.

Murray, John. *Collected Writings of John Murray*. Edinburgh: Banner of Truth, 1976.

------. *NIC: The Epistle to the Romans*. Grand Rapids: Eerdmans, 1965.

------. *Principles of Conduct*. 1957. Reprint, Grand Rapids: Eerdmans, 1981.

O

Oehler, Gustav Friedrich. *Theology of the Old Testament*. 1873. Reprint, Minneapolis: Klock & Klock Christian Publishers, 1978.

Origen. *Against Celsus*.

Owen, John. *An Exposition of the Epistle to the Hebrews*. Reprint, Marshallton, DE: National Foundation for Christian Education, n.d.

P

Pink, Arthur W. *An Exposition of the Sermon on the Mount*. 1950.

Bibliography

Reprint, Grand Rapids: Baker, 1979.

Plummer, Alfred. *The Pastoral Epistles*. NYC: Hodder & Stoughton, n.d.

Poythress, Vern. *The Shadow of Christ in the Law of Moses*. Phillipsburg, NJ: Presbyterian & Reformed, 1991.

R

Reisinger, John. *Christ Lord and Lawgiver Over the Church*. Frederick, MD: New Covenant Media, 1998.

Ridderbos, H. N. *Matthew* in *The Bible Student's Commentary*. Translated by Ray Togtman. Grand Rapids: Zondervan, 1987.

Richardson, Alan, ed. *A Dictionary of Christian Theology*. Philadelphia: Westminster, 1969.

Robertson, O. Palmer. *The Christ of the Covenants*. Phillipsburg, NJ: Presbyterian and Reformed, 1980.

Ryrie, Charles Caldwell. *Dispensationalism Today*. 1965. Reprint, Chicago: Moody, 1977.

S

Schaff, Philip. *Creeds of Christendom*. Grand Rapids: Baker, 1983.

Schnackenburg, Rudolph. *The Church in the New Testament*. New York, Herder & Herder, 1965.

Schreiner, Thomas R. *ECNT: Romans*. Grand Rapids: Baker, 1998.

------. *The Law & Its Fulfillment: A Pauline Theology of Law*. Grand Rapids: Baker, 1993.

Scofield, C. I. *Law and Grace*. Winona Lake, IN: BMH Books, 1973.

------, ed. *The Scofield Reference Bible*. 1909. Reprint, New York: Oxford University Press, n.d.

Sloyan, Gerard S. *Is Christ the End of the Law?* Philadelphia: The Westminster Press, 1978.

Smith, Ralph. *Old Testament Theology*. Nashville: Broadman & Holman Publishers, 1993.

Stonehouse, Ned B. *The Witness of Matthew and Mark to Christ*. Philadelphia: Presbyterian Guardian, 1944.

Stott, John R. W. *The Message of Ephesians*. Downers Grove, IL: InterVarsity Press, 1979.

Streeter, B. H. *The Four Gospels*. London: Macmillan, 1924.

Strickland, Wayne, ed. *The Law, the Gospel, and the Modern Christian*. Grand Rapids, 1991.

T

Tasker, R. V. G. *The Gospel According to St. Matthew* in *TNTC*. 1961. Reprint, Grand Rapids: Eerdmans, 1978.

Tousaint, Stanley, and Charles Dyer. *Essays in Honor of J. Dwight Pentecost*. Chicago: Moody Press, 1986.

Trever, John C. *The Dead Sea Scrolls*. 1965. Reprint, Grand Rapids: Eerdmans, 1977.

V

Verduin, Leonard. *The Reformers and Their Stepchildren*. Grand Rapids: Eerdmans, 1964.

Vidler, Alec R. *Christ's Strange Work*. London: Longmans and Green, 1944.

Vincent, Thomas. *The Shorter Catechism Explained from Scripture*. Reprint, Edinburgh: Banner of Truth, 1980.

Vos, Geerhardus. *Biblical Theology: Old and New Testaments*. 1948. Reprint, Grand Rapids: Eerdmans, 1977.

W

Waldron, Sam. *The Lord's Day*. Grand Rapids: Time for Eternity, n.d.

Walton, John. *Covenant: God's Purpose, God's Plan*. Grand Rapids: Zondervan, 1994.

Ward, Norbert, ed. *Beloved Brethren: Circular Letters of the Philadelphia Baptist Association from 1774 to 1807*. Nashville, Baptist Reformation Review, [1970's].

Warfield, B. B. *Selected Shorter Writings*. Phillipsburg, NJ: Presbyterian & Reformed Publishing Co., 1973.

Wells, Tom. *Christian: Take Heart*. Edinburgh: Banner of Truth, 1987.

Wesley, John. *Sermons: On Several Occasions*. London: Wesleyan Conference Office, 1876.

Westerholm, Stephen. *Israel's Law and the Church's Faith*. Grand Rapids: Eerdmans, 1988.

Williams, George H. *The Radical Reformation*. Philadelphia: Westminster, 1962.

------, and Angel M. Mergal, eds. *Spiritual and Anabaptist Writers*. Philadelphia: Westminster, 1957.

Wilson, Stephen G. *Luke and The Law*. Cambridge: Cambridge University Press, 1983.

Z

Zaspel, Fred G. *The Continuing Relevance of Divine Law*. Hatfield, PA: Interdisciplinary Biblical Research Institute, 1991.

------. *The Theology of Fulfillment*. Hatfield, PA: The Interdisciplinary Biblical Research Institute, 1993.

ARTICLES

A

Allison, Dale C. "Jesus and Moses (Mt 5:1-2)." *The Expository Times* 98 (1987).

B

Bacon, B. W. "Jesus and the Law: A Study of the First 'Book' of Matthew." JBL 47 (1928).

Bahnsen, Greg. "The Theonomic Reformed Approach to Law and Gospel." In *The Law, the Gospel, and the Modern Christian*.

Baker, J. P. "Offices of Christ." *New Dictionary of Theology*. Edited by Sinclair B. Ferguson et al. Downers Grove, IL: IVP, 1988

Banks, Robert. "Matthew's Understanding of the Law: Authenticity and Interpretation in Matthew 5:17-20" *JBL* 93 (1974): 226-242.

C

Carson, D. A. "New Testament Theology." *Dictionary of the Later New Testament and Its Developments*. Edited by Ralph P. Martin and Peter H. Davids. Downers Grove, IL: IVP, 1988.

------. "Jesus and the Sabbath in the Four Gospels." In *From Sabbath to Lord's Day*. Edited by D. A. Carson. Grand Rapids: Zondervan, 1982.

Cotrell, Jack. "Baptism in the Reformed Tradition." In *Baptism and the Remission of Sins*. Edited by David W. Fletcher. Joplin, Missouri: College Press, 1990.

Cranfield, C. E. B. "St. Paul and the Law." *SJT* 17 (1964).

F

Ferguson, Sinclair B. "An Assembly of Theonomists?" In *Theonomy: A Reformed Critique*. Edited by William S. Barker and W. Robert Godfrey. Grand Rapids: Zondervan, 1990.

Frame, John. "Westminster Catechism." *Evangelical Dictionary of Theology*. Edited by Walter A. Elwell, Grand Rapids: Baker, 1984.

Franck, Sebastian. *A Letter to John Campanus*. Quoted in George H. Williams and Angel M. Mergal, eds., *Spiritual and Anabaptist Writers*. (Phila.: Westminster, 1957), 151.

G

Goldingay, John. "The Old Testament and Christian Faith: Jesus and the Old Testament in Matthew 1-5." Parts 1 and 2. *Themelios* 8 (1982, 1983).

Gorman, Frank H. "When Law Becomes Gospel: Matthew's Transformed Torah." *Listening* (1989).

Grassi, Joseph A. "Matthew as a Second Testament Deuteronomy." *Biblical Theology Bulletin* 19 (1989).

H

Hammerton-Kelly, R. G. "Attitudes to the Law in Matthew's Gospel." *Biblical Research* 17 (1972).

Herbermann, Charles G. et alt., eds., *The Catholic Encyclopedia*. NYC: The Gilmary Society, 1913.

Hoch Jr., Carl B. "The New Covenant: Its Problems, Certainties and Some Proposals." *Reformation and Revival Journal* 6, no. 3 (summer 1997).

J

Johnson, Alan F. "Jesus and Moses: Rabbinic Backgrounds and Exegetical Concerns in Matthew 5 as Crucial to the Theological Foundations of Christian Ethics." In *The Living and Active Word of God*. Edited by Inch and Youngblood. Winona Lake: Eisenbrauns, 1983.

Johnson, S. Lewis. "The Paralysis of Legalism." *Bib Sac* 120 (1963), 112.

K

Kaiser, Walter C. "Leviticus 18:5 and Paul: Do This and You Shall Live [Eternally]?" *JETS* 14 (1971), 19-28.

------. "The Theology of the Old Testament." In *The Expositor's Bible Commentary*, Vol. 1. Edited by Frank E. Gaeblein. Grand Rapids: Zondervan, 1982, 292-294.

------. "The Promise Theme and the Theology of Rest." *Bib Sac* (April 1973).

L

Lincoln, A.T. "Sabbath, Rest, and Eschatology in the New Testament." In *From Sabbath to Lord's Day*. Edited by D. A. Carson. Grand Rapids: Zondervan, 1982.

M

Martin, John A. "Dispensational Approaches to the Sermon on the Mount." In *Essays in Honor of J.Dwight Pentecost*. Edited by Stanley D. Toussaint and Charles H. Dyer. Chicago: Moody, 1986.

Mayhue, Richard L. "Covenant of Grace or New Covenant?" *The Master's Seminary Journal* 7, no. 2, (fall 1996), 251-257.

Moo, Douglas. "Jesus and the Authority of the Mosaic Law." *JSNT* 20 (1984), 3-49.

------. "The Law of Christ as the Fulfillment of the Law of Moses." In *The Law, the Gospel, and the Modern Christian*, 319-382.

------. "The Law of Moses or the Law of Christ." In *Continuity and Discontinuity*. Edited by John S. Feinburg. Westchester, IL: Crossway Books, 1988, 203-213.

Moule, C. F. D. "Fulfillment-Words in the New Testament: Use and Abuse." *NTS* 14, 314.

N

Nixon, Robin. "Fulfilling the Law: The Gospels and Acts." In *Law, Morality and the Bible*. Edited by Bruce Kaye and Gordon Wenham. Downers Grove, IL: InterVarsity Press, 1978.

O

Oberholtzer, Thomas Kem. "The Kingdom Rest in Hebrews 3:1-4:13." *Bib Sac* 145, no. 578 (April 1988).

R

Rayburn, R. S. "Covenant, The New." *Evangelical Dictionary of Theology*. Edited by Walter A. Elwell. Grand Rapids: Baker, 1984.

Richardson, Alan. "Biblical Theology." *A Dictionary of Christian Theology*. Edited by Alan Richardson. Philadelphia:

Westminster, 1969.

S

Sampey, John Richard. "Sabbath." *The International Standard Bible Encyclopedia*. Grand Rapids: Wm. B. Eerdmans, 1939.

Slater, T. "Law, Divine, Moral Aspect of." *The Catholic Encyclopedia*. Vol. 9. Edited by Charles G. Herbermann et alt. NYC: The Gilmary Society, 1913.

Strickland, Wayne. "The Inauguration of the Law of Christ with the Gospel." In *The Law, the Gospel, and the Modern Christian*, 258.

Swanson, Scott A. "Can We Reproduce the Exegesis of the New Testament? Why Are We Still Asking?" *Trinity Journal* 17, no. 1, 67-76.

T

Turner, Max B. "The Sabbath, Sunday, and the Law in Luke/Acts." In *From Sabbath to Lord's Day*. Edited by D. A. Carson. Grand Rapids: Zondervan, 1982.

V

VanGemeren, Willem. "Systems of Continuity." In *Continuity and Discontinuity*. Edited by John S. Feinburg. Westchester, IL: Crossway, 1988.

W

Ware, Bruce A. "The New Covenant and the People(s) of God." In *Dispensationalism, Israel and the Church*. Craig A. Blaising and Darrell L. Bock.

Westerholm, S. "Sabbath." *Dictionary of Jesus and the Gospels*. Edited by Joel B. Green and Scott McKnight. Downers Grove, IL: InterVarsity Press, 1992.

Y

Yarbrough, Robert W. "Biblical Theology." *Evangelical Dictionary of Biblical Theology*. Edited by Walter A. Elwell. Grand Rapids: Baker, 1996.

Z

Zens, Jon. "Is There a Covenant of Grace?" *Baptist Reformation Review*. (autumn 1977), 44.

Scripture Index

Genesis
1:1-2:3 .... 212, 213
1:31-2:1 212
1-2 225
2 ..... 212, 217, 220
2:1-2 213
2:1-3 . 212, 214, 215
2:2 11
2:2-3 ..... 225, 232
2:2-3a 213
2:3 .... 11, 233
2:15 216
2-3 227
3 213
3:6 141
3:15 232
3:15ff 221
3:16-17 216
3:17-19 221
3:21 214
4:3 216
4:5 141
4:8-11 141
5:29 ..... 216, 221
6:1-7 141
6:5 141
9:6 159
9:8-17 276
9:12 218
9:13 218
9:17 218
9:22-25 141
11:4ff 141
12 .... 60, 285
12:2 285
12:3 ...... 285, 286
12:7 ...... 286, 291
12-17 60
13:15 286
13:16 286
15 .... 60, 285
15:5 286
15:7 286
15:16 141
16:5ff 141
17 10
17:6 286
17:8 286
17:11 218
17:19 286
19:4ff 141
19:31ff 141
27 141
39:5 285

Exodus
2 92
3:6 279
4:19 93
12:12 141
15:17 221
16 .... 216, 217
16:23 293
16:29 216
16:30 216
19:3 93
19:3-6 278
19:5 145
19:12 93
19:13 93
19:14 93
19-20 216
20 .... 170, 176
.... 177, 179
.... 202, 203, 217
20:1 152
20:1-2 278
20:2-17 ... 129, 217
20:8 ...... 198, 217
20:8-11 ... 217, 220
20:10 219
20:14 159
21:15 74
21:17 74
21:24 100
22:19 158
23:12 ..... 218, 219
23:14ff. 220
24:8 282

24:12	93
24:13	93
24:16	95
24:18	93
31:12-18	218
31:13	218
31:14	219
31:14-15	219
31:17	212
33:14	221, 222
34:21	218, 219, 226
34:27-28	144, 151
34:29	93
35:2-3	218, 220
35:3	219

Leviticus

16:29	220
16:30	220
18:5	145, 146
18:23	158
19:3	220
19:12	100, 106
19:18	100, 107, 154
19:30	220
19:34	100
20:9	74
20:16	158
21:9	74
23:1-3	219
23:4ff	220
23:24-25	220
23:34	220
24:5-9	227
25	220
25:1ff	220
25:2	221
26	145
26:1-8	145
26:2	220
26:42	217
26:45	217

Numbers

15:32-36	219
15:39-40	217
28:9-10	223

Deuteronomy

3:20	221
4:20	221
5:6-21	129
5:12	217
5:12-15	220
5:15	220
6:16	93
8:3	93
9:9	93
10:20	93
12:9-10	221
17:7	193
18:15	17
18:15-19	34, 96, 132
18:19	132
19:16-21	194
21:18-21	74, 194
22:13-19	159
22:21	194
22:24	194
23:3-6	100, 107
23:25	226
24	100, 105
24:1	106
24:1-4	105, 159
24:7	194
25:4	159
25:19	221
26:5	285
27:21	158
27:26	145, 146
32	293

Joshua

1:13	221
11:23	221
14:15	221
21:43	286
21:43-45	60
21:44	222
24:3-4	286

Judges

3:11	221

Scripture Index

3:30 221
8:34 217

1 Samuel
17:33 221
21:1-6 226

2 Samuel
7:1 221
7:11 221
12:24 286
17:8 221
23:2 34

1 Kings
3:8 286
8:56 221
17:7 216

1 Chronicles
22:9 221

2 Chronicles
19:2 100
20:7 61
36:21 219

Nehemiah
9:14 .. 216, 217, 293

Esther
3:1 14
7:1-10 14

Psalms
2:4 67
2:7 49
19:1-3 33
77:13-15 286
92 223
94:13 222
95 .... 222, 223
95:11 . 212, 221, 222
95:7b-11 232
103:18 217
116:7 222
132:8 222
132:14 222
139:21-22 100
149 286

Proverbs
7 206

7:7 206
7:25 206
7:26-27 206

Ecclesiastes
12:1 217
12:6 217
12:13-14 217

Isaiah
2:1-3 133
9:6-7 223
11 222
11:9-11 237
27:9 282
42:4 ...... 133, 273
51:4 133
52:7 223
53 202
55:12 223
56 196
56:4-6 218
57:2 223
58 196
59:20-21 282
65 222
66:1 222

Jeremiah
11:16 64
13:6 216
14:21 217
17:21 219
25:11 219
30:10 223
31 46
31:31-34 170
31:31ff 43
31:32 ... 46, 50, 133
31:33... 50, 133, 170
..... 177, 184, 187
31:33-34 282
31:34a 50
31:34b 50

Lamentations
1:3 221
5:5 221

Ezekiel
- 18:23 273
- 20:10-26 219
- 20:12 218
- 20:20 218
- 22:8 219
- 22:26 219
- 22:31 219
- 34:25 223
- 36:27 133
- 37:26 223
- 46:1-3 223
- 44 196

Hosea
- 11:1 .... 94, 114

Amos
- 1-2 141
- 1:9 217

Micah
- 4:2 133

Malachi
- 4:4 217

Matthew
- 1:1 94
- 1:21 .... 94, 224
- 1:22 .. 102, 103, 112
- 1-2 91
- 1-4 92
- 1-5 92
- 2 92
- 2:5 112
- 2:15 .... 94, 103
- 112, 114
- 2:16-18 .... 94, 114
- 2:17 ...... 103, 112
- 2:17-18 112
- 2:20 93
- 2:23 .. 103, 112, 114
- 3:3 103
- 3:11 54
- 3:15 112
- 3:16 94
- 3-7 91
- 4:2 93
- 4:4 .... 93, 103
- 4:7 .... 93, 103
- 4:10 93
- 4:14 .. 102, 103, 112
- 5. .... 79, 84
- 98, 101, 102
- 103, 111, 115
- 128, 132, 159
- 5:1 93
- 5:1-2 92
- 5:3-10 93
- 5:4 102
- 5:6 116
- 5:8 102
- 5:10 116
- 5:17... 85, 88, 96, 99
- .. 109, 110, 118
- ... 118, 120, 126
- ... 134-136, 138
- ... 157, 203, 207
- 5:17a 109
- 5:17-18 ... 101, 125
- 5:17-19 .. 69, 84, 98
- 5:17-20 ..... xiii, 78
- ... 79, 90, 91
- 96, 109, 133
- 150, 153, 199
- 5:17ff 172, 199
- 5:18 .... 89, 110
- 115, 123
- 5:18-20 123
- 5:19 ... 87, 116, 124
- 126
- 5:20 ...... 116, 128
- 5:21 104
- 5:21ff. 70, 81
- 181, 292
- 5:21-22 .... 99, 104
- .. 126, 127
- 5:21-47 69
- 5:21-48 .. 88, 96-99
- 111, 116
- ... 119, 120
- 125, 126, 134

5:22 .... 70, 95, 119	9:9-13 117
5:22-23 105	9:13 110
5:26 119	9:16 121
5:27 ...... 104, 205	9:17 121
5:27ff 70	10:34 ..... 109, 110
5:27-28 ... 100, 105	10:42 285
.. 127, 181, 205	11-13 91
5:28 .... 70, 95	11:13 113
.... 119, 205	11:19 110
5:31 159	11:28 ..... 230, 236
5:31ff 70	11:28ff 225
5:31-32 100	11:28-30 250
.. 105, 127	11:29 ..... 119, 131
5:32 .... 70, 95, 119	12 95
5:33ff. 70	12:1 230
5:33-34 100	12:1-6 134
.. 106, 127	12:1-8 117, 226, 231
5:34 .... 70, 95, 119	12:3-4 94
5:34-36 106	12:5 229
5:38ff 70	12:5-6 94
5:38-39 100	12:6 .... 63, 94, 229
.. 106, 127	12:7 230
5:39 .... 70, 95, 119	12:8 .... 94, 95, 117
5:39-42 107	.. 131, 228, 229
5:43-44 ... 100, 107	12:8-14 231
5:43b 69	12:17 ..... 103, 112
5:43ff 70	12:39-41 94
5:44 .... 70, 95, 119	12:41 ... 63, 94, 229
5:48 ...... 128, 132	12:42 ... 63, 94, 229
5-7 ...... 78, 79, 92	13:35 ..... 103, 112
6:14 200	13:48 111
7:23 95	14-18 91
7:23-24 126	15:1-20 117
7:24 119	15:4 ...... 181, 290
.. 125, 131	15:10-20 134
7:24-27 .... 95, 126	15:21ff. 290
.... 133, 155	16 51
7:26 .. 119, 125, 131	16:18 .... 38, 51
7:28 70	17:1-9 94
7:28-29 ..... 35, 95	17:1-10 95
8:1 93	17:5 .... 34, 94
8:17 ...... 103, 112	.. 119, 132, 155
8-10 .... 91, 95	19 74
9:1-8 117	19:1-9 117

19:8	106
19:17	74
19:17-19	181
19:18	74
19:18-19	290
19:19	74
19-25	91
20:28	110
21:4	103, 112
21:4-5	112
21:43	65
22:31	102, 103
22:39	154
22:45	94
23:32	112
24:2	110
24:15	103
24:35	124
25:46	45
26:28	236, 282
26:54	112
26:56	112
26:61	110
26-28	91
27:9	103, 112
27:40	110
28:18	67, 96, 253
28:18-20	96
28:19-20	131
28:20	96, 119, 155

Mark.

1:7-8	54
1:8	55
2:18-22	230
2:23-28	134, 226
2:27	213, 228
2:27-28	249, 290
2:28	131, 229, 250
3:2	241
3:1-6	231
7:10	181, 290
7:14-23	134
9:2-8	17
9:7	17
10:19	182, 290
14:24	282
15:28	193
15:42	234

Luke

1:72	217, 282
2:24	102
2:29-30	224
2:49	49
3:16	54
3:21-38	286
4	102
4:12	102
4:16ff	224
4:16-21	235
6:1	226
6:1-5	226
6:6-11	231
6:7	241
7:1	156
13:10	231
13:16	231
14:1	241
14:1-6	231
16:16	116
16:16-18	113
16:17	89, 157
18:20	182, 290
20:20	241
20:39	278
22:20	45, 281, 282
22:37	193
23:56	290
24:19	132
24:27	44

John

1:11	110
1:17	140
1:18	34
1:28	54
1:29	232
1:33	54
3:16	19
3:31	110

Scripture Index

3:34-35	19	15:15	14
4:25	132	15:16	178
4:34	232	15:22	110
5:1-18	231	16:8	274
5:14	232	16:12-13	121
5:17	214, 232	16:12-14	155
5:43	110	16:12-15	36, 160
5:46	44	16:13	40
6:14	110, 132	16:28	110
6:37-40	232	17:2	253
6:38	49	17:4	49, 232
6:56	56	17:6	20
7:16	35	17:8	35, 37, 155
7:37	235	17:18	37, 155
7:40	132	17:20	37, 155
7:42	110	18:37	110
8:11	290	19:30	232
8:14	110	20:21	20
8:42	110	21:24	38
8:53	63		

Acts

9:1-41	231
9:4	232
9:39	110
10:10	110
10:35	124
10:36	293
11:27	110
12:27	110
12:46	110
12:47	110
14	18
14:3	110
14:8-9	18
14:16	35
14:18	35, 110
14:20	56
14:23	110
14:24	35
14:24-26	36
14:28	110
14-16	35
15:5	56
15:13	19
15:14	14

1	56
1:5	55
2:23	49, 193
2:42	260
2:46	260
2:47b	65
3:25	282
4:28	49
7:8	282
8	202
8:31	202
9:24	241
11	166
11:7-8	166
11:18	9
11:27	53
13:1	53
13:14	12
13:25	156
13:44	12
14:26	156
15	150
15:10	150
15:19	150

Reference	Page(s)
15:32	53
16:13	12
17:2	12
18:4	12
18:19-21	245
18:22-23	246
18:25-26	246
19:8	246
20:7	12, 252
20:33	290
21:9-10	53

Romans

Reference	Page(s)
1:1	16
1:2	31, 53
1:18	193
1:18-19	140
1:18-21	33
1:18-25	142
1:18-32	193
1:18ff	140
1:19	140
1:24	193
1:25	141
1:26	193
1:28	140, 193
1:32	140
1-2	140
2:14	140
2:15	140, 141
2:26	140
2:27	141
3:9	140
3:21	53, 147
3:21-26	149
3:31	120, 136
4:2	200
4:5	234
4:18	102
5:13	30, 146
5:20	30
6:3	63
6:14-15	137
7:4	31
7:6	31
7:7	290
8:3	150
8:9	178
8:14	178
8:16	178
8:18-24	225
9:4	25, 281
9:6b	10
9:12	102
9:19-20a	15
9:24-25	62
9:31-32	150
9-11	64
10:4	31, 136, 148, 174
10:5	145
11	63
11:1-6	63
11:2-3	53
11:7-11	63
11:11-15	63
11:15	64
11:16	64
11:21-22	66
11:27	282
12:1-8	179
12:2	180
12:6	263, 264
13:4	158
13:9	157, 290
13:9-10	182
14	15, 150, 247, 251
14:1ff	150
14:1-6	236, 241, 242
14:4	15, 16
14:5	12, 236, 245, 255
14:5-6	12, 243
14:5-8	15
14:6	13, 15, 16, 255
14:6-9	16
14:9	15, 16

Scripture Index

14:14 134
14:18 16

1 Corinthians

5:7 235
5:9-13 193
6 107
6:9-10 290
6:9-11 194
6:18 158
7:2 158
7:19 ...... 137, 154
7:22-23 16
9:9 .... 157, 159
9:19-20 136
9:19-21 136
9:20 ...... 153, 160
9:20-21 ... 133, 153
9:21 .... 66, 193
9:21a 136, 153
9:21b 136, 153
10:1-2 63
11 255
11:2 217
11:17-26 254
11:20 . 253, 254, 255
11:23-26 255
11:25 .. 45, 281, 282
12 55
12:12 .... 54, 55
12:12-13 . 54, 56, 63
12:13 .... 54, 55, 56
12:27 55
14:37 .... 20, 40
15:27 68
16:1-2 .... 251, 252
16:2 12

2 Corinthians

1:20 224
3 ..... 127, 150-152
3:6 .... 43, 281
3:6-7 145
3:7 ... 144, 150, 151
3:11 ...... 150, 151
3:13 ...... 150, 151
3:14 281
4:1-6 20
5:17 ...... 178, 234
6:2 234
6:14-18 62

Galatians

1:6-9 240
1:8-9 ..... 242, 256
1:10 16
1:14ff 40
2:11-21 248
3 146
3:3 242
3:8 31
3:10 145
3:12 145
3:13 146
3:15 281
3:16 146
3:17 .... 23, 30
  .. 146, 147, 282
3:18 146
3:18b-19a 1496
3:19 .... 30, 147
3:19b 146
3:19-25 150
3:19-28 135
3:21 147
3:21-24 147
3:23 ...... 146, 150
3:23-25 31
3:24 ...... 146, 150
3:25 135
3:27 63
4:4 226
4:5 150
4:8-11 .... 240, 248
4:9 241
4:9-11 .... 150, 236
4:10 ...... 12, 136
   .... 241, 242
4:10-11 .... 13, 245
4:11 ...... 241, 242

4:21-31 150
4:24 281
5:1 .... 136, 242
5:1-12 150
5:2 241
6:2 .... 66, 133, 148
6:12 136

Ephesians
1:10 225
2 .... 55, 56
2:10 ...... 178, 234
2:12 .... 25, 281
2:13 141
2:14 174
2:14-16 203
2:14-22 52
2:15 150
2:20 ..... 38, 40, 53
.... 54, 166
3:4-5 53
3:11 49
4:4-6 260
4:8-11 54
4:28 291
5:5 291
5:5-8 178
5:25-33 159
6:1 182
6:1-3 157
6:2-3 . 182, 183, 291
6:5-8 16

Philippians
1:1 16
2:2 156
2:9-11 ..... 67, 253
3:8-9 149

Colossians
1:25 156
2:9-12 196
2:11 235
2:14 ...... 150, 151
2:16 .... 13, 150
...... 236, 241
2:16-17 .... 12, 135

.... 225, 244
2:17 ... 13, 122, 123
...... 235, 236
3:5 291
3:20 291
3:22-24 16
4:12 16

1 Thessalonians
2:13 40
2:15 53
4:1-2ff 40
4:9 36

2 Thessalonians
1:11 156
2:8 193
2:15 .... 38, 40, 155
3:6 .... 38, 40
3:12 40
3:14 40

1 Timothy
1:8ff 197
1:8-10 191
1:8-11 .... 177, 190
... 194, 195
1:9 197
1:9-10 291
1:10 193
4:2 271
5:17-18 159
5:18 157
6:3 40

2 Timothy
1:9 49
2:24 16
3 202
3:1-5 195
3:6-9 195
3:16 ... 85, 200, 208
3:16-17 ... 200, 201
3:17 201

Titus
1:1 16
1:12 53
2:1-10 162

2:4-5	162
2:9-10	162

Hebrews

1:1	34
1:1-2	50, 155
1:1-2a	46
1:2	26, 34, 234
1:3	34
1:4	34
2:2	26
2:3	37
2:3b	47
3:1-4:13	233
3:5-6	137
3:7–4:13	213, 232
4	224, 235
4:1-11	12
4:2	232, 233
4:3	102
4:3-4	232
4:4	214
4:5	232
4:6	232, 233
4:9	232, 233
4:10	233, 236
4:11	233
6:1-2	198
6:18	235
7:12	137, 150, 154
7:18-19	167
7:19	150
7:22	281, 282
8:6	145, 281
8:6-9:1	150
8:7	45
8:7-12	282
8:8	43, 281
8:9	133, 281
8:10	281
8:13	45
9:1	45
9:4	281, 282
9:12	234
9:15	281
9:16	281
9:17	281
9:18	45, 282
9:18ff	282
9:20	282
10:1-9	150
10:1-14	235
10:9	45, 49
10:11	234
10:12	234
10:16	282
10:29	282
11	61
11:8	61
11:9	61
11:10	62
11:13	61
11:13-16	61
11:39-40	61
12:24	281
13:4	158, 291
13:7	217
13:15	63
13:20	45, 282, 283

James

1:25	158
2:5	155
2:8	154, 160
2:10	152
2:10-11	183
2:11-12	292

1 Peter

1:12	39
1:20	49
2:4-5	53
2:5	63
2:9-10	62
2:16	17
3:7	159

2 Peter

1:1	17
2:8	193

1 John

2:24	56

2:27 36
3:2 .... 164, 280
3:4 148
3:12-15 292
3:24 56
4:13 56
5:21 157

Jude

3 155

Revelation

1:10 .... 12, 252
.... 254, 255
1:11 40
2:1 40
3:21 286
5:9 285
6:9-11 286
7:9 286
11:19 281
14:11 236
14:13 .. 40, 233, 237
19:9 40
21:1-8 286
21:3 ...... 237, 286
21:4 237
21:5 40
21:8 292
21:14 38
22:3 237
22:5 237
22:13 224

General Index

Abraham 9, 24, 29, 31
.... 60, 61, 64, 65
   children of 9
Allison, Dale C. 92, 118
Anabaptists 2, 3, 8
.... 27-29, 83, 86
   view of Scripture .. 29, 30
Analogy of faith 264, 265
Antichrist 193
Antinomianism 128
Apostles 36-40
   as ambassadors of Christ ..
              36, 37, 40
Aquinas 80
Augustine 80
Bahnsen, Greg 84, 97, 98
.... .102-104, 107, 116
.... 120, 124, 125, 131
Banks, Robert ... 87, 118, 125
   in contemporary discussion
                  89
Baptism 2, 3, 10
   in the Spirit ...... 54 -56
   into Moses 63
Baptists 32, 169
   Philadelphia association of
                  267
Barcellos, Richard 1, 3, 5
...... 144, 169, 170, 175, 177
... 187-191, 197, 200-203, 210
   contrast 173
Barker, William S. 107
Barnhouse, D. G. 214
Beastiality 158
Biblical Theology 2, 21, 29, 265
   defined 21
Body of Christ 75
Boice, James M. 214, 218
Bolton, Samuel 81
Brown, John 156
Brown, Michael L. 231
Bruce, F. F. 151
Bunyan, John 293
Calendar 241

Jewish 241
Calvin, John 81, 128
Capital Punishment 158
Carson, D. A. 78, 87, 106
.... 117, 229, 230, 232
Chafer, L. S. 85, 98, 148
Chantry, Walter 128
Childs, Brevard 117
Christian liberty 243, 246, 247
Christians
   character of 178
   unity of 259, 266
   weak and strong 243
Chrysostom 79
Church . 11, 50-53, 59, 60, 62
   as "invisible" 66
   as "universal" 66
   as "visible" 65
   composition of 32, 63, 65
   history of 23
   images of 62
   in Abrahamic covenant 277
   its foundation 52-56
Churches of Christ
   and creeds 261
Circumcision 10, 241
   as sign of the Abrahamic
     covenant 196
Commentaries
   critical 239
   devotional 239
Confessions 2, 259
   .... 261, 265, 268
   as barriers to unity ....
              259, 270
   deviations from 268
Continuity and discontinuity . 5
Covenant 9, 24, 25, 43
.... 45, 165, 275
   Abrahamic . 276, 277, 285
   administrations of 10
   .... 44, 48, 49
   defined 4, 5
   difficulties in discussing . 4

essence of 163
human covenants 281
in redemptive history . 281
Mosaic 276, 278
Noahic 276
sign of 9-11
usage in NT 45, 47-49, 281
Covenants
plurality of 281
teleological relations of . . .
. . . . 275, 276
unity of 276
Covenant of Grace 3, 45
Covenant Theology . . 2, 9, 23
. . . . 32, 51, 59, 63
Coxe, A. Cleveland 79
Creation ordinance 247
Creeds 2, 259-261
. . . . 263, 268, 274
as barriers to unity 259, 270
changing of 268
loose subscription to . . . . .
. . . . 266-268
multiplication of 266
object of 261
simplification of 266
subscription to . . 209, 210
. . . . 266, 267, 270
'unwritten' 260, 261
Crime 177
Dabney, R. L. 129
David, Peter 155
Davies, W. D. 118
Days
importance of . . 241-245
. . . . . 248, 249, 252, 256
imposition of 248
. . . . 256, 257
summary of Paul's under-
standing 248, 256
Decalogue
See Ten Commandments
. . . . 11, 141, 143
. . . . 144, 150-152

Dispensationalism . . . 2, 43, 44
. . . . 59, 200, 208
Driver, Samuel R. 144
Dunn, James D. G. 88
Early Church 79
Estep, William 83
Eternal Covenant 45
Faith
content of 272
Fairbairn, Patrick 98
Faustus 87
Fee, Gordon 99
Ferguson, Sinclair 107
Formula of Concord 148
France, R. T. 87, 91
Friedlander, Gerald 88
Fulfillment 80, 84-87
. . . . 95, 96, 99, 111-117, 119
. . 121, 123, 124, 126, 132, 135
Reformed view of 116, 117
Gaebelein, A. C. 148
Galatian church 240, 241
. . . . 244, 248
Garner, Robert 235
God 15
faithfulness of 163
finality of his judgments 15
glory of 19, 20
love of 19
promises of 60-62
purposes of 49
Godfrey, W. Robert 107
Gorman, Frank 92
Gospel 20, 31, 32, 44, 271, 273
Luther's view of 31
Gould, Ezra P. 228
Grassi, Joseph 92
Green, Michael 97
Guelich, Robert 109
Haman 14
Hamerton-Kelly, R. G. 89
Hendriksen, William . . 82, 101
. . . . 104, 106, 125
Henry, Carl F. H. 78

General Index

Hiebert, D. Edmond 226
Holy Spirit 35-39, 178
House, Paul R. 219
Irenaeus 79
Israel 8, 30, 57, 59, 60
.... 62-65, 203, 277
   as a type of the church 62
   in Abrahamic covenant 283
   identification of 10
   rejection of 63, 64
Jeremias, Joachim 78, 101
Jesus
   authority of 95, 109
   compared to Moses 91-94
   ...... 97, 109, 114, 119
      122, 123, 126, 131, 153
   compared to OT figures 94
   transfiguration of .. 95, 96
Jesus Christ 17, 46, 47
   as agent of God 15
   as fulfillment of OT .. 197
   .... 199, 207
   as God-man 67
   as king 173, 191
   as lawgiver 17, 67
   .... 166, 173
   as new Torah 167
   as priest 173, 191
   as prophet 18, 34
   ..... 173, 191
   as Redeemer 44
   as revelation of God 2
   ..... 18-20, 34, 35, 166
   attractiveness of 271
   authority of 35
   death of ... 15, 16, 19, 23
   . 27, 45, 57, 174, 203, 272
   Deity of 67
   lordship of 11, 67,68
   .... 70, 253-255
   love of 19
   on Lord's Day 12
   relation to Mosaic law . 69
   .... 71, 174, 185

   resurrection of 253
   .... 255, 256
   sufficiency of ... 240, 242
   teaching of 19, 20
   transfiguration of 17
Johnson, Alan 101
Johnson, S. Lewis 135
Joshua 95
Justification 24
Kaiser, Walter 152, 221
.... 222, 223
Kaye, Bruce 99
Keil & Delitsch 215
Kevan, Ernest 82, 98
Kidner, Derek 213
Kissinger, Warren 78
Kline, M. 218
Larkin, Clarence 148
Law 2, 5, 30, 44, 69, 127
.... 161, 167, 191, 205
..... 207, 246, 248, 271, 273
   abolition of 109, 110
   abrogation of 149
   Anabaptist view 83
   and grace 199, 200
   as eschatologically fulfilled
   .... 86, 87
   as national and societal ....
   .... 205, 206
   as Old Covenant 142
   .... 145, 151
   as prophecy 86, 87
   as written on hearts .. 170
   before Moses ... 140, 142
   "ceremonial" 82
   "civil" 82
   critical views 89
   Dispensational view of ....
   .... 85, 86, 117
   Early Church view . 79, 80
   for whom intended ......
   191-194
   fulfillment of ... 112, 127

in contemporary discussion
.... 89, 90
Luther's view of 30
Medieval Church view . 80
"moral" 81, 82
necessity of 66
of Christ 66, 72, 75
.... 166, 180, 273
Reformed view of . 81, 82
.... 121, 125, 131
Theonomists' view of 84, 85
threefold division of . . 164
.... 165
traditional discussion of 170
tripartite view of ....
.... 150-152, 156
used to mean "covenant" . .
.... 26, 27
Law of Christ 39
Lenski, R. C. H. 97
Lincoln, A. T. 222, 232
Longenecker, Richard
in contemporary discussion
.... 89
Lord's Day 12, 244-247
.... 251, 252, 254-256
Lord's Supper 253-255
Lord's Table 63
Love
as basis of unity 270
Luther, Martin . . 81, 106, 107
Lutheran churches 262
Manichaeans 87
Marcionites 87
Marpeck, Pilgram 28, 29
view of Scripture 29
Martin, John 78, 85
Martin, Ralph 155
Martyr, Justin 236
Master 15, 16, 17
McArthur, Harvey 78-80, 83, 88
McClain, Alva 148
McKnight, Scot 228
Medieval Church 80

Meier, John P. 102
Moo, Douglas 87, 105, 106, 136
.... 155, 226, 231, 236
Moral law 67, 72, 161
.... 163-166, 177, 182
application of 176
and evangelism . 271, 273
as love 164, 182
as seen in Christ 72
defined 161, 162
Mosaic law
external nature of 177
Moses 19, 24, 198
Moule, C. F. D. 114
Munsterites 83
Murray, John 121
Mystery
in the NT 164
Name
defined 19
National Constitution
Mosaic covenant as . . 278
New Covenant 23-25, 43, 48, 57
...... 170, 174, 275, 277, 279
contrasted with the Old ...
.... 48, 50, 172, 175
defined 75, 76
difficulties in discussing . 4
implications of 12
New Covenant Theology . . 1,2
...... 169, 175, 187-189, 196
...... 200, 201, 204, 207, 210
difficulties in discussing . 3
goals of 22
its 'canon of ethics' ... 209
on Sabbath 196
on Sermon on the Mount
.... 204
relation to church history . .
.... 22, 23
New Testament 7
logical priority of 1, 7
.... 10-12, 29, 166, 239
moral content of . . 71, 72

General Index

writers of 20
Nixon, Robin 99
Oberholtzer, Thomas Kem 233
Oehler, G. F. 215
Old Covenant 24, 26, 28
. . . . 48, 176, 275
   application of . . . 187, 188
   permanence of 173
Old Testament
   application of . . . 202, 203
   logical priority of 9, 10, 14
   present usefulness of . 202
   regeneration in 206
   transformation of 202
Origen 80
Paedobaptists 32
Parable of the Caterpillar . . 171
   application of . . . 172, 173
   . . . . 175, 176, 184
Passover 62
Paul
   his lists of ungodly persons
   195
   his lists of vices 195
Pentecost 65
People of God . . . 9, 50, 52, 62
   Gentiles as part of 9
   identification of 11
Peter 52
Pilgrims 261
Pink, A. W. 129
Plymouth Brethren
   and creeds 261
Poythress, Vern . . . 87, 92, 105
. . . . 120, 121, 151
Presuppositions 21, 207
   effects of 13, 14
Promises of Abrahamic covenant
. . . . 285
Prophet 165
Prophets 53, 54
Puritans 68, 72, 271, 275
Qumran 101
Redemption 163

God's purposes in 44
Reformed churches 262
Reisinger, John 188, 189
   on Sermon on the Mount
   205
Revelation
   as cumulative 164
   general 33
   7
   of God's character 18
   progressive 7, 162
   . . . . 163, 166, 239
Ridderbos, H. N. 82
Robinson, John 262
Roman church 243
Sabbath . . 11, 13, 95, 109, 134
. . 143, 144, 152, 196, 198, 204
. . 239-241, 244, 245, 252, 267
   abolition of 250
   as the seal or sign of Old
   Covenant 196, 218
   fulfilled in Christ 250
   Jesus' lordship over 249, 250
   purpose of 249
Sacrifices 62
Sanctification
   usage in NT 48
Schreiner, Thomas 99, 104-107
Scripture
   inspiration of 21, 201
Scofield, C. I. 85, 148
Sermon on the Mount 204, 205
Slavery
   to Jesus Christ 2, 14
Slaves 14-17
Sloyan, Gerard S. 88
Smith, Ralph 214
Spiritualists 27, 28
Stott, John 40
Strickland, Wayne . 77, 86, 117
Stuart, Douglas 99
Synagogue
   Christian attachment to . . .
   . . . . 245, 246

Systematic Theology 2, 48
.... 49, 269
   Relation to biblical ... 21
Tasker, R. V. G. 111
Ten Commandments 11, 18, 19
.... 67, 71-74, 164, 170
...... 176, 177, 179, 182-184
...... 187, 188, 190, 197, 206
   and evangelism 271
   application of ... 202, 203
   as fulfilled in Christ .. 172
   as revelation of God . 2, 19
   as used in NT 293
   as written on hearts .. 172
   190
   external nature of 177
   for whom intended .. 195
   frequency of, in NT .....
   184-188
   transformation of 172
   .... 184, 189
   unity of 189, 190
Tertullian 79
Testament
   used to mean "covenant"
   26
Theophylact 79
Thirty-Nine Articles 264
Toussaint, Stanley D. 78
Tradition 38, 155, 264
Trinity 48
Truth
   as basis of unity 270
Turner, Max B. 228
Typology 59, 62, 75, 173
.... 183, 190, 191, 197
   in Abrahamic covenant 277
von Rad, G. 213, 214
Vos, Geerhardus 82
Warfare 8
Warfield, B. B. . 144, 217, 228
Wenham, Gordon 99
Wesley, John 77
Westerholm, Stephen 115

Westminster Standards 73
.... 74, 264
Wilson, Stephen G. ... 88, 228
Xerxes 14
Zaspel, Fred 188
Zwingli, Ulrich 2

pg. 65 - Jews & Gentiles the church